ASEAN AND THE SECURITY OF SOUTH-EAST ASIA

International Politics in Asia Series
Edited by Michael Leifer, London School of Economics

China and the Arms Trade
Ann Gilks and Gerald Segal

Soviet Foreign Policy in Southeast Asia
Leszek Buszynski

ASEAN AND THE SECURITY OF SOUTH-EAST ASIA

MICHAEL LEIFER

ROUTLEDGE
London and New York

First published 1989
by Routledge
11 New Fetter Lane, London EC4P 4EE

© 1989 Michael Leifer

Printed in Great Britain by
Billing & Sons Ltd, Worcester

British Library Cataloguing in Publication Data

Leifer, Michael
    ASEAN and the security of South-East
    Asia.
    1. South-east Asia. National security.
    Attitudes of governments
    I. Title
    327'.0959
    ISBN 0-415-01008-X

Contents

Acknowledgements

Financial support for travel in the course of preparation of this book has been provided by the Suntory-Toyota International Centre for Economics and Related Disciplines and the Staff Research Fund of the London School of Economics and Political Science. Its completion would not have been possible without the opportunity to spend a year as visiting Professor of Political Science at the National University of Singapore. I thank my colleagues there for their intellectual company. The final draft of the manuscript was typed with care by Margaret Bothwell.

Responsibility for the content and conclusions of this volume rest, of course, exclusively with the author.

Introduction

The Association of South-East Nations (ASEAN) was established on 8 August 1967 at a meeting in Bangkok between the Foreign Ministers of Indonesia, the Philippines, Singapore and Thailand and the Deputy Prime Minister of Malaysia. Security was uppermost in their minds but not conspicuously addressed. It was contemplated in practical terms as a by-product of institutionalised regional reconciliation. To that end, the five founding governments hoped in time to attract to their ranks all the states of South-East Asia. That goal has not been realised. Indochina lay beyond their prospect until the end of the Vietnam War in 1975, but then fundamental political differences interposed to divide established conservative from successor revolutionary governments. That divide became entrenched as a result of the protracted conflict over Kampuchea (once Cambodia). In the circumstances, Burma deemed it politic to keep its distance from the Association. It was only in January 1984 that membership was augmented by the admission of the Sultanate of Brunei, but without changing ASEAN's subregional scope.

ASEAN's declared primary goals of promoting 'economic growth, social progress and cultural development' through regional co-operation have been realised also only to a very limited extent. For example, by 1987 trade among the six member states, whose combined populations comprise some 300 million, had amounted to no more than 17 per cent of their total trade. Preferential tariff arrangements had accounted for around 2 per cent of that intra-ASEAN trade. Despite its subregional scope and a modest record of economic co-operation, ASEAN has displayed a quality of political cohesion and a diplomatic accomplishment unanticipated at the outset. The Association has attained a notable international standing in comparison with other Third World regional organisations of larger membership and longer duration. One indication of that standing has been the annual dialogue conducted between ASEAN's Foreign Ministers and counterparts from the United States, Japan, Australia, New Zealand, and Canada, as well as a corresponding representative from the European Community. Such dialogues are unique to ASEAN, whose record as a diplomatic community has encouraged regional co-operation in adjacent South Asia which only assumed institutional form in the mid-1980s. Their attraction prompted the Soviet government to seek dialogue partner status in January 1987.

ASEAN's international reputation as a diplomatic community derives from an evolving practice of bureaucratic and ministerial consultation. Such a practice has enabled member governments to co-ordinate their regional policies with relative harmony and to some political effect. Regarded widely with unconcealed scepticism at the outset, ASEAN began to attract international attention and respect from 1975 when its members responded to the successes of revolutionary Communism in Indochina by registering a common political identity and purpose. More significantly, since January 1979 the governments of ASEAN have undertaken a sustained diplomatic challenge to Vietnam's invasion and occupation of Kampuchea.

ASEAN's engagement in the Kampuchean conflict indicates an abiding preoccupation with the problems of regional security. In addressing those problems over Kampuchea, however, ASEAN has exhibited an evident paradox. Whenever governments co-operate with security in mind, it is usual for their collective enterprise to assume some military form. ASEAN, as a corporate entity, has been a notable exception to this rule. Defence co-operation, beyond exchanges of intelligence, does take place among ASEAN states but primarily on a limited bilateral basis and then only outside of the formal institutional structure of the Association. The restricted nature of that co-operation supports the insistence of its governments that their multilateral arrangements have neither embodied the obligations nor assumed the structure of an alliance.

In pursuing the elusive goal of regional security, ASEAN has moved beyond an initial and continuing practice of intra-mural dispute management. Its governments have become jointly involved over Kampuchea in trying to redress the regional balance of power. Ever since Vietnam's invasion, the collective energies of the Association have been directed primarily towards denying its dominance in Indochina. In consequence, a subregional association, whose members have categorically rejected an alliance option, has assumed a role which traditionally has required the instrumentality and means of an alliance. In ASEAN's case, those means have been limited to diplomatic measures. Accordingly, a security role has been pursued in informal coalition with extra-regional powers which provide material and coercive capability. The net effect of such an enterprise has been mixed because it has exposed differences of strategic perspective among member governments. As a result, the institutional experience of the Association comprises both solidarity and strain.

Before addressing the experience and record of ASEAN in pursuit of regional security, it is instructive to take brief note of the changing condition of its environment over the past two decades and more. When ASEAN was formed, decolonisation had largely run its course in South-East Asia. State succession had mainly followed colonial territorial bounds. Other than in North Vietnam, political succession had passed to conservative leaderships. In South Vietnam, however, a revolutionary political challenge with implications for the whole of Indochina and beyond were still being denied by U.S. military intervention. The Vietnam (or Second Indochina) War provided the prime reference point for regional politics. It was responsible for sustaining a pattern of competitive global and regional relationships in Asia brought into being by the Cold War. Cold War imagery of an aggressive monolithic international Communism whose prime regional agency was China coloured the outlooks of ASEAN's governments. External threat was contemplated, however, primarily with reference to the exploitation of internal political weakness, reflecting an imperfect condition of post-colonial statehood. The common concern was the external fuelling and stoking of regional insurgencies. For this reason, although not of one mind over the Vietnam War and the U.S. role, its intervention enjoyed, at the very least, the tacit support of all of ASEAN's governments.

By February 1972, however, the global structure of international relations was in flux with consequences for South-East Asia. President Nixon's historic visit to China repudiated the *raison d'être* of the U.S. containment policy in Asia and paved the way for the ultimate end to the Vietnam War. Sino-U.S. rapprochement in the context of acute Sino-Soviet hostility and with a direct bearing on Sino-Vietnamese ties, meant that ASEAN states were obliged to cope with a new and more complex competitive structure of linked global and regional relationships.

In the circumstances, South-East Asia did not become any less vulnerable to competitive external intervention. Such intervention may have reduced in relative scale and intensity, but the net effect of the new structure was to draw the battle lines for the conflict over Kampuchea and then to sustain it in a condition of active stalemate. That conflict has served as both cause and symptom of a condition of regional polarisation to which ASEAN has been a prime party.

That polarisation provides the environmental context in which the governments of ASEAN continue to engage in the pursuit of regional security, if they are not of one mind over its priorities. Their institutional experience and record in that enterprise over more than two decades will be explored and assessed in the following chapters.

1

Common and Contending Security Ideas

The five founding governments of ASEAN were drawn together by a recognition of the self-defeating and wasteful nature of contention among neighbouring states of a corresponding conservative political disposition. That correspondence reflected in external affiliations had been given greater substance by Indonesia renouncing a radical nationalism and returning to conventional diplomatic practice. The assumption of power in March 1966 of a military based anti-Communist administration in the largest and most populous regional state had the effect of expanding significantly a pattern of conformity in political outlook already encompassing Thailand, Malaysia, Singapore and the Philippines. The five states shared a common vulnerability to internal threats aggravated by external predators taking advantage of a conflict ridden regional environment. Regional partnership was intended to control conflict, to ease the management of fragile political systems and so to mitigate vulnerability.[1]

The ostensible purpose of establishing ASEAN was to promote economic, social and cultural co-operation but regional security was the prime preoccupation of its founders. That common preoccupation did not express itself in a full consensus over its definition and how to confront its problems. In their physical and human geography as well as historical experience, the states of ASEAN comprise a rich diversity characteristic of South-East Asia. That diversity has given rise to important differences of strategic perspective and political interest within the Association which have limited its efficacy. For that reason, ASEAN's experience and attainment in security co-operation are best evaluated in the prior light of contending as well as common ideas which have informed the views and conduct of its member governments.

1

ASEAN has been described by a former Foreign Minister of Malaysia and a participant in its formation as 'a development out of the pains of *konfrontasi*'[2] The most immediate and practical common security goal of the founding governments was to expand and institutionalise the process of reconciliation which had paved the way for a political settlement to Indonesia's coercive challenge to the legitimacy of Malaysia between 1963 and 1966. Practical utility was recognised in being able to manage and even overcome regional disputes and more deep-seated contention through forging a structure of special relationships. This approach to regional security in its external dimension was joined to the instrumentality of economic development as a way of coping with its internal one. It reflected a basic consensus among governments conscious of the fragile fabric of their post-colonial societies. They had all experienced internal political challenges which had attracted popular support partly because of economic deprivation. Common threat was defined with reference to internal subversion and insurgency only, not to any single external source. The relevance of economic development to regional security was based on the half-truth that poverty is the prime cause of political discontent because it provides a fertile soil in which revolutionary forces can flourish. It was not a novel view. Its post-Pacific War origins may be found in the calculations which led to the establishment of the Colombo Plan in 1950. Corresponding calculations underpinned the conventional wisdom from the outset that social and political discontent could be more directly and energetically addressed by the governments of ASEAN if regional tensions could be reduced or overcome through regional co-operation. Thus, although reducing external threats among past regional adversaries and new found regional partners was a dominant purpose in itself for forming ASEAN, an important collateral reason was to prevent a diversion of national energies and resources from security-relevant economic development. By cultivating intra-mural accord and so reducing threats among themselves, the ASEAN states would be able to devote themselves through the instrumentality of economic development to the common cause of political stability. The ideal end product would be political stability on both an individual and collective basis denying, for example, the emergence of those domestic circumstances which had encouraged Indonesia's practice of Confrontation of Malaysia with attendant external involvement.

In entering into regional co-operation, the governments of

ASEAN would appear to have had in mind a general approach which may be rationalised as 'collective internal security'. Such a term has never appeared in the political vocabulary of any ASEAN government but it fits the general intention of the Association's founders. The original concept of collective security, identified with the ill-fated League of Nations, was meant in application to protect member states from acts of aggression by any of their number. It was conceived as an operational device for an intra-mural structure of security with membership envisaged in universal terms. Collective internal security was intended to do the same and more for ASEAN but not through the medium of sanctions as provided for in the League of Nations Covenant. A process of reconciliation institutionalised through regional co-operation was intended to counter any revival of serious contention between member governments. An attendant ability to address problems of domestic political stability through the mechanisms of economic development was expected to produce corporate as well as individual benefits. External adventurism would be discouraged. The contagion of internal political disorder would be prevented from spreading from an infected state to contaminate the body politic of regional partners, and from providing a point of entry to South-East Asia for competing external powers. This inferred theory of political prophylaxis expressed the idea of the indivisibility of security integral to the original concept of collective security. Overrationalised in this exposition, the common approach to regional security on the part of ASEAN governments reflected a genuine consensus. That consensus was over the most appropriate way that a regional association, deficient in military capability and in no position to engage in collective defence, might make a contribution to regional security.

The founding assumption about the positive relationship between economic development and security was not unique to ASEAN. It had informed the joint outlook of those three governments (of Malaya, the Philippines, and Thailand) which had inspired the formation in July 1961 of the short-lived Association of South-East Asia (ASA). ASA foundered politically within only two years, primarily because of a territorial dispute over part of Northern Borneo between the Philippines and Malaya and then its constitutional successor, Malaysia. It was temporarily revived in 1966 on the same doctrinal terms. In a joint communique issued in March, its Standing Committee expressed the view that 'Economic progress was the foundation of political stability which was the best guarantee for political independence.'[3] That joint outlook survived the political demise of ASA when it was superseded by ASEAN. It was embraced and articulated with enthusiasm by General Suharto's Indonesia. His government invested that outlook with conceptual expression through the doctrine of national resilience.

National resilience is a slogan first employed by General (later President) Suharto and became an article of political faith in Indonesia from the late 1960s. It is not an exceptional doctrine, as President Suharto's exegesis indicates:

> 'National resilience' means internally: the ability to ensure the necessary social changes while keeping one's own identity, with all its vulnerability, and externally, it is the ability to face all external threats, regardless of their manifestations. 'National Resilience', therefore, covers the strengthening of all the component elements in the development of a nation in its entirety, thus consisting of resilience in the ideological, political, economic, social, cultural and military fields. Since 'national resilience' emanates from the need to foster continuously the development process of a nation, it naturally follows that the degree of emphasis accorded to particular problems at a given period or stage of development will be determined by the particular condition and requirements of that nation itself. If each member country develops its own 'national resilience', gradually a 'regional resilience' may emerge, i.e. the ability of member-countries to settle jointly their common problems and look after their future and well-being together.[4]

The term national resilience was intended to identify and encapsulate those qualities of self-sufficiency and resourcefulness which regional co-operation would help to promote and realise in each member state. It was intended also as a means of reconciling a limited practical approach to regional security for which there was consensus within ASEAN and an ideal prerogative one indicated in the preamble to the founding Bangkok Declaration which had been accepted only nominally by most regional partners. In Suharto's rationale, it was anticipated that national resilience attained on an individual basis would assume wider expression and application in aggregate form as regional or ASEAN resilience. The premise for contemplating such wider expression was the assumed positive indivisible relationship between development and security on an individual and on a collective basis. To the extent that an institutionalised structure of regional reconciliation might be transformed into a corresponding structure of regional stability then a longstanding disposition of extra-regional predators to fish in the troubled political waters of South-East Asia would be reduced. In consequence, regional partners would be able to assume a greater collective responsibility for managing regional security without needing to engage in conventional collective defence.

Consideration had not been given to ASEAN assuming any collective military responsibility for regional security. Founding governments had been only too aware of the danger of provoking a menacing response through a premature attempt to confront the problems of regional security head on in military form. An alliance had been out of the question partly because of deficiencies in corporate capability and because Indonesia did not wish to be seen to compromise its non-aligned status. Moreover, the consensus over coping with internal threats was not matched by agreement on external defence. Indeed, because ASEAN was neither disposed nor in any position to undertake collective defence, four of its founding governments retained long-established security relationships with extra-regional powers. A claim to exercise a managerial regional role had been indicated, however, in the preamble to the Bangkok Declaration inaugurating ASEAN. Part of that preamble expressed the determination of member states 'to ensure their stability and security from external interference in any form or manifestation in order to preserve their national identities in accordance with the ideals and aspirations of their people.'[5] Such a prerogative approach to regional security, expressed also with reference to excluding foreign military bases, was not an indication of either operational capability or practical intent.

Its enunciation represented in part a gesture of deference by four regional partners to Indonesia, whose membership had invested ASEAN with a measure of credibility. The prerogative approach reflected a strain in the Republic's foreign policy which provided continuity between the very different political systems of President Sukarno and President Suharto.[6] A regionally autonomous structure of order under Indonesia's guidance was an abiding aspiration but not one shared by its fellow member governments. Indonesia's regional vision challenged the logic of the balance of power which in South-East Asia had always been influenced by extra-regional forces. Such a perspective separated Indonesia from its regional partners, which still valued access to extra-regional sources of countervailing power. Singapore's government, for example, which was acutely apprehensive of any locally based regional dominance, strongly upheld the latter view. Such apprehension could be borne because Indonesia's prescription for regional order was devoid of operational utility when ASEAN was established. Its public endorsement did not impose the obligation of united action. The preamble to the Bangkok Declaration registered a claim and no more. For that reason, it could be upheld by governments which harboured misgivings about Indonesia's intent because of the declared linkage between national and regional resilience as well as the memory of Confrontation.

Despite serious reservations by some ASEAN governments about the implications of such linkage for the regional balance or distribution of power, the rhetoric of national resilience came to be accepted as the symbolic common denominator of corporate declaratory aspiration. If one overlooks the rhetorical dimension, the linked notions of national and regional resilience pointed to a security role of a practical kind for ASEAN defined with reference to intra-mural relations. Regional co-operation was not intended to serve the interest of common security through the projection of common power but through the mitigation and management of conflict and attendant economic development. That premiss, if not formally articulated, was dominant from the formation of ASEAN, even though during its early years the actual record of co-operation was marred by open discord and political disarray. The practice of regional co-operation took some time to approximate the theory, and then only in a limited way, as a consequence of alarming political changes in Indochina during 1975.

As the five governments began to develop the habit of political co-operation, ASEAN stood in a peripheral position to the locus of regional turbulence in Indochina. The practical security ideas which informed the day-to-day workings of ASEAN had no direct relevance to overcoming that turbulence. Indeed, the ASEAN states were only spectators to a series of fundamental changes with a direct bearing on the resolution of conflict in Indochina and on the regional balance of power. It was in this context of political impotence to influence events beyond its walls, that a second approach to regional security by ASEAN took form coloured by those ideas of Indonesian provenance incorporated in its founding declaration. It was prompted by the People's Republic of China, which took a seat in the United Nations in October 1971.

At a meeting in Kuala Lumpur in the following November, the foreign ministers of ASEAN enunciated a declaratory policy for regional security of an extra-mural scope. That policy was intended in the first instance to provide an alternative to an earlier unilateral initiative by Malaysia. In September 1970, during the meeting of heads of government of non-aligned states held in Lusaka, incoming Prime Minister Tun Abdul Razak had proposed that the region of South-East Asia be neutralised partly through the provision of guarantees by the major powers. That proposal provoked an unsympathetic response from Malaysia's regional partners. The formally non-aligned government of Indonesia, in particular, reacted with concern lest Malaysia's initiative serve as a means for corporate accommodation to China, which was viewed as the Republic's main external threat. In addition, strong objection was taken to a proposal whose terms conferred virtual policing rights on extra-regional powers. Such an arrangement was regarded as being in direct contradiction to Indonesia's vision of a regionally policed system of regional order.

In the event, the foreign ministers meeting, in an *ad hoc* capacity and not under ASEAN's auspices, reached an agreement on an alternative formula to the neutralisation proposal. A collective commitment to neutralisation, in principle, was overshadowed by and subordinated to support for a formula to establish a regional 'Zone of Peace, Freedom and Neutrality' (Zopfan).[7] This formula avoided the legal rigour of the concept of neutralisation and excluded any prerogative role in South-East Asia for major powers. Devoid of operational relevance, this vague alternative proved to be an acceptable compromise. Its terms did not impose any practical obligations on member governments. As a statement of general aspiration only, none of those governments had a strong reason to quarrel publicly with the proposition that South-East Asia should be insulated from the intruding rivalries of external powers and that its political destinies should rest in the charge of its resident states. The proposition was also not in conflict with ASEAN's working consensus over collective internal security. None the less, the corporate endorsement of the Zone of Peace gave security ideas of Indonesian provenance a higher profile and correspondingly reinforced ASEAN's claim to prescribe for regional order as indicated in the Bangkok Declaration. Such corporate prescription, however, took ASEAN out of its political depth because such a claim could not be underpinned by corporate capability. It was devoid of immediate utility other than to serve as a reference point for and symbol of intra-ASEAN solidarity. In point of fact, it could only serve as a basis for such solidarity as long as it was devoid of operational intent. When it became an object of such intent, then intra-mural differences over strategic perspective took their toll of ASEAN solidarity. In the meantime the Zopfan formula was held in abeyance as revolutionary change in Indochina reached a culmination during 1975.

The ASEAN states responded to revolutionary change in Indochina by convening their first meeting of heads of government on the island of Bali in Indonesia in February 1976. The Bali meeting was significant for a decision to place political co-operation on a formal footing. The collective internal security role of the Association was reaffirmed within a Declaration of ASEAN Concord which incorporated, almost in passing, the Zone of Peace formula.[8] Institutional progress was indicated by a decision to establish a permanent central secretariat but defence co-operation under ASEAN's auspices was rejected quite categorically. In practical terms, the operational security doctrine of ASEAN had not advanced substantively since its initial expression in 1967. The Association had approached security co-operation through political co-operation but it was prevented by its ideological identity from expanding geographically to provide a wider framework for such co-operation. To the revolutionary successor states of Indochina, ASEAN's provenance and credentials were tainted. For their part, the member governments saw only difficulty in a wider structure of relationships involving Communist participation. There was an absence of serious interest on either side in expanding the bounds of regional partnership.

Under these circumstances, a more limited collective initiative was undertaken to strengthen regional security. That initiative incorporated an extra-mural focus, at least in principle. The Declaration of ASEAN Concord had made reference to the settlement of intra-regional disputes by peaceful means. To serve this end, a Treaty of Amity and Co-operation was concluded at Bali.[9] Its terms were conventional, drawing its primary inspiration from the Charter of the United Nations. Provision was made for a High Council with powers of recommendation but the treaty placed prime emphasis on the sanctity of national sovereignty. Such an emphasis had informed the workings of ASEAN from the outset but it had never been articulated in such an explicit manner. A notable feature of the treaty was that it contained a provision for accession by regional states outside of ASEAN. As such, it was intended to serve as a political bridge beyond the bounds of the Association, particularly to a united Communist Vietnam. The envisaged support for such a bridge was an accord on state practice, especially a common respect for the national sovereignty of all signatories. The treaty was designed to provide a basic code of conduct for stable state relationships which Vietnam might be persuaded to endorse in the interests of regional accommodation and order. It represented an attempt to expand the bounds of interrelated political and security co-operation without confronting the intractable problem of expanding ASEAN's membership. A reference in the preamble to the treaty to the Kuala Lumpur Declaration in November 1971 indicated a complementary link with the Zone of Peace formula. As such, it constituted an attempt to sink regional foundations for regional order, a vital prerequisite to any prerogative approach to that condition.

The Treaty of Amity and Friendship was a modest undertaking but it did not attract the interest of the revolutionary governments of Indochina. On the contrary, the attempt by the ASEAN states to establish a regional meeting point over security concerns met with strong resistance. The Vietnamese and Laotian governments in particular not only ignored the opportunity to adhere to the treaty (as did that of Kampuchea) but also repudiated publicly the Zone of Peace formula. By putting forward an alternative proposal for regional order at the meeting of heads of government of non-aligned states in Colombo in August 1976, they succeeded in excluding the Zone of Peace from the final communique, despite its presence in the corresponding communique of the preceding summit in Algiers. In effect, Vietnam and Laos had set out to deny recognition to ASEAN as an appropriate vehicle for managing regional security beyond its intra-mural scope. Its declaratory position was deemed unacceptable because of its tainted credentials.

The experience of those ASEAN governments (Indonesia, Malaysia and Singapore) represented at Colombo caused them frustration and alarm. The blatant challenge to the regional credentials of the Association had the effect of strengthening corporate solidarity. In the process, an extra-mural security function of ASEAN was made manifest. It had been identified early on by Thanat Khoman, Thailand's Foreign Minister at ASEAN's formation, who had devised the term 'collective political defence'. He had employed it first in the late 1960s when searching for alternatives to reliance on the United States which had already begun to revise its policy for Vietnam.[10] Seven years later, a corporate ability to close ranks against an external source of intimidation was demonstrated when ASEAN became the object of hostile attention. Irrespective of the efficacy of so-called collective political defence, the attitude of Vietnam's representatives at Colombo demonstrated the difficulty of trying to extend beyond ASEAN the bounds of even limited co-operation over regional security. The only practical option was for member governments to explore the prospects for a *modus vivendi* with Vietnam on a bilateral basis. Opportunity to do so arose when the government in Hanoi began to exhibit growing concern over joined contention with Kampuchea and China and in consequence set out to repair regional relationships. But as the preliminary rounds to the Third Indochina War over Kampuchea got under way, ASEAN found itself once again relegated to the role of a spectator to regional events of major political moment. Its venture in seeking to expand the scope of its security ideas beyond an initial developmental approach had proved abortive. Yet, when the issue of conflict between Vietnam and Democratic Kampuchea was joined in violence, the central philosophy of the treaty employed in that venture became relevant to the diplomatic position adopted by ASEAN requiring the instrumentality of collective political defence.

Vietnam's invasion of Kampuchea on 25 December 1978, facilitated by a prior treaty of friendship with the Soviet Union, marked a turning point in ASEAN's attempt to assume a regional security role. One compelling reason why the governments of ASEAN felt obliged to oppose openly Vietnam's forward policy in Indochina was their concern to uphold the sanctity of national sovereignty, enthroned in their Treaty of Amity and Co-operation. The five governments could not afford to endorse by default such a blatant regional violation of the cardinal rule of the society of states without damaging the credibility of ASEAN. To have done so would have indicated tolerance for a precedent with disturbing implications for the security of all member states. A corporate challenge to Vietnam was required also for reasons of intra-ASEAN cohesion. More than principle had been violated as a result of Vietnam's invasion and occupation of Kampuchea – so had the security environment of Thailand. The presence of Vietnamese troops in an independent capacity along the border between Kampuchea and Thailand was historically unprecedented. That military presence, in addition to one in neighbouring Laos, foreshadowed the consolidation of a new centre of regional power by a traditional adversary of a profoundly more disturbing nature than that forged by French colonialism during the nineteenth century. At stake for Thailand, in particular, was whether or not Vietnam would consolidate its position as the dominant power in Indochina. That question raised the proverbial issue of the balance of power. Vietnam had sought to revise the balance in its favour through an act of force. ASEAN, however, was not capable of responding as a conventional security partnership. It could not contemplate matching force with force. Diplomatic challenge or collective political defence was its only recourse in displaying solidarity with Thailand. And such a challenge on its own was not appropriate or adequate to the task assumed.

Because Thailand had been confronted by a security threat which ASEAN could not counter physically, its government sought access to more efficacious sources of countervailing power. Indeed the projection of such power, particularly by China, served to underpin and sustain ASEAN's diplomatic challenge to Vietnam. The imperative of challenge accelerated the momentum of political co-operation among member governments, enhancing in turn ASEAN's international standing. However, because its diplomatic challenge could not stand on its own and was dependent on external military support, the theory and the practice of regional security collided. ASEAN became a party to a structure of external intervention justified with reference to respect for national sovereignty, the essential prerequisite for any system of regional order either between the ASEAN states or for the whole of South-East Asia. But that intervening structure, required in the specific interests of Thai security, stood in direct contradiction to the Association's ideal design for regional order; namely a Zone of Peace, Freedom and Neutrality. A consequence of that contradiction was to introduce tensions into a set of special relationships strengthened through political co-operation. Collective political defence in the corporate (but specifically Thailand's) interest had mixed security benefits.

There were misgivings, particularly on the part of Indonesia and Malaysia, who have regarded China and not Vietnam as their main source of external threat. The prospect of Vietnam as the dominant power in Indochina was viewed by them with mixed feelings. They were more apprehensive that an open-ended commitment to principle would distort their own national security priorities. At the root of such misgivings was a general fear that ASEAN's engagement in the conflict over Kampuchea would serve to entrench the rivalries of external powers so returning South-East Asia to the condition which it had experienced during the first two Indochina wars. Regional subordination and not regional autonomy would be South-East Asia's enduring fate.

From January 1979, despite such misgivings, the governments of ASEAN have demonstrated an ability to speak and act most of the time with one voice over Kampuchea. The Association has drawn on regional credentials to play a major diplomatic role in denying international legitimacy to the administration carried into Phnom Penh literally in the saddle bags of the Vietnamese army. In addition, Vietnam has been placed in a position of relative diplomatic isolation. The ability to make such an impact as a diplomatic community has been a product only in part of the development and display of a collegial identity. As indicated above, ASEAN's diplomatic role has been effective also because of the overall impact of a wider structure of alignments directed against Vietnam to which it became a party. The nature of that structure, which incorporated a burgeoning tacit alliance between Thailand and China, has served to impose a strain on corporate dealings within ASEAN over its regional role. It would be an exaggeration to describe ASEAN as a house divided against itself over Kampuchea. None the less, the governments of the Association have been privately and sometimes publicly at odds over how to reconcile their individual security interests with the collective diplomatic stance sustained since January 1979.

The conflict over Kampuchea has been a mixed blessing for ASEAN. It has demonstrated the strengths and weaknesses of an Association which has never been able to contemplate a conventional security role yet which has sought to prescribe for regional order. Its strengths have been displayed in corporate solidarity through political co-operation. Its weaknesses have arisen less from deficiencies in aggregate capability than from failings of consensus because the acute problem of regional security which has confronted ASEAN over Kampuchea has leant itself to a differentiation of member governments' interests. At issue has been the question of whether or not Vietnam will become the dominant power in Indochina. Coping with that prospect, irrespective of ASEAN's own capability to deny it, is totally different from forging an intra-mural consensus over collective internal security or from enunciating a declaratory regional design. Before Vietnam's invasion of Kampuchea, it had not been deemed necessary for ASEAN to tackle such a problem in a direct sense. After the success of revolutionary Communism in Indochina during 1975, the only practical course for corporate action was to try to promote a measure of regional co-existence in the face of a *fait accompli* which could not be challenged by ASEAN. Such a course of action did not divide member governments then because alternative options reflecting divergent strategic perspective were not available.

In the case of Kampuchea, the advent in April 1975 of an obdurately independent Communist state came to be acceptable in balance-of-power terms in Bangkok. That state assumed the role of a territorial buffer interposed between Thailand and a unified Vietnam, denying its assertion of dominance over the whole of Indochina. Such a situation was tolerable also in Jakarta. The inter-Communist balance of power in the peninsula appeared to be holding in check the competing influences of both China and Vietnam without provoking contention between Thailand and Indonesia. It was only after Vietnam had invaded Kampuchea and revised that balance to Thailand's and China's disadvantage, that the governments of ASEAN were confronted with a regional security issue of truly divisive significance. In January 1979 those governments adopted a common stand justified with reference to principle; namely, respect for Kampuchea's sovereign status. Their diplomatic response foreshadowed the assertive role which the Association would play as a party to the protracted conflict. In taking such a stand ASEAN engaged itself in the practice of the balance of power, despite lacking both the appropriate military capability and the common strategic perspective required for such an undertaking. That engagement drew it into a wider coalition ranged against Vietnam whose other members provided the coercive and material capability which ASEAN lacked. That coalition by its very nature has represented at best complementary rather than common interests.

For ASEAN, one consequence of embarking upon a diplomatic confrontation of Vietnam as a member of a wider coalition has been to place its declared regional security goals in contradiction to one another. In order to uphold the sanctity of national sovereignty, ASEAN has been obliged to compromise over its declaratory formula for regional order. That formula has the ideal purpose of insulating South-East Asia from the intruding rivalries of external powers. But in prosecuting a diplomatic challenge to Vietnam, the ASEAN states have become parties to a structure of regional conflict fuelled and sustained by competing external powers. In the face of contradictions in declared policy goals, ASEAN governments have been obliged to uphold one set in preference to the other. The sanctity of national sovereignty is the most sacred corporate value. Over Kampuchea it has been joined to the imperative of intra-ASEAN solidarity in support of Thailand, thus taking pride of place.

Paradoxically, provision for intra-mural solidarity has had the effect of testing it. The intra-mural differences which have arisen as a consequence have been accommodated rather than reconciled. The requirement for accommodation in order not to prejudice corporate accomplishment points to a structural flaw in ASEAN as an embryonic security organisation with a regional ambit. It has been less than fully equipped to assume such a role only in part because of limitations in its aggregate military capability. At least as significant has been the inability to forge a unifying strategic perspective based on a common definition of external threat. Continued divergence on that score stands in the way of a truly common approach to regional security.

The security ideas identified with ASEAN reflect the intergovernmental character of the Association. In intra-mural scope they express consensus among regional partners over upholding the political identity and integrity of each member state, irrespective of stature. Security co-operation takes the practical form of dispute management in the context of a common commitment to economic development conceived as an instrument for promoting political order. Intra-mural co-operation is based on a shared sense of vulnerability with reference to internal threat which may be exploited from afar. That intra-mural perspective does not have a corresponding extra-mural expression. Accordingly, prescription for regional order has assumed a declaratory form in the main, accommodating a longstanding vision held by Indonesian governments. More practical prescription for regional order arising from intra-mural priorities has stressed the sanctity of national sovereignty. The violation of such sanctity in the case of Kampuchea has required not only resort to the instrumentality of collective political defence but also participation in an alignment extending beyond South-East Asia. Such participation has gone against the grain of declaratory policy, to the dismay of Indonesia in particular. In a sense, ASEAN has become ensnared in the Kampuchean conflict, to which it is only a diplomatic party and then not of central significance. Its corporate stand has served as a basis for solidarity and for displaying a quality of diplomatic community but in the process an underlying intra-mural tension has developed. Yet, any attempt to disengage from that conflict to the evident advantage of Vietnam would almost certainly be even more damaging to the cohesion and viability of the Association.

Thailand could not be expected to place the cohesion of ASEAN before provision for its own security, for which it undertakes recourse to extra-regional sources of countervailing power.[11]

Despite weaknesses inherent in its structure and reflected in contending security ideas, ASEAN has become a regional actor of some consequence. It has established itself as an important factor in the political calculations of both regional and extra-regional states. Its record of political co-operation and diplomatic practice has made it a corporate party to the settlement of regional problems. This preliminary discussion of both common and contending regional security ideas has been intended to serve as a point of entry for exploring ASEAN's institutional evolution and role as a diplomatic community. It has been in this role that the Association has sought to provide for the security of South-East Asia.

Notes

1. See Franklin B. Weinstein, 'The Meaning of National Security in Southeast Asia', *Bulletin of Atomic Scientists,* November 1978; Mohammed Ayoob 'Regional Security in the Third World', in Mohammed Ayoob (ed.) *Regional Security in the Third World*, Croom Helm, London, 1986, Chapter 1.

2. Tan Sri M Ghazalie Shafie, *ASEAN: Contribution to Stability and Development*, address at Fletcher School of Law and Diplomacy, 11 November 1981, Ministry of Foreign Affairs, Kuala Lumpur, 1982.

3. *Straits Times*, 3 March 1966

4. *Regionalism in South-East Asia*, Centre for Strategic and International Studies, Jakarta, 1975, p. 8

5. ASEAN Declaration, reprinted in Association of South-East Asian Nations, *ASEAN Documents Series, 1967–1985*, ASEAN Secretariat, Jakarta, 1985, p. 17

6. For a discussion of that continuity with reference to the management of regional order, see Michael Leifer, *Indonesia's Foreign Policy*, Allen & Unwin, London, 1983

7. *ASEAN Documents Series*, 1967–1985, op. cit., p. 21

8. *Ibid.*, pp. 22–5

9. *Ibid.*, pp. 26–8

10. In *Foreign Affairs Bulletin*, Ministry of Foreign Affairs, Bangkok,

August–September 1968; and in an interview in *Far Eastern Economic Review*, 12 June 1969

11. See Muthiah Alagappa, *The National Security of Developing States: Lessons from Thailand*, Auburn House Publishing, Dover, MA, 1987, p. 105

2

The Evolution of ASEAN:
Faltering Steps in Regional Reconciliation

ASEAN was the institutional product of regional conflict resolution. When the Association was established in August 1967, only twelve months had elapsed since a political settlement had put an end to Indonesia's Confrontation of Malaysia.[1] In Jakarta and Kuala Lumpur, it was agreed that the settlement would stand a better chance of enduring if buffered by a wider structure of regional co-operation. Initial accord was lacking, however, on the appropriate terms of reference for such a structure. Malaysia's Prime Minister, Tunku Abdul Rahman, still harboured misgivings about Indonesia because President Sukarno had not yet been silenced politically. Ultimate accord owed much to the diplomatic initiative and role of Thailand's Foreign Minister, Thanat Khoman, who believed that regional co-operation would contribute to regional security. Bangkok served therefore as the logical venue for ASEAN's inaugural meeting. Thailand had not become embroiled in Confrontation. Its government had been engaged in mediation not only between Indonesia and Malaysia but also between Malaysia and the Philippines, whose claim to Sabah in Northern Borneo had antedated and then become part of Indonesia's confrontation policy.[2] The problem of regional reconciliation was not confined to Malaysia's experience of contention with Indonesia and the Philippines, however. Every member state brought bilateral problems within the walls of the Association.

The government of Thailand provided the venue and much diplomatic impetus for the collective act of regional reconciliation, but it too was not free of latent tensions with a prospective regional partner. The Thai government was concerned that its counterpart in Kuala Lumpur was sympathetic to irredentist sentiment within

Malaysia towards the co-religionist Muslim-Malay population who inhabited Thailand's southernmost provinces. The political boundary between a predominantly Buddhist Thailand and Malaysia had been established as a result of colonial demarcation. The Thai government was apprehensive lest Malaysia take steps to move that boundary northwards to coincide with the line of religious-cultural division between Buddhists and Muslims.[3] Correspondingly, the Malaysian government believed that the government in Bangkok had been less than vigorous in co-operating to eliminate the military wing of the Malayan Communist Party which had retreated to redoubts along the Thai–Malaysian border from the mid-1950s. The Thais were suspected of tolerating a Communist buffer zone as an obstacle to irredentism. On the surface, the bilateral relationship was sound, but it was not free of difficulty because of the common border.

The fifth founding member of ASEAN, the island-republic of Singapore, was the least secure despite the settlement of Confrontation. Its government viewed its closest neighbours, Indonesia and Malaysia, as potential adversaries. Singapore had been ejected from Malaysia in August 1965, less than two years after it had joined the new federation. Political separation and an unsolicited independence had been the imposed solution to the emotionally charged problem of how to accommodate the predominantly ethnic Chinese island within a federal structure based on Malay-Muslim political dominance. Separation had occurred before the external threat of Confrontation, directed also at Singapore, had begun to diminish. The unique circumstances of an enforced independence generated an acute sense of vulnerability among the political leaders of the island-state.[4] Singapore was wedged physically between two tense bilateral relationships. Its interposing location seemed even more precarious when during early 1966 the diplomacy of reconciliation was conducted exclusively between Jakarta and Kuala Lumpur.

A fresh start in regional co-operation seemed ready made for a vulnerable Singapore as a way of coping with geopolitical adversity. The opportunity of membership in ASEAN, however, was viewed with mixed feelings. It was welcomed as a way of managing bilateral tensions within a wider institutional context which might also compensate economically for the loss of a hinterland. It was adopted also with misgivings because of a suspicion that ASEAN was intended to serve as a vehicle for Indonesia's regional ambitions, possibly in collusion with

Malaysia. Singapore's apprehensions expressed in an acute form a fundamental problem confronting any regional association with a pre-history of contention among its members. Regional co-operation was undertaken in ASEAN's case in order to transform contention into partnership but institutional form in itself was not a sure recipe for conflict resolution and mutual trust.

At the outset, ASEAN was faced with overcoming the legacy of contention which had obstructed the progress of a prior but more limited undertaking in regional co-operation. The Association of Southeast Asia (ASA), established in July 1961 by Thailand, Malaya, and the Philippines, had fallen victim to such contention. Before it could assume a viable institutional identity, the Philippine claim to Sabah caused a suspension of its activities.[5] Filipino opportunism in establishing a united front with Indonesia in opposition to the advent of Malaysia made ASA a casualty of wider conflict.

That conflict gave rise to a tripartite diplomacy which produced an even more short-lived enterprise in regional association which ignored the moribund ASA. As a result of a series of conferences which convened in Manila during 1963, the governments of Malaya, the Philippines and Indonesia agreed to establish a so-called confederal entity dubbed 'Maphilindo' in acronymic correspondence to the names of its three participants. Maphilindo was a diplomatic device ostensibly intended to reconcile contending interests over the legitimacy and territorial bounds of Malaysia. Genuine reconciliation proved impossible to attain, however. The advent of the confederation served only to paper over fundamental differences of political interest. In the event, Maphilindo foundered with the formation of Malaysia on 16 September 1963. It did not assume any kind of institutional existence beyond its declaratory establishment.

The structure of regional conflict which disrupted ASA and which gave rise to the spurious and short-lived Maphilindo was mixed. The Philippine claim to Sabah was sustained by a heady domestic politics which made for difficulty in regional co-operation. But it was not necessarily an insuperable obstacle to its revival. The Philippines and Malaya/Malaysia were led by governments of matching political and economic dispositions and external affiliations. They enjoyed corresponding perspectives on regional security. Moreover, President Marcos, who came to office in January 1966, had not been tied personally to the Sabah claim. More fundamental an obstacle had been the radical political culture of Indonesia under the leadership of President Sukarno, who had repudiated ASA because of its anti-Communist and pro-Western disposition. A fresh start in wider regional co-operation through ASEAN became possible only with the enthusiastic participation of an Indonesia transformed in political identity. That its population and territory were larger than those of all the other members combined lent substance to the initiative.

Confrontation had been halted as a consequence of fundamental political change within the Republic, set in train by an abortive coup launched in the early hours of 1 October 1965. The challenge to the legitimacy of Malaysia had drawn much of its dynamic force from the competitive structure of Indonesia's political system of Guided Democracy. When that structure was dismantled at the expense of both Indonesia's Communist Party and President Sukarno with the conservative Armed Forces led by General Suharto as the prime political beneficiary, Confrontation ceased to perform the same domestic political function. It was then no longer necessary to manage the turbulence of Indonesia's political life with reference to an external threat.[6] The succeeding military establishment did not have any need of an adventurist foreign policy that only alienated those Western governments with the resources and motive to assist Indonesia to recover from a condition of economic decay. That military establishment was vehemently anti-Communist but none the less shared Sukarno's proprietory approach to regional order. They still had misgivings about Malaysia because of Britain's hand in its formation, as well as about Singapore because of its predominantly ethnic-Chinese identity and economic role. They were also conscious of a regional mistrust of Indonesia and therefore envisaged better prospects for pursuing regional ambition by attracting the willing co-operation of neighbouring states, including recent adversaries.

Political change in Indonesia, reflected in revised international priorities, was decisive in facilitating a new start in regional co-operation. The point was well made by the late Adam Malik, who was Indonesia's Foreign Minister when ASEAN was formed:

> Although from the outset ASEAN was conceived as an organisation for economic, social and cultural co-operation, and although considerations in these fields were no doubt central, it was the fact that there was a convergence in the political outlook of the five prospective member nations, both with regard to national priority objectives as on the question

of how best to secure these objectives in the emergent strategic configuration of East Asia which provided the main stimulus to join together in ASEAN.[7]

In this statement made more than seven years after the advent of ASEAN, Malik was undoubtedly stretching the degree of consensus attained among representatives of the founding governments who assembled in Bangkok in August 1967. He was correct, however, in identifying the importance of a convergence of political outlook. That convergence, to which Indonesia was a party, widened the basis of conformity necessary for revival of regional co-operation.

Convergence of political outlook did not mean a ready-made consensus about how to proceed. The formation of ASEAN required extensive negotiations over a period of twelve months. Indonesia's military establishment, led by General Suharto, wanted a fresh start in regional co-operation, but governments in Malaysia, the Philippines, and Singapore reacted to that prospect with some reserve. Malaysia had been willing to rediscover ties of kith and kin with Indonesia in negotiating an end to Confrontation, but its Prime Minister Tunku Abdul Rahman was not ready to dispense with ASA, which had reconvened officially in March 1966 with a meeting in Bangkok. He required convincing that an undertaking alternative to one with which he was personally identified would be worthwhile. General Suharto's public commitment to 'revive the idea of Maphilindo in a wider sphere'[8] had not encouraged him because of its association with Confrontation. It had been made early in a period of political transition in Indonesia to demonstrate that its new rulers would not compromise an independent foreign policy by joining a regional enterprise such as ASA that was only recently derided because of its client-state associations. President Sukarno was still fighting for his political life, and General Suharto was determined not to allow him to charge that Indonesia had been humbled by agreeing to join a tainted association.[9] For the established members of ASA, however, Indonesia's terms for a fresh start in regional co-operation were controversial and politically disturbing. Although repudiating Confrontation and not pushing for a wider Maphilindo in name, Indonesia's government insisted on stamping its own imprint on the new venture in regional co-operation. More to the point, that imprint drew direct inspiration from the ideology of Maphilindo, which was identified with the radical rhetoric of Sukarno and his controversial Foreign Minister,

Dr Subandrio. It had stressed a regionally self-reliant approach to the management of security and was implicity critical of those regional states that made provision for security through dependence on external powers.

Representatives of the five prospective members of ASEAN met to discuss its terms of reference, initially in the Thai resort of Bangsaen. Indonesia's Foreign Minister proceeded to disinter the themes of Maphilindo. He argued for an approach to regional security virtually identical to that embodied in the documents produced by the tripartite conferences held in Manila during 1963. As a result, prospective regional partners revived doubts about the political *bona fides* of the Republic's new leaders. A proprietory view of regional order expressed in an insistence on the subordinate role of all external powers and which questioned the legitimacy of foreign (i.e. Western) military bases in the region was difficult to accept for those states which had been on the receiving end of Confrontation. They had resisted Indonesia's blandishments because of access to external sources of countervailing power which were still regarded as of direct practical relevance to national security. The prospect of accommodating a local preponderance of power was in no way appealing. That underlying concern had been made explicit shortly after independence by Singapore's first head of state, Yusof bin Ishak. He remarked: 'So many of our neighbours and we ourselves would not have a separate existence if purely Asian forces were to settle the shape of decolonized Asia.'[10] For its part, the government of the Philippines resented the challenge to its security relationship with the United States which maintained major military bases on the island of Luzon.

In the event, despite strong objections from Singapore and the Philippines, as well as reservations from Malaysia, Indonesia's insistence on incorporating some of the themes of Maphilindo prevailed. Their resistance was overcome because Adam Malik managed to persuade them that domestic political considerations governed Indonesia's attitude, in particular the need to neutralise Sukarno and his supporters. By then, Tunku Abdul Rahman had been more assured of the genuine nature of Suharto's political commitment by cross-border co-operation against Communist insurgents in Northern Borneo. Other regional partners were equally accommodating, encouraged by Thailand's Foreign Minister who had been responsible for a negotiating draft inspired by Indonesia's priorities. As a result, the conventional wisdom of a regional outlook which spanned both the Sukarno and Suharto administrations was incorporated in the preamble to the ASEAN Declaration. It was affirmed *inter alia* that the countries of South-East Asia shared a primary responsibility for strengthening the economic and social stability of the region and that they were determined to ensure their stability and security from external interference in any form or manifestation. In addition, it was maintained that all foreign bases were temporary and were not intended to be used directly or indirectly to subvert the national independence and freedom of states in the area.[11] Those prerogative provisions included in the preamble at Indonesia's behest did not express a true concordance of interests, however. Their endorsement is best understood as an intra-mural concession; not as an expression of genuine consensus about how to manage regional order. Such declaratory concession to Indonesia's priorities was intended to accelerate a process of regional reconciliation on the unstated assumption that the post-Sukarno government in Jakarta would conduct its foreign policy with practical deference to the political sensibilities of its new-found regional partners. For its part, Indonesia compromised over nomenclature. An initial proposal for a 'South-East Asian Association for Regional Co-operation' was withdrawn in favour of ASEAN, a term devised by Adam Malik which gave the impression of continuity with ASA. One contemporary observer commented: 'In essence, the creation of ASEAN means that ASA rather than disappearing has simply been enlarged and given a new name.'[12]

In form, ASEAN constituted an amalgamation of the membership of ASA and Maphilindo, Indonesia's approaches to Burma and Cambodia having been rebuffed. It also incorporated a mixture of ideas from the two moribund regional enterprises. If incorporating Maphilindo themes had caused a measure of consternation, they were tolerated as a declaratory expression of Indonesia's regional vision in order to channel the underlying ambition of the Republic within a structure of diplomatic constraint. In that respect, the formation of ASEAN bears some resemblance to the development of the Inter-American System, which achieved institutional form as the Organisation of American States. The political encapsulation of the United States within a structure of regional organisation was contemplated as both a way of catering for the natural political ambition of the most powerful regional state and of trying to contain its objectionable interventionist disposition. Indonesia was the object of this kind of calculation which was well understood in Jakarta in August 1967.

The initial outlook for regional co-operation was mixed, despite the diplomatic achievement of getting the multilateral enterprise under way. Regional reconciliation proceeded hand in hand with a general uncertainty about the prospect for regional environment. The moment of formation was virtually coincident with Britain's initial decision to disengage militarily from east of Suez and with the high point of U.S. military intervention in Vietnam. The prospect of an end to the Vietnam War was a factor in the calculations that led to ASEAN.[13] With no end in sight, however, ASEAN was hardly a security alternative for governments in Bangkok and Manila, both military parties to the U.S. effort to uphold the separate political identity of South Vietnam. Indeed, Thailand despatched its first contingent of troops to Vietnam in the month following ASEAN's formation. The primary declared purpose of the Association was 'to accelerate the economic growth, social progress and cultural development in the region through joint endeavours in the spirit of equality and partnership'. This purpose was indicative of the limited practical expectations of the member governments as well as of a concern to avoid becoming a centre of regional controversy. In order not to lend credence to charges that a substitute for the ill-fated South-East Asia Treaty Organisation (SEATO) was in the making, active collaboration was restricted to 'matters of common interest in the economic, social, cultural, technical, scientific and administrative fields'. A secondary interest was expressed in promoting regional peace and stability but only on the basis of a common adherence to conventional international norms without accompanying anti-Communist rhetoric. Those norms were 'respect for justice and the rule of law in the relationship among countries of the region and adherence to the principles of the United Nations Charter'. This commitment to the ideal values of the society of states did not imply any accord to realise those aspirations about regional order which had been included in the preamble to the ASEAN Declaration at Indonesia's insistence.

ASEAN was established as a conventional intergovernmental grouping in direct lineal descent from both ASA and Maphilindo. If some of the ideas which informed the declaratory aspirations of the Association were derived from the rhetoric of Maphilindo, the practical goals and the institutional form derived directly from the model and limited experience of ASA. The founding document was a multilateral declaration and not a treaty establishing a legal regime embodying a commitment to some form of political integration. Sovereignty was not at issue, except that the object of the corporate exercise was to reaffirm it. Intergovernmental form was confirmed at the outset when it was agreed that the Association would be managed by an annual meeting of foreign ministers to be convened in member states on a rotating basis. Doubt about the institutionalisation of that practice was indicated in the provision for meetings to 'be convened as required'. The policy role of such meetings was not clearly defined to begin with, but over time the rotating annual assembly of foreign ministers has assumed ultimate responsibility for all policy guidelines for the Association. With only one interruption in 1970, annual meetings of foreign ministers have been held with regularity, and from 1976 they have taken place at mid-year. Before February 1976, when political co-operation was placed on a formal footing at the first meeting of heads of government, a number of *ad hoc* meetings of ASEAN foreign ministers were convened to deal with specific regional issues. Up to then, however, such meetings had not been dignified with the prefix ASEAN. From February 1976 the foreign ministers of the Association have met both on an *ad hoc* basis according to regional circumstances, as well as annually, but as formal partners putting forward a single corporate view on behalf of ASEAN.

Provision was not made in the ASEAN Declaration for meetings of heads of government. Indeed, multinational summitry on the European model has not become standard practice. In February 1976 the first meeting of ASEAN heads of government convened on the Indonesian island of Bali, where it was agreed that further meetings would be called 'as and when necessary'. In August of the following year, a second such meeting was held in Kuala Lumpur to commemorate the tenth anniversary of ASEAN's formation. A third meeting was long delayed partly because of continuing differences between Malaysia and the Philippines over Sabah. A firm decision to convene such a meeting was not taken until after the overthrow of President Marcos in February 1986. Because of a longstanding obligation to hold a third summit in Manila, it had been deemed impolitic to tarnish the corporate reputation of the Association by appearing to lend support to the decaying political system of the Philippine President. Summitry has been approached with some caution because of apprehension that an inability to demonstrate concrete achievement on such an occasion would ill serve the interests of ASEAN.[14] A third summit was held in Manila in December 1987 to inaugurate the Association's third decade but the annual meeting of foreign ministers has retained the political importance indicated in the founding declaration. In Manila the heads of government agreed to meet every three to five years, but only 'if necessary'. From the time of the Bali summit it became standard practice for sets of other ministers, especially those with economic responsibilities, to meet at regular intervals but they all report to the annual meeting of foreign ministers which has remained at the apex of ASEAN's institutional structure. In practice, however, such meetings usually endorse rather than formulate policy guidelines. Such guidelines have been worked out since 1971 through a prior process of consultation and bargaining conducted by senior officials, involving permanent heads of respective foreign ministries. The Senior Officials Meeting has become the prime vehicle of intra-ASEAN co-operation, albeit without being accorded a formal place in the Association's institutional structure.

At the outset it was agreed also that an annually rotating Standing Committee would 'carry on the work of the Association in between meetings of Foreign Ministers'. That committee comprises the foreign minister of the state due to act as host for the forthcoming annual ministerial meeting, who serves as chairman, as well as the resident ambassadors and high commissioners of the other member states. That peripatetic arrangement has stood the test of time and has not been disturbed by the establishment of a permanent ASEAN Secretariat in Jakarta in June 1976. That Secretariat has enjoyed only a limited service responsibility relating to economic and technical co-operation and public information. A clear indication of its subordinate place within the institutional structure of the Association is that its head carries the title of Secretary-General of the ASEAN Secretariat and *not* of ASEAN. Moreover, he does not serve as a channel of communication with non-member governments. The Secretary-General held office initially for two years at a time, extended to three from 1986. The post circulates among the member states, although the incumbent works from Jakarta and is normally an expendable member of a national bureaucracy. The Secretary-General of the ASEAN Secretariat is responsible to the Association's annual ministerial meeting when in session and to its Standing Committee at all other times. His staff are seconded from member bureaucracies for limited tours and are organised into three bureaus dealing respectively with economics, science and technology and socio-cultural affairs.

In its activities the ASEAN Secretariat has not in any way

superseded national secretariats located in the foreign ministries of member states as provided for in the founding declaration. Their role was identified as 'to carry out the work of the Association on behalf of that country and to service the Annual or Special Meetings of Foreign Ministers, the Standing Committee and such other committees as may hereafter be established'. These separate bureaucratic structures headed by Directors-General have played the prime role in servicing the principal meetings and committees with the ASEAN Secretariat relegated to a subordinate position. That role has been reinforced by the peripatetic existence of the Standing Committee, which is reconstituted every year. That practice makes for institutional discontinuity to the advantage of the separate foreign ministries.[15]

The functional activities of ASEAN have expanded considerably since its formation. Besides the key policy committee of senior officials, eight committees with functional economic and technical responsibilities, with a host of subcommittees are distributed among member states. There is also a separate structure of committees responsible for conducting negotiations with external economic dialogue partners who comprise Australia, Canada, the European Community, Japan, the United States, and New Zealand. This expansion of activities has not given rise to any fundamental change in the organisational and political forms of the Association. For example, the opportunity to strengthen the role of the Secretariat was not taken when in July 1984 the foreign ministers considered the report of an ASEAN Task Force set up in 1982 to review and assess the performance of the Association and to recommend measures for improving it.[16] That report drew inspiration from the institutional experience of the European Community. And it was almost certainly for that reason that its recommendations were in the main unacceptable to member governments deeply suspicious of centrist tendencies. A commitment to strengthen the Secretariat was expressed only in an increase in staff and funds but not in any change in its limited role. The institutional structure and decision-making process were left untouched.[17] In corporate decision-making, ASEAN has abided by the principle of consensus which has meant that policy initiatives can arise only on the basis of a common denominator. This practice has been justified with reference to a regional cultural style which has enthroned consensus as the *modus operandi* of the Association.

At its formation, ASEAN was identified as representing 'the collective will of the nations of Southeast Asia to bind themselves together in friendship and co-operation'. This expression of ideal relationships took some time to evolve in practical terms and has been confined primarily to political co-operation exemplified by the sustained predominant role assumed by ASEAN's foreign ministers. Political co-operation has not been extended to include defence co-operation of even an informal multilateral kind. In September 1982 Singapore's Prime Minister, Lee Kuan Yew, advocated the introduction of multilateral military exercises but failed to attract a positive response from his regional partners. In the main, defence co-operation has been conducted on a bilateral basis but always outside of the ASEAN format. A conventional security role has not been sought, despite initial speculation to the contrary; certainly, the formal anatomy of ASEAN would not suggest one. Within its extensive committee structure there is no provision for formal liaison between government representatives with defence responsibilities although intelligence chiefs do hold an unpublicised annual meeting prior to that of the foreign ministers. The paradoxical quality of ASEAN indicated above has been present from the outset and sustained in that a conspicuous preoccupation with regional security has not been reflected explicitly in the bureaucratic structure of the Association. None the less, ASEAN in the course of its political and institutional evolution has come to play a security role of a kind. The capability it has displayed in this respect has arisen from a collegial identity acquired through political co-operation. But that identity and the attendant acquisition of regional credentials took some time to establish. Initially there was a tendency to write off the Association as a substitute for the ill-fated South-East Asia Treaty Organisation.

SEATO was the organisational structure for the Manila Pact of 1954 designed to contain Communist China. It was inspired by U.S. calculations of interest and backed by U.S. military capability. Although SEATO was disbanded in June 1977, the pact has not been revoked and Thailand and the Philippines remain signatories.[18] In security terms, however, ASEAN was in lineal descent to ASA, which had also attracted the charge that it was a substitute for SEATO. ASA was intended to be an embryonic alternative rather than a substitute for SEATO. Its model was employed to provide an operational security doctrine for ASEAN. In January 1959, during a visit to the Philippines, Malaya's Prime Minister, Tunku Abdul Rahman, had advanced a proposal for a South-East Asia Friendship and Economic Treaty. His proposal represented an attempt to break away from a military approach to problems of regional security, exemplified by the Manila Pact and SEATO which had failed to demonstrate its efficacy. The ideal objective was to confront problems of political stability through collective attention to their economic causes. The modest tripartite enterprise, which included Thailand and which emerged as a result of this initiative, was limited because of its scale and premature formation. Its declared aims were limited to economic and cultural co-operation but they were never expressed in even modest tangible achievements because ASA passed the greater part of its short-lived existence as a house divided.[19]

Despite its chequered existence and doubtful credentials (its members were either directly or indirectly linked to SEATO) ASA served as the practical model for ASEAN at its formation. It was much more practical as a guide for regional co-operation than Maphilindo from which the Association drew declaratory inspiration. That inspiration when transposed to the preamble of the ASEAN Declaration did not provide a tangible basis on which to begin regional co-operation. Despite its failings, ASA offered a better basis in collective consensus from which to proceed with regional co-operation with security in mind. As indicated above, the underlying premiss of ASA had incorporated an approach to regional security, albeit of an intra-mural kind. Co-operation among prospective regional partners was regarded as more than an end in itself. It was deemed relevant to tackling the domestic roots of insecurity. In the case of ASEAN, beyond overcoming Confrontation and collateral disputes, there was a corresponding goal: the institutionalisation of conflict management in order to permit a single-minded allocation of national resources to economic development. To the extent that there was assumed to be a positive relationship between economic development and political stability, regional co-operation within ASEAN could serve a security function. The founding governments of ASEAN were not of one mind over how to cope with the external dimension of regional security. They were agreed, however, on the common threat posed by internal revolutionary challenge. They were agreed also that its significant incidence in any one member state could not necessarily be isolated and contained and that such political contagion might spread to other member states. In other words, on the basis of a common concern that political instability would not necessarily be divisible among proximate partners, the modest, ostensibly non-political objectives of ASA were carried over intact to ASEAN. It was in this sense that ASEAN sought to address the security problems of its members, other than those external threats countered by its formation.

It was by adopting the premisses of ASA that ASEAN began its corporate existence. It did not address itself to conventional collective defence against any potential external aggressor. Its bureaucratic structure did not make any provision for such protection. Security was approached on a collective basis by way of regional reconciliation and a common agenda of concern over internal security problems to be coped with by giving national priority to economic development. However simplistic and idealised a view, ASEAN's security role was contemplated initially in these terms and as such the Association began its existence as a collective internal security organisation along the lines indicated in the previous chapter. In Jakarta, if not in all ASEAN capitals, it was assumed also that a judicious management of intra-mural tensions and containment of political instability through devotion to economic development would restrict the opportunity for predatory extra-regional powers to fish in troubled regional waters. To that extent, common attention to internal security would make provision for its external dimension beyond that engendered by regional reconciliation.

Whatever aspirations may have been entertained about the security role of ASEAN, the Association began its working life as a very modest inter-governmental enterprise. Its members consciously played down any such role in a region dominated by the Vietnam War. Their initial activities were limited to examining the prospects for economic co-operation, in part through reviving some of the abortive projects of ASA. Above all, the central priority was to cultivate a habit of harmony within the extended set of multilateral relationships. This goal proved to be difficult to attain. Acute tensions emerged within the ranks of the Association during its very first year so that the very viability of ASEAN appeared to be at risk. Hostility revived between governments in Kuala Lumpur and Manila whose relationship as partners within ASA had been upset before the formation of Malaysia because of the claim to Sabah. That issue survived the settlement of Confrontation which on Indonesia's part did not involve a claim to territory. As Confrontation was being brought to an end, however, there did seem to be a willingness in Manila to settle the Sabah issue by negotiations. Diplomatic relations broken off on the establishment of Malaysia were restored in June 1966, with ambassadors exchanged in the following month.

Although President Marcos had avoided any mention of the Sabah claim in his state of the nation address in January 1967, the dispute continued to disturb the relationship with Malaysia concurrent with multilateral discussions about the formation of ASEAN. For example, against the advice of its foreign ministry, the Philippine government refused an invitation to send observers to witness the first direct elections in Sabah, which were conducted in April. This decision was taken on the ground that the presence of Filipino observers might prejudice the validity of the claim to Sabah. In the event, the elections, attended by Indonesian observers, assumed the character of a plebiscite. The result, in favour of the local component of the ruling federal Alliance Party served to reaffirm Sabah's commitment to membership of Malaysia. Despite this episode, Malaysian–Philippine reconciliation within the wider framework of ASEAN appeared to go ahead uninterrupted.

Shortly after their joint participation in the formation of ASEAN, the governments in Kuala Lumpur and Manila confirmed the terms of an anti-smuggling agreement. The Philippines had long pressed for such an accord to help counter the extensive illegal trade across the Sulu Sea. That agreement, which was concluded in the Malaysian capital in September 1967, was a diplomatic success for the government in Manila. Malaysia agreed to permit the establishment of three Philippine customs liaison offices in Sabah. That the Philippines were prepared to conclude a treaty whose practical terms more than implied recognition of Malaysia's sovereignty over Sabah seemed to suggest, however, that if the territorial claim was not to be dropped officially for the time being, it would cease to be an irritant in relations between the two states. Indeed, when President Marcos and his wife paid a state visit to Malaysia in January 1968, the tone of the occasion seemed to confirm the extent of genuine reconciliation between the two ASEAN partners.

The quality of the restored relationship changed dramatically for the worse with the revelation in March of what became known as the Corregidor Affair. This was the name given to a bloody episode in a secret military camp on the island which had been the site of a memorable last stand by Filipino and U.S. soldiers against the invading Japanese in 1942. At the camp, an unknown number of Filipino Muslims recruited allegedly to train as insurgents for infiltration into Sabah were killed by their officers. A sole survivor maintained that the recruits had been shot when they had mutinied in reaction to harsh discipline and non-payment of wages. The full facts have never been established, although it is probable that the ill-fated undertaking, which ended in bloodshed, was intended to redirect Filipino–Muslim energies away from separatist sentiment then surfacing in the south of the country.

When the first accounts of the Corregidor Affair were made public, the Malaysian government responded with alarm reinforced by the prior arrest in Sabah of twenty-six armed Filipinos. In reaction, the Philippine government appeared to try to cover up its political embarrassment at home and abroad by reviving attention to the Sabah claim. In the ensuing acrimony, ASEAN was not the first resort of the two governments. It was not used either for containing tension or for dispute settlement. Malaysia, for its part, instructed its mission to the United Nations to report the matter to Secretary-General U Thant, while the Philippines adopted the view that the episode was purely an internal affair. The deliberate, if reactive, revival of the claim was discussed in a series of bilateral meetings held in Bangkok from June 1968 but they served only to aggravate the tense relationship. By mid-July those talks reached an acrimonious impasse breaking up when Malaysia's delegation walked out. The Permanent Head of Malaysia's Foreign Ministry pointedly remarked that the persistent pursuit of the claim to Sabah by the Philippines 'will [also] destroy any co-operation in the regional and international spheres such as ASEAN'.[20] The Philippine government responded to Malaysia's refusal to hold further talks by announcing the withdrawal of its ambassador and his staff from Kuala Lumpur.

ASEAN eventually became involved in the intra-mural dispute during the second meeting of its foreign ministers, which convened in Jakarta in August 1968. The Association was able to proceed with this meeting in part because the agenda was concerned with little more than fleshing out its bureaucratic structure. Apart from establishing an *ad hoc* committee to study financial aspects of ASEAN projects (many carried over from ASA), four permanent functional committees were set up. The joint communique comprised a terse text that barely amounted to two pages, including ritual statements of appreciation and political intent. It is relevant to record, however, that 'the Ministers reaffirmed their faith in the ASEAN Declaration as the expression of their collective will to attain stability and peace in the region as a prerequisite for the well-being and prosperity of the ASEAN people'.[21] Evidently, the issue of regional security was much on the minds of the five ministers in a year punctuated by the Tet Offensive in South Vietnam and the attendant decision by President Johnson to enter into negotiations with the Vietnamese communists. In addition, the British government had given notice in January 1968 of an accelerated military withdrawal from east of Suez. The Soviet Union had displayed capability and regional interest in March by deploying for the first time a naval squadron into the Indian Ocean from the South China Sea.

Against a background of disturbing regional events, Adam Malik, Indonesia's Foreign Minister and chairman of ASEAN's Standing Committee seized the opportunity of the ministerial meeting to encourage reconciliation between alienated regional partners. In Jakarta, Tun Abdul Razak, Malaysia's Deputy Prime Minister, met privately with the Philippine Foreign Minister, Narciso Ramos. The outcome of this meeting was an agreement to have a 'cooling-off' period in the dispute between their two governments. An ASEAN occasion had served as an opportunity for dispute management between two member states. Indeed, Ramos announced that he would recommend a reversal of the decision to withdraw his government's diplomats from Kuala Lumpur. Any optimism over the role of ASEAN in helping to mitigate tensions between two of its members was short-lived, however. Such optimism had taken insufficient account of the paramount importance of domestic politics and of the limited stake of some governments at the time in the emergence of ASEAN as a regional institution.

The effect of Indonesia's mediation in an ASEAN context was dissipated when a legislative initiative within the Philippines Congress defining the baselines of the Republic's territorial sea incorporated an amendment to the effect that it had acquired dominion and sovereignty over Sabah. President Marcos signed the act in September 1968 and made a statement that the Philippines enjoyed sovereignty over the territory. He pointed out that although his government did not contemplate physical incorporation of Sabah, the Republic's national boundaries would be revised accordingly when the right to exercise sovereignty had received international recognition. A consequent Malaysian request for confirmation that the government of the Philippines continued to recognise and respect the Federation's sovereignty and territorial integrity, including Sabah as a constituent state, met with a negative response. That response provoked a heated exchange, which made nonsense of the idea of a cooling-off period. Relations were aggravated further when a Philippine delegate to an ASEAN committee meeting on Commerce and Industry held in Manila questioned the competence of his Malaysian counterpart to represent Sabah. He was acting in accord with a general policy directive from the Philippine Foreign Minister who reaffirmed the challenge in October before the General Assembly of the United Nations. The practice of questioning the competence of Malaysian delegates to speak for Sabah prompted their withdrawal from all ASEAN meetings until it was discontinued. It also provoked a deliberate contest between representatives of the two countries for the chairmanship of the International Labour Organisation, which was won by Malaysia. A junior minister at the time has recorded that

> Malaysia decided to 'humiliate' the Philippines because it had been assured by Indonesia that the Philippines would cease the practice of challenging Malaysia's competence for the sake of regional harmony. But in spite of it *[sic]* the Philippines persisted, ignoring Indonesia's desire to play a mediator role.[22]

In the meantime, the Malaysian government had adopted more concrete measures to indicate the extent of its political displeasure. Shortly after President Marcos had signed the controversial act, the Malaysian government announced that it was abrogating the anti-smuggling agreement with the Philippines and that it was recalling its ambassador and staff from Manila. A prospect of sanctions was introduced into the diplomatic contention when Malaysia secured a display of force from its British alliance partner. Six RAF hunter jet fighters deliberately flew over Sabah's capital en route from Hong Kong to their base in Singapore, while a flotilla of British warships sailed through Philippine waters close to Sabah, although giving advance notice of their passage. In the meantime, the government of Singapore within the same alliance structure as Malaysia and Britain, took the opportunity of affirming support for the position of the government in Kuala Lumpur.[23]

Despite the element of sabre rattling and the semblance of crisis, the revived contention between Malaysia and the Philippines did not go beyond diplomatic form. None the less, this expression of conflict over Sabah was sufficient to disrupt the bilateral relationship and to interfere with the development of ASEAN.

Moreover, both governments became caught up with overriding domestic political considerations, with parliamentary elections called in Malaysia for May 1969 and presidential elections due in the Philippines in the following November. An ASEAN initiative taken at an *ad hoc* meeting of foreign ministers held in Bangkok in December 1968 had failed to find an acceptable formula for Philippine recognition of Malaysia's sovereignty. In the circumstances, the role of the Association in providing a forum for reconciliation was suspended until President Marcos had secured re-election. In the meantime, Malaysia had been subject to unprecedented political turbulence through racial riots arising from the results of its general elections. The overall impact of recurrent acrimony reinforced by domestic factors from the time of the public revelation of the Corregidor Affair was to leave ASEAN in a condition of political disarray, pointedly demonstrated by an inability to convene the third annual ministerial meeting of the Association until December 1969. By that time, growing concern at the prospect of adverse changes in the regional balance of power had been heightened by President Nixon's statement about the revised terms of U.S. security obligations in Asia made in the preceding July on the island of Guam.

In Jakarta in August 1968 it had been agreed that ASEAN's third ministerial meeting would take place in Malaysia. It convened eventually in mid-December 1969 in the holiday resort of the Cameron Highlands. Moved by anxiety over the prospect for regional security generated by U.S. reappraisal of policy and commitment, President Marcos instructed his new Foreign Minister, Carlos Romulo, to send an emissary to Kuala Lumpur to pave the way for his attendance. The evening before the ministerial meeting, Romulo had a private discussion with Malaysia's Prime Minister, Tunku Abdul Rahman. The very next morning at the opening session of the ASEAN meeting, the Tunku announced that Malaysia and the Philippines had agreed to restore diplomatic relations without any preconditions, out of consideration for the need for regional co-operation. That act of reconciliation provided the central item in the joint communique issued by the ministerial meeting. It recorded that the restoration of diplomatic relations had been agreed 'because of the great value which Malaysia and the Philippines placed on ASEAN.'[24] That statement may be taken at face value only up to a point given the adverse consequences for the Association of the public squabble over Sabah which had occurred in a context of disturbing regional changes. None the less, public reconciliation at the ministerial meeting served to demonstrate that the Association had some facility for keeping its corporate house in order. Indeed, from that time, ASEAN has never been beset by quite the same degree of public intra-mural discord, even though the Philippine claim to Sabah continued to cast a shadow over the corporate life of the Association.

Before considering other episodes of intra-mural tension which have hampered the institutional evolution of ASEAN, it is relevant to run ahead of events in order to indicate briefly the continuing significance of the Philippine claim for the cohesion of ASEAN. It is important to note that the bilateral relationship between Malaysia and the Philippines did not begin to recover fully from the strain induced by the Corregidor Affair and its aftermath until the political downfall of President Marcos in February 1986. That strain was aggravated from the Malaysian side during the 1970s when Muslim rebellion in the south of the Philippines was supported from Sabah as an act of retaliation during the tenure of Chief Minister Tun Mustapha Harun. The unresolved Sabah claim served to dampen Malaysia's enthusiasm for the first meeting of ASEAN heads of government. That summit convened in February 1976 only after Indonesia's government had secured an assurance from its Philippine counterpart that the Sabah issue would not be raised.[25] The Malaysian government was also cautious over endorsing in advance the Treaty of Amity and Co-operation which was signed at that meeting. Its reluctance arose from a concern that the peaceful settlement provisions of the treaty might be employed by the Philippines to engage Malaysia against its will in a legal process over the claim.

A second meeting of ASEAN heads of government convened in Kuala Lumpur in August 1977 to commemorate the tenth anniversary of the Association's formation. On that occasion, President Marcos made a public statement which gave the strong impression that his government would drop its claim to Sabah in the interest of ASEAN unity. A seeming confirmation of good intent was his subsequent visit to Sabah in the company of its Chief Minister, Datuk Harris Salleh. That visit was widely construed as recognition of Malaysia's sovereign position. The matter did not rest there, however. The Malaysian government insisted that such recognition be expressed through a revision of the Philippine Constitution which in its new form, under the martial law regime inaugurated in September 1972, had included a statement in its preamble which could be interpreted as claiming jurisdiction over

Sabah. President Marcos proved unwilling to accommodate Malaysia over this demand. Any flexibility on his part disappeared as his political base became increasingly fragile because of insurgent Communist success and economic decline which accelerated after the assassination of opposition leader Benigno Aquino in August 1983.

The protracted impasse over the revival of the Philippine claim which occurred less than a year after ASEAN's formation entrenched a discordant relationship into the structure of the Association. For example, no Malaysian Prime Minister visited Manila from the time of the public revelation of the Corregidor Affair until the third summit in December 1987, even though it became a working convention for new heads of ASEAN governments to pay courtesy calls on their more established counterparts. The continuing strain in Malaysian–Philippine relations was a factor in delaying a third meeting of ASEAN heads of government. The claim to Sabah was even raised during the course of the notorious Presidential elections in the Philippines in February 1986 which led to the political downfall of Marcos. It was only with the assumption to office of Mrs Corazon Aquino that bilateral discussions were revived at the level of foreign minister to try to settle the claim. The matter was not laid to rest, however, when a new Philippines constitution endorsed by referendum in February 1987 excluded any implicit claim to Sabah. In November 1987 President Aquino initiated legislation redefining the archipelagic baselines of the Philippines without reference to Sabah in a deliberate attempt to improve relations with Malaysia before the third ASEAN summit. Unfavourable reaction in Congress made it necessary to introduce revised legislation incorporating conditions to be met by Malaysia before the claim would be dropped officially.

The territorial dispute between Malaysia and the Philippines was only one of a number of tests of the unity of ASEAN evident in its early years. The island-state of Singapore was also at the centre of intra-mural tensions which arose from the related circumstances of its separation from Malaysia and then Malaysia's rapprochement with Indonesia. On attaining an unexpected independence in August 1965, its government exhibited an acute sense of vulnerability. Because of the Republic's minute scale, circumscribed location, regional entrepot role, and prevailing ethnic-Chinese identity, the government of Singapore was hypersensitive to any presumed slights and challenges to its new-found international status. Only too aware of innate limitations in defence capability, it decided to adopt an abrasive international posture in order to convince potential predators of Singapore's indigestible qualities. A self-styled 'poison-shrimp' policy was pursued in order to secure respect from Malaysia and Indonesia in particular. The communal antagonism which had surrounded Singapore's enforced independence and then the public rhetoric of Malay blood-brotherhood which accompanied the termination of Confrontation was responsible for such an outlook and policy. These experiences informed the defensive mentality of Singapore's leadership, who were resentful and suspicious of their exclusion from the negotiations which brought Confrontation to a close. One episode which exemplified that defensiveness occurred in February 1966 when a Singapore army battalion returning from Sabah found that its barracks was still occupied by a Malaysian battalion. At a time when the unravelling of the federal link was proceeding, the government of Singapore expressed concern lest Malaysia seek to retain a permanent and controlling military presence on the island through a unilateral interpretation of the Separation Agreement between the two states. Without discounting the extent to which the episode was deliberately exploited to serve a domestic political function, the reaction of Singapore's government was symptomatic of a fundamental tension in the relationship with Malaysia which found expression also in the collapse of the Combined Defence Council set up on separation.[26]

Despite Singapore's participation in ASEAN from the outset, it took many years for the two governments on either side of the Johore Strait to establish anything like a working relationship. Indeed, it may be suggested that such a relationship was not established, and then only imperfectly, until after Dr Mahathir Mohamad became Prime Minister of Malaysia in July 1981. Well after the formation of ASEAN, the legacy of Singapore's stormy interlude with Malaysia interposed in the relationship. Politicians from both states appeared incapable of refraining from commenting publicly on matters within one another's domestic domain. In August 1970 the first official visit to Malaysia since separation by Prime Minister Lee Kuan Yew had to be called off at the last moment. Over-zealous immigration officers in Singapore had ordered that the lengthy hair of two visiting Malay youths be cut in keeping with the prevailing social ethic in the Republic that long hair was a sign of moral degeneracy. That action provoked a furore across the causeway in a symptomatic expression of resentment. It required a two-year cooling-off period for Mr Lee's visit to be reinstated. In the meantime, irritation was expressed by the Malaysian side at Singapore's unwillingness to defer to initiatives from Kuala Lumpur. For example, such irritation became manifest when Singapore refused to support Malaysia's proposal for neutralising South-East Asia and a joint challenge by Malaysia and Indonesia to the customary legal status of the Straits of Malacca and Singapore.

A more serious public altercation occurred, this time between the governments of Singapore and Indonesia, shortly after the second ASEAN ministerial meeting. In one sense, the issue was a legacy of Confrontation. Two Indonesian marines who had been found guilty of committing acts of sabotage in Singapore during that period were sentenced to death and then hanged in October 1968. Their deaths assumed heightened political significance because General Suharto, then acting President, had felt obliged for domestic reasons to intercede publicly to seek clemency. This plea, which was augmented by that of Malaysia's Prime Minister, Tunku Abdul Rahman, went unanswered because of the belief in Singapore that to do so would suggest a willingness to give in to external pressure. The execution of the two marines provoked public disorder in Jakarta. The embassy of Singapore came under attack, while the local Chinese community served as a scapegoat for the wrath of the capital's mob.

It may be suggested that the hanging of the marines indicated an adolescent quality in Singapore's early conduct of foreign policy. The crude logic of the 'poison-shrimp' policy had obliged the government to turn a deaf ear to General Suharto's personal plea for clemency which had been effective in a corresponding case in Malaysia. The government of Singapore took its decision guided by a compulsive concern not to leave anyone in any doubt about the validity of the island-state's recently acquired international status. There did not seem to be consideration given to the impact of the decision to proceed with the executions on the cohesion of ASEAN. Indeed, the whole episode indicated the absence of any serious recognition that the Association might serve the security interests of Singapore through providing a regional structure of consultation and co-operation. By contrast, Indonesia, in a much less vulnerable position and with very much more of a proprietory political interest in the development and viability of the newly born institution, could afford to adopt a magnanimous attitude. In the circumstances, General Suharto concealed a deeply felt sense of personal slight.

The uproar in Jakarta which followed the executions reflected this sense of slight and a conviction within the ruling military establishment that its original assessment of Singapore as a regional anomaly had been correct. Popular pressure on the government to take strong retaliatory action was resisted, however. A measure of public disorder in Jakarta was countenanced as a means of satisfying national honour, while the bodies of the two marines were received in Indonesia with full military honours and then buried in the national heroes' cemetery. A formal commitment to suspend trade relations with Singapore was not applied beyond a nominal gesture.

Indonesia's Foreign Minister, Adam Malik, realised that there were more important issues at stake than the bilateral relationship with Singapore and that the Republic's larger interests would be better served by avoiding a diplomatic breach reminiscent of Sukarno's Confrontation. General Suharto supported Malik in this course, influenced undoubtedly by Indonesia's priority of economic reconstruction and by an abiding concern to avoid any unnecessary disruption to ASEAN. Accordingly, Indonesia's government took the initiative in engaging in dispute management. Malik went out of his way to try to limit diplomatic damage. The episode was not permitted to stand in the way of a progressive normalisation of the bilateral relationship, although it did delay the first official visit to Jakarta by Prime Minister Lee until May 1973. On that occasion, he thought it fitting to make a personal act of contrition by scattering flower petals on the graves of the two executed marines in the Kalibata heroes' cemetery. It was only by that time that the government of Singapore had come to appreciate fully the seriousness of President Suharto's personal commitment to ASEAN and regional co-operation. That commitment has since been recognised as of fundamental importance to the security of the island-state. As a consequence, Lee Kuan Yew has taken great pains to cultivate a close personal relationship with President Suharto.

The relationship between Singapore and Indonesia soon settled down. That with Malaysia took longer to stabilise because separation had been such a traumatic political event. The two entities had once been bound together within a common colonial structure with a legacy in economic links and personal and family ties. Indeed, Singapore's entry into Malaysia in 1963 had been represented as the restoration of a natural unity violated by colonial edict in 1946. Separation less than two years after merger gave rise to problems of political adjustment on both sides in coming to terms with the independence of the island-republic, whose existence seemed to fly in the face of all conventional wisdom. Such problems did not apply to the same extent in the case of Indonesia, however, where Singapore was more readily tolerated as a political fact of life in part because it was no longer a member of Malaysia. Despite striking disparities in size and population between Singapore and Indonesia, reflected in divergent strategic perspectives, it proved to be easier to establish a working relationship. From Singapore's perspective, the ruling military establishment in Jakarta came to be viewed increasingly as sober pragmatists applying a policy of regional co-operation in the interest of economic development. Correspondingly, through the vehicle of sound diplomatic representation, the government of the island-state came to be respected for the intellectual qualities of its political leadership and for its impeccable anti-Communist credentials. The two states moved into accord on important policy issues, despite periodic irritants in the relationship. For example, Singapore was only prepared to despatch a junior minister to a conference on Cambodia held in Jakarta in May 1970, whereas all other ASEAN partners were represented at foreign minister level. Mention has been made above of Singapore's refusal to countenance the joint challenge by Indonesia and Malaysia to the customary legal status of the Straits of Malacca and Singapore. Yet, despite such differences a meeting of political minds was forged on other significant regional issues. Moreover, a close relationship between intelligence communities served to reinforce the progressive importance placed on managing tensions between the conspicuously unequal republics.

The two governments shared strong misgivings, if for different reasons, about Malaysia's unilateral proposal for neutralising South-East Asia. They also shared an apprehension of the consequences of establishing diplomatic relations with the People's Republic of China which the government of Malaysia sought to encourage. The government of Singapore made it known in a skilful gesture that it would accept a Chinese diplomatic mission only after one had been set up in Jakarta. Increasingly in Singapore, ASEAN came to be recognised as a valuable regional resource because of Indonesia's strong commitment to the Association. It must be stressed, however, that more than eight years after the establishment of ASEAN the government of Singapore was still prepared to test its cohesion over an issue of difference with

Indonesia. When Indonesia's forcible annexation of the eastern half of the island of Timor in December 1975 was subject to a hostile resolution before the General Assembly of the United Nations, Singapore's representative abstained instead of supporting a regional partner. That position was not sustained. Singapore subsequently joined with the other members of ASEAN in endorsing the incorporation of East Timor by Indonesia. A political point had been made, however, to demonstrate that the rhetoric of ASEAN solidarity would not be permitted to obstruct the defence of security interests. Indonesia's annexation had revived an acute sense of national vulnerability which provoked a characteristic momentary gesture. That gesture did not interrupt the practical development of working political co-operation which became in time the distinguishing feature of the intra-ASEAN relationship.

Open differences between Malaysia and the Philippines and between Singapore and both Malaysia and Indonesia served to mar the early years of ASEAN. Added to those open differences were less public tensions between Malaysia and Thailand. Although not punctuated by the same measure of recrimination which characterised post-separation exchanges across the causeway linking Singapore to Malaysia, undoubted discord obtained. That discord arose from adverse security perspectives affecting attitudes to policing the common border between Malaysia and Thailand. The principal security threat across that border as perceived in Kuala Lumpur was posed by the Malayan Communist Party which had launched an insurrection in 1948. By the mid-1950s that insurrection had been well contained by British counter-insurgency action. The remnant of a primarily ethnic-Chinese party had retreated to the northern border where they set up a sanctuary zone on the Thai side. Although the Thai government had first approached its colonial British counterpart in 1948 to negotiate a border control agreement, an underlying motive was to secure recognition of a military regime established through a coup whose leader had been tainted by collaboration with the Japanese during the Pacific War. None the less, a Thai–Malayan border agreement was concluded during 1949 which provided for hot pursuit by Malayan police patrols as well as for a cross-border para-military presence. By the mid-1950s forces from the two countries were engaged in joint operations as the border became 'the major residual problem of the Emergency'.[27]

Tension in the relationship between Kuala Lumpur and Bangkok arose in part because the active remnant of the Malayan Communist

Party was perceived in the Thai capital as posing only a minimal threat to national security. The direction of their political ambition was southwards. Accordingly, Thai security forces did not approach the Communist insurgents with the same sense of urgency as their Malayan counterparts. Moreover, of greater concern to the Thai authorities was separatist sentiment in the four southernmost provinces where Malay-Muslims were the dominant community. The political boundary between Malaya/Malaysia and Thailand had been established only in 1909, cutting directly across the geographical pattern of Muslim settlement. Thai political sensitivity to Malay-Muslim national awareness stimulated by the burgeoning of Malay nationalism south of the border was heightened by the emergence in 1948 of a South Siam secession movement. This movement never succeeded in posing an effective political challenge. However, the suspicion that it and subsequent companion movements had attracted support from south of the border served to discourage the Thai government from instructing its security forces to engage in more than nominal co-operation with Malayan counterparts. Indeed, the Malayan Communist Party was even regarded as a useful obstacle to Muslim separatism or Malay irredentism. This conflict of security interests did not make for an ideal political relationship. Indeed, even after Malaysia and Indonesia were engaged in reconciling their differences during the mid-1960s, Thai Foreign Ministry officials made known their concern over Malaysia's irredentist proclivity.

The element of tension in the Thai–Malayan/Malaysian relationship was well contained publicly through the medium of both ASA and ASEAN. Indeed, for Malaysia in the early days of ASEAN, the relationship with Thailand was the closest within the Association after that with Indonesia. But the issue of their common border has interposed to trouble that relationship. For example, in July 1976 a Malaysian para-military presence was instructed to withdraw from its longstanding position just north of the border following an armed incursion from the Malaysian side. Although the breakdown in cross-border co-operation proved to be only temporary and had been initiated by a civilian government in Bangkok seeking accommodation with its counterpart in Hanoi, it reflected a resentment of the absence of parity in rights of hot pursuit, permitted only from the Malaysian side. That disparity in rights of hot pursuit served to sustain suspicion of Malaysia's political intent. The refusal by Malaysia's government to denounce publicly, or to be seen to be taking action against, Muslim separatists was justified on the ground that it could not afford to alienate its Malay constituency in the face of political challenge from the radical opposition Party Islam. In Bangkok that justification has been viewed with scepticism and misgivings, encouraging suspicion between regional partners. Any strain generated must, of course, be viewed in a wider political context taking into full account the range of interests which the two governments have held in common, exemplified by an ability to come to terms over maritime boundaries and the sharing of the sea bed. Those interests were brought sharply into focus from 1975 in the wake of revolutionary political change in Indochina and more intensely so following Vietnam's invasion of Kampuchea at the end of 1978. Moreover, since the assumption to high office in Kuala Lumpur of Dr Mahathir Mohamad in July 1981, an even closer accord in security perspective has emerged with Thailand perceived more acutely as a zone of forward defence for Malaysia. It is important, however, to keep in focus (not only with respect to Malaysian–Thai relations) the overriding inter-governmental nature of ASEAN and the propensity for friction which is part of the normal condition of inter-state relationships.

A significant factor in this normal condition in the case of the ASEAN states is the geopolitical position of Malaysia. Malaysia occupies a unique place within the Association because it shares land and/or maritime boundaries with every other member state. Fundamental differences with Indonesia over the incorporation of most of Northern Borneo in the new federation were resolved before the formation of ASEAN in August 1967. ASEAN was established in part to provide an institutional frame for cementing regional reconciliation. Malaysia's differences with Thailand and Singapore have been contained to manageable proportions, even though in the latter case a dispute has arisen over the location of the maritime boundary in the Strait of Johore. A visit to Singapore in November 1986 by the President of Israel prompted an open revival of antagonism which placed a major, if temporary, strain on relations with Malaysia. Only in the case of the relationship between Malaysia and the Philippines, however, have persisting differences over the claim to Sabah obstructed bilateral political consultation at the highest level.

As ASEAN evolved politically in response to regional changes and challenges, other intra-mural differences served to point up the inter-governmental nature of the Association. Such differences over strategic perspective will be discussed below in considering

ASEAN's regional security role. There is, however, a further point of intra-mural tension which requires addressing at this juncture which has involved Malaysia and which is a product of its unique geopolitical position within the Association.

Standing outside of ASEAN until January 1984 when it resumed sovereign international status was the minuscule Sultanate of Brunei. Its stormy relationship with Malaysia before becoming a member of ASEAN merits some consideration in order to provide a complete picture of those intra-mural tensions which have been either resolved or accommodated within the walls of the Association. Indeed, Brunei's eventual accession as the first additional member since its formation demonstrated the measure of ASEAN's success in managing such tensions.

The Sultanate of Brunei is a territorial vestige of a historical empire in Northern Borneo whose suzerainty once extended to the southern islands of the Philippine archipelago. Britain's protection enabled it to survive territorial absorption in the form of two enclaves linked only by water. These enclaves are surrounded on their landward sides by Sarawak, transferred in status from a British colony to a constituent state of the Federation of Malaysia on its formation in September 1963. The Sultan, Sir Omar Ali Saifuddien, ruling as an absolute monarch had initially contemplated membership of Malaysia. That option was rejected in the wake of an abortive rebellion in December 1962 which provided the pretext for Indonesia to challenge the federal proposal. The sense of vulnerability induced by that experience was not mitigated by the course of negotiations between Brunei and the government in Kuala Lumpur over terms of entry into the new federation. The failure of those negotiations left a legacy of discordance. That discordance was aggravated from Brunei's side by the revival of a claim to the adjacent territory of Limbang in Sarawak, which interposed between the two enclaves comprising the Sultanate. Limbang had long been a source of contention because the British ruler of Sarawak, Raja Charles Brooke, had seized it from Brunei in 1890 two years after a protectorate agreement had been concluded with London.

Following the formation of ASEAN, Malaysia undertook a diplomatic initiative within the General Assembly of the United Nations challenging the international status of the Sultanate.[28] Its representatives argued that independence was being denied by Britain and that an act of self-determination should take place. In this diplomatic exercise, the government of Malaysia placed itself on the same side as the political party which had mounted the rebellion in Brunei in December 1962. Concurrently, covert activities were conducted to foster political unrest within the Sultanate which only served to intensify antipathy between Bandar Seri Begawan and Kuala Lumpur. These activities began during the tenure of Malaysia's Prime Minister, Tun Abdul Razak and continued into that of his successor, Datuk Hussein Onn who was unaware that they were taking place. Apart from an interest in Brunei's ample oil and natural gas resources, the Malaysian operations were also prompted by a concern that the vestige of empire might become a centre of political instability, threatening the security of its neighbours. The example of East Timor served to reinforce this conviction. Brunei was regarded as a political anomaly. As a ruling monarchy whose affairs were conducted much like a family business, there was little confidence in its longer-term viability. From the perspective of Brunei's ruling family, however, Malaysia and Indonesia were menacing neighbours. ASEAN, in which they occupied a prominent place, was viewed with corresponding suspicion.

Although Brunei moved close politically to Singapore after it had separated from Malaysia because of a common sense of vulnerability, the Sultanate kept its distance from ASEAN until the early 1980s. Partly because of Malaysia's policy, the government of Brunei resisted British attempts to cast it adrift politically. It only conceded a willingness to resume full sovereign status when Britain agreed to a five-year grace period before a treaty of friendship restoring a residual foreign affairs power would become operative. In addition, undisclosed terms were worked out for a battalion of British Gurkha Rifles to remain in Brunei after sovereignty was resumed. A willingness to contemplate independence was a consequence of a significant improvement in relations between Brunei and Malaysia when Prime Minister Datuk Hussein Onn took pains to overcome the deep suspicion between the two states. Indonesia's government made a corresponding effort to cope with the revival of apprehension in Bandar Seri Begawan provoked by its annexation of East Timor in December 1975. Encouraged by the government of Singapore, which had come to regard membership of ASEAN as a political asset, Brunei responded positively to an invitation to join the Association on independence. The five year grace period from January 1979 before the resumption of sovereignty was employed to secure familiarity with the working practices of the Association through attendance at its committees. For example, Prince Mohamad Bolkiah who became Foreign Minister in January 1984 attended ministerial meetings in the capacity of an observer from June 1981, giving the Sultanate a *de facto* membership of the Association even before the final constitutional link with Britain was severed.

The government of Brunei was persuaded of the merits of ASEAN as an institutional mechanism for validating a tenuous independence instead of regarding the Association as merely the vehicle of political predators. Brunei became a member of ASEAN for reasons corresponding to its joining the United Nations, the Commonwealth, and the Organisation of the Islamic Conference – namely, to ensure as extensive international respect as possible for its national sovereignty. The political evolution of ASEAN had served this purpose, making Brunei's membership of the regional body more relevant than that of any other international institution. Such reasoning arose, in part, from ASEAN having made the sanctity of national sovereignty the centrepiece of its public philosophy. It had been articulated in the Treaty of Amity and Co-operation concluded between heads of government in February 1976. Moreover, that principle had served as the basis for ASEAN's stand from January 1979 in challenging Vietnam's invasion and occupation of Kampuchea. The collective commitment displayed encouraged Brunei to risk joining in regional co-operation with some of its former adversaries on attaining independence in January 1984. By that time, the founding members had developed a much stronger political stake in the Association. Through an evolving practice of official and ministerial consultation, ASEAN had emerged as a diplomatic community that was increasingly taken into serious account beyond the bounds of South-East Asia. From Brunei's perspective, the evident stake of the founding members in ASEAN's cohesion and viability constituted a hostage to its political fortunes. Any revealed challenge to the sovereign status of the Sultanate by any member of the Association would be certain to reflect on its international standing and credibility.

When Brunei joined ASEAN in January 1984, membership constituted more than a matter of form. It indicated a clear policy choice with a security objective in mind. Membership was contemplated as serving the security interests of the Sultanate because the five founding states would be obliged to be restrained in political intent towards their new regional partner. The nature of the political evolution of ASEAN had enabled the government of Brunei to regard the Association as a collective security organisation whose members were constrained by self-denying ordinance from behaving in a threatening manner towards one another. Membership of the same regional grouping as neighbouring states which had been hostile in the past was regarded as a practical if less than certain way to protect a vulnerable independence; a condition resisted for many years.[29]

The experience and outlook of Brunei have not been matched by every other ASEAN state to the extent that membership in itself has been deemed to make a major contribution to national security. For the more established states, the security role of the Association has not been contemplated in quite the same way. Only Singapore has shared a sense of vulnerability corresponding to that of Brunei with reference to more immediate regional sources of threat. Thailand, in different geopolitical circumstances, has looked beyond ASEAN to immediate threat and for access to countervailing power. In the wake of Confrontation, however, all prospective members of ASEAN viewed the Association as a framework for both ambition and restraint which would channel and contain the restless political energy of Indonesia.

The more general apprehension of its new-found regional partners was well understood in Jakarta from the outset. To that extent, its ministerial and diplomatic representatives went out of their way to limit the profile of the Republic in the deliberations of the Association. But if the post-Sukarno leadership of Indonesia displayed political sensitivity to regional misgivings, it approached the problem of regional security in a positive manner. From its earliest years, the government of General Suharto articulated an aspirant security role which had general application beyond catering for particular national vulnerabilities. Security was conceived of primarily as a domestic problem. The principal source of common threat was deemed to be internal in nature arising from those economic and social circumstances which facilitated subversion and insurgency. Development was identified as both the means with which to cope with such challenges and through which to underpin a stable political order. Inter-governmental co-operation within ASEAN would serve this purpose in a number of possible ways. Apart from the obvious benefits of economic co-operation, however limited, the very process of regional reconciliation would prevent a wasteful diversion of national energies and resources into conflict and away from development. Indonesia's regional vision was based on the assumption that the attainment of political stability could be promoted on a regional basis, thus insulating South-East Asia from the rivalries of extra-regional powers. The ideal is that resident states should assume responsibility for managing regional security by putting their own houses in order.

As indicated above and in the previous chapter, within Indonesia security was contemplated as the product of a desirable domestic condition described as national resilience with regional application. If little more than a rhetorical way of depicting an ideal self-reliance, the concept did express the conviction that security was best approached through the mechanisms of development and that intra-ASEAN co-operation would promote it both nationally and regionally. In practice, economic co-operation among ASEAN states has been marked by only modest achievement, despite recurrent meetings of economic ministers to discuss overcoming trade barriers. Attempts to promote trade liberalisation have been met with strong intra-mural resistance reflected in the relatively small percentage of intra-ASEAN trade in the total trade of member states; calculated at no more that 17 per cent.[30] Regional economic co-operation which was given the highest priority in ASEAN's founding declaration, has not made a major practical contribution to the security-related process of development. More effective has been the cultivation of a habit of political co-operation which has played a part in encouraging external business confidence.

After a difficult start, the process of regional reconciliation picked up momentum, although the habit of political co-operation took longer to establish. The early modest achievement of ASEAN lay in the ability of its members to stay together. There was no other tangible accomplishment to speak of. By the turn of the 1970s there was no indication that the Association might become the core of an expanding network of regional relationships with a managerial role. Such a goal was not only exceedingly ambitious during the Second Indochina War, but it was also controversial among member governments. Well before ASEAN had its cohesion tested over the appropriate response to Vietnam's invasion of Kampuchea, it was obliged to address divisions over the appropriate approach to regional order. At issue, if hypothetical still, was whether regional order should be fashioned exclusively by resident states or through external associations. That issue confronted ASEAN as the members of the Association became obliged to face up to disturbing changes in the balance of external influences bearing on their regional environment.[31] At that point, the Association was barely more than an annual conference attended by ministers whose international reputations were not matched by their domestic political standing. The utility of ASEAN for regional security was then the recognisable political opportunity cost of not soldiering on. As Prime Minister Lee Kuan Yew pointed out when addressing its meeting of foreign ministers in April 1972: 'Perhaps the most valuable achievement of ASEAN since its inception was the understanding and goodwill created at the various ASEAN meetings which had helped to lubricate relationships which could otherwise have generated friction.'[32]

Notes

1. For a full account of the course of Confrontation, see J.A.C. Mackie, *Konfrontasi: The Indonesia–Malaysia Dispute 1963–1966*, Oxford University Press, Kuala Lumpur, 1974.
2. See Lela Garner Noble, *Philippine Policy Towards Sabah*, University of Arizona Press, Tucson, 1977; Michael Leifer, *The Philippine Claim to Sabah* Interdocumentation Co., Zug, 1968.
3. Muthiah Alagappa, *The National Security of Developing States: Lessons from Thailand*, Auburn House Publishing, Dover, MA, 1987, Chapter 5.
4. Chan Heng Chee, *Singapore: The Politics of Survival* Oxford University Press, Singapore, 1971.
5. For accounts of the limited institutional experience of ASA, see Bernard K. Gordon, *Towards Disengagement in Asia*, Prentice-Hall, Englewood Cliffs, 1969; and Arnfinn Jorgensen-Dahl, *Regional Organisation and Order in South-East Asia*, Macmillan, London, 1982.
6. Franklin B. Weinstein, *Indonesia Abandons Confrontation*, Modern Indonesia Project, Cornell University, Ithaca, NY, 1969.
7. 'Regional Co-operation in International Politics', in *Regionalism in Southeast Asia*, Centre for Strategic and International Studies, Jakarta, 1975, p. 161.
8. *Government Statement Before the Gotong-Royong House of Representatives on 16th August 1966*, Department of Information, Jakarta, 1966.
9. Gordon, *Towards Disengagement*, op. cit., p. 113.
10. *The Times*, 9 December 1985.
11. *ASEAN Documents Series*, 1967–1985, ASEAN ·Secretariat, Jakarta, 1985, p. 21.
12. Gordon, *Towards Disengagement*, op. cit., p. 98.
13. Ali Moertopo 'Political and Economic Developments in Indonesia in the context of Regionalism in South-East Asia', *Indonesian Quarterly*, April 1978.
14. See Chin Kin Wah and Narciso G. Reyes, *Two Views on Summit Three*, Institute of Strategic and Industrial Studies, Kuala Lumpur, 1986.

15. See David Irvine, 'Making Haste Less Slowly: ASEAN from 1975', in Alison Broinowski (ed.) *Understanding ASEAN*, St Martin's Press, New York, 1982, p. 54.

16. For the content of that report, see Muthiah Alagappa, 'ASEAN Institutional Framework and *Modus Operandi*: Recommendations for Change', in Noordin Sopiee *et al.* (eds), *ASEAN at the Crossroads*, Institute of Strategic and International Studies, Kuala Lumpur, 1987, pp. 206–7; Chan Heng Chee, 'ASEAN: Subregional Resilience', in James W. Morley (ed.), *Security Interdependence in the Asia Pacific Region*, D.C. Heath, Lexington, 1986, Chapter 5.

17. See 'Press Release on the Recommendations of the ASEAN Task Force at the Seventeenth ASEAN Ministerial Meeting, Jakarta 9–10 July 1984', in *ASEAN Documents Series*, 1967–1985, *op. cit.*, pp. 90–1.

18. Leszek Buszynski, *SEATO: The Failure of an Alliance Strategy*, Singapore University Press, Singapore, 1983.

19. Bernard K. Gordon, *The Dimensions of Conflict in Southeast Asia*, Prentice Hall, Englewood Cliffs, NJ, 1966, p. 160.

20. *Foreign Affairs Malaysia* (Ministry of Foreign Affairs, Kuala Lumpur) 1, nos. 9–10: p. 102.

21. *ASEAN Documents Series*, 1967–1985, op. cit., p. 39.

22. Dato Abdullah Ahmad, *Tengku Abdul Rahman and Malaysia's Foreign Policy, 1963–1970*, Berita Publishing SDN, BHD, Kuala Lumpur, 1985, p. 78.

23. Chin Kin Wah, *The Defence of Malaysia and Singapore*, Cambridge University Press, Cambridge, 1983, pp. 256–9.

24. *ASEAN Documents Series*, 1967–1985, op. cit., p. 208.

25. Noble, *Philippine Policy*, op. cit., p. 39.

26. Michael Leifer, 'Astride the Straits of Johore: The British Presence and Commonwealth Rivalry in South-East Asia', *Modern Asian Studies* 1, part 3 (July 1967).

27. Anthony Short, *The Communist Insurrection in Malaya*, Frederick Muller Limited, London, 1975, p. 493.

28. Michael Leifer, 'Decolonization and International Status: The Experience of Brunei' *International Affairs* (April 1978).

29. See the discussion in Michael Leifer, 'Brunei: Domestic Politics and Foreign Policy', in Karl D. Jackson *et al.* (eds), *ASEAN in Regional and Global Context*, Institute of East Asian Studies, University of California, Berkeley, CA, 1986, Chapter 12.

30. *Sunday Times*, Singapore, 28 June 1987.

31. A useful account of ASEAN's early evolution is to be found in Roger Irvine, 'The Formative Years of ASEAN: 1967–1975', in Broinowski, *Understanding ASEAN*, op. cit., Chapter 2.

32. *ASEAN Documents Series*, 1967–1985, op. cit., p. 42.

3

The Evolution of ASEAN: Emergence as a Diplomatic Community

The early years of ASEAN were marked by intra-mural tensions and mistrust. Its main attainment was institutional survival. Concurrently, the regional environment became subject to changes well beyond the influence of the Association. In January 1968 the British Labour administration announced an accelerated timetable for military disengagement from east of Suez. A successor Conservative administration in June 1970 revised that policy in form, not in substance. A soft commitment to consult with South-East Asian defence partners was substituted for a hard one to engage in common action under the terms of the superseded Anglo-Malaysian Defence Agreement.[1] Corresponding limited military deployments by Britain, Australia and New Zealand under new Five Power Defence Arrangements did not survive the mid-1970s intact.

Britain's decision to accelerate its military disengagement appeared to be followed deliberately in March 1968 by the first appearance in the Indian Ocean of a small Soviet naval flotilla, entering by way of the Straits of Malacca and Singapore. The deployment was in all probability a measured response to Anglo-American cooperation in developing a communications facility on the Indian Ocean atoll of Diego Garcia. The Soviet naval presence was widely interpreted, however, as a considered attempt to fill a naval vacuum created by Britain's abdication of a historical role.

More dramatic in political impact was the demonstration of the limits of U.S. power by the Tet Offensive in Vietnam in January–February 1968. President Johnson's decision not to seek re-election and to find a negotiated solution to the Second Indochina War marked a decisive turning point. The direction of

U.S. policy was confirmed when Richard Nixon was elected President after having promised to end the war. In his first year of office, Nixon astounded America's Asian partners by a statement on the island of Guam in July in which he made it clear that the United States would no longer carry the burden of conventional defence against internal Communist challenge. The so-called Nixon Doctrine engendered nervousness within ASEAN as it became clear that a major reappraisal of U.S. policy in Asia was under way. That reappraisal assumed more dramatic form with the onset of Sino-U.S. rapprochement encouraged by a growing antagonism between the Soviet Union and China.

Regardless of the motivation, the initial clandestine visit of National Security Adviser Dr Henry Kissinger to Beijing caused consternation in ASEAN capitals. It not only signalled recognition of a new regional role for China in the wake of the convulsions of the Cultural Revolution, but also had an immediate effect on the prospects of China's seat in the United Nations being transferred to the government of the People's Republic. Thus, before President Nixon made his historic visit to China in February 1972, the ASEAN states found themselves obliged to take a position in the General Assembly of the United Nations. Indeed, it marked the first occasion on which ASEAN delegations had caucused together. In the context of a bewildering diplomatic buffeting, the members of the Association were unable to define a common stand. Natural concern at the changing balance of external influences bearing on South-East Asia had not been indicated in the communique published by the Third ASEAN Ministerial Meeting held in Malaysia in December 1969. The communique issued by the Fourth Ministerial Meeting held in the Philippines in March 1971 was no different in its expression of pious aspirations and in its failure to confront substantive matters of common concern. There was conspicuous omission also in that communique to any reference to the widening war in Indochina which had overcome Cambodia in the wake of Prince Norodom Sihanouk's deposition in March 1970.[2]

By April the pace and success of the Vietnamese Communist military advance in support of the radical Khmer opponents of the new Lon Nol administration was such that the expectation arose that the capital, Phnom Penh, might fall. Although its motives were mixed, arising from intra-bureaucratic conflict, Indonesia's government took a public initiative by calling a conference in Jakarta 'to find a constructive formula on how to stop the deteriorating situation in Cambodia'. That initiative was undertaken outside of the corporate structure of ASEAN and the scope of anticipated representation was extended beyond South-East Asia. Apart from expressing concern over the condition of Cambodia, perceived as the soft underbelly of Indochina, the occasion was contemplated also as an opportunity to demonstrate that Indonesia had resumed an independent and active foreign policy. In the event, the Jakarta Conference on Cambodia which convened in May 1970 was a diplomatic failure. Representation was limited because Communist and non-aligned invitees declined to attend. Indeed, the credentials of the occasion were compromised by permitting Yem Sambaur, Foreign Minister in Lon Nol's administration, to deliver an explanatory address to delegates drawn exclusively from the Western international alignment. Its credibility suffered also from its platitudinous outcome in which even the United States seemed disinterested. More to the point for this discussion, the conference was not distinguished by a display of ASEAN solidarity. Only the government of Malaysia appeared to respond with any real enthusiasm to Indonesia's initiative. Moreover, Singapore pointedly sent only a junior minister indicating a sense of reserve about the diplomatic occasion and also about the source of the diplomatic initiative. Its government was, in effect, signalling an objection to any reversion to regional assertiveness by the larger republic.

If the Jakarta Conference on Cambodia was something of a diplomatic non-event exhibiting evidence of intra-ASEAN disunity, more conspicuous disarray emerged when regional partners were obliged to vote on the question of which government should represent China in the United Nations. The ASEAN states were unable to adopt a common position, neither on the initial resolution that the expulsion of Nationalist China was an important matter requiring a majority of two-thirds, nor on the subsequent resolution to seat the People's Republic. On the first resolution Indonesia, the Philippines and Thailand voted in favour; Malaysia and Singapore voted against with the blocking majority which defeated the resolution. On the subsequent resolution, discordance among the ASEAN states was more marked. Malaysia and Singapore voted in favour, the Philippines voted against, and Indonesia and Thailand abstained.[3]

It is noteworthy that not only Singapore, with a predominantly ethnic-Chinese population, but also Malaysia voted in favour of the

People's Republic of China. Malaysia voted to seat the People's Republic despite residual challenge by an insurgent Communist Party whose support was drawn mainly from the country's ethnic-Chinese community and which looked to Beijing for ideological guidance. Malaysia's position, incongruous on the surface, complemented its unilateral initiative in 1970 that South-East Asia should be neutralised in part through provision of guarantees by the major powers. The external responses to this initiative had been mixed. Washington did not indicate any interest or sympathy because of the implicit threat to its military base rights in the Philippines. Moscow had no interest whatsoever in an alternative proposal to its own scheme for a system of collective security in Asia put forward by Leonid Brezhnev in June 1969. Neutralisation implied a balanced exclusion of external powers, whereas the Soviet Union sought to play a more direct role in Asian affairs, especially given the prospect of Sino-U.S. reconciliation.[4] Only China had indicated a positive interest in Malaysia's proposal because its geopolitical position meant that neutralisation if applied would not have the same excluding effect as on either the Soviet Union or the United States.

Direct contact with Malaysia – with whom diplomatic relations did not yet exist – was made when a senior emissary attended a trade fair in Canton in June 1971. From Malaysia's point of view, apart from asserting a greater independence in foreign policy, and compensating for Britain's military disengagement, a dominant motive was to establish a diplomatic opening to China in order to serve a domestic political purpose. Threat was conceived of primarily in internal terms but was linked to external support. In order to cope with that threat, the government wished to demonstrate to the country's resident Chinese community and to its insurgent Communist Party that its legitimacy was recognised and endorsed by its counterpart in Beijing. Neutralisation which deferred to China's international stature was intended to serve as a nexus for a revised relationship.[5] For other members of ASEAN, however, especially Indonesia, Malaysia's attempt to reach a practical accommodation with China foreshadowed an alarming precedent and a threat to its vision of regional order. That vision articulated by General Suharto had 'contemplated a co-operating Southeast Asia, an integrated Southeast Asia to constitute the strongest bulwark and base in facing imperialism and colonialism of whatever form and from whatever quarter it may come [*sic*]'.[6] Instead of providing for South-East Asian states to assert themselves as the central factor in the regional balance, Malaysia had appeared to concede a regional policing role to external powers, including China, which was regarded by Indonesia's military establishment as the principal long-term source of external threat. Malaysia's policy implied a regional power vacuum which could only be filled in an orderly manner through external involvement. Such thinking was an anathema in Jakarta.

The diverse positions adopted by ASEAN delegations in the General Assembly of the United Nations also reflected differences of interest over the weight attached to the relationship with the United States. Ironically, in view of President Nixon's impending visit to Beijing, the State Department had applied considerable pressure on friendly delegations in an attempt to deny the People's Republic's claim to the China seat. Malaysia, whose neutralisation proposal represented a diplomatic opening to China, and Singapore, which was sensitive over the emotional disposition of its majority community, resisted U.S. entreaties. The Philippines put its alliance relationship first, while Thailand and even Indonesia abstained from a concern not to offend the U.S. government. Regardless of motivation, the ASEAN states were out of step with one another on an issue directly related to regional security.

The assumption by the People's Republic of China of its UN seat in October 1971 had a number of disturbing consequences. In Thailand, it justified an incumbency coup which temporarily arrested a trend towards detente with China initiated by Foreign Minister Thanat Khoman, who was relieved of his office. In Indonesia, corresponding concern was expressed within the politically dominant military establishment that China's influence would extend more directly to South-East Asia and would be facilitated, if it became operational, by Malaysia's neutralisation proposal. That concern was demonstrated by the despatch of a number of senior military officers to accompany Foreign Minister Adam Malik to an *ad hoc* meeting of ASEAN's Foreign Ministers in Kuala Lumpur towards the end of November 1971. That meeting had been arranged at the beginning of October by heads of ASEAN delegations attending the UN General Assembly and before the final vote was taken on the tenure of China's seat. The decision had been reached because of the general realisation that fundamental changes affecting South-East Asia were taking place.

The meeting in Kuala Lumpur, which was not officially an ASEAN occasion, displayed a strong measure of consensus but was directed against Malaysia's neutralisation proposal. That proposal had been presented formally to regional partners at the annual ministerial meeting held in Manila in March 1971. Adam Malik had spelled out Indonesia's objections the following September, arguing that 'neutralisation that is the product of one-way benevolence on the part of the big powers, at this stage, would perhaps prove as brittle and unstable as the interrelationship between the major powers themselves'.[7] Malik rejected the concept of neutralisation in its Malaysian formulation because it suggested that the future of South-East Asia would be determined by the ministrations of the major powers. Apart from annoyance that Malaysia had been so presumptuous as to prescribe unilaterally for regional order, the proposal foreshadowed an external condominium over South-East Asia which directly contradicted principles enshrined in the preamble to the ASEAN Declaration. Indonesia sought to encourage a collective return to the ideas of that founding document which Malaysia had appeared to repudiate. Adam Malik had argued in September 1971:

> I strongly believe that it is only through developing among ourselves an area of internal cohesion and stability, based on indigenous socio-political and economic strength, that we can ever hope to assist in the early stabilisation of a new equilibrium in the region that would not be the exclusive 'diktat' of the major powers.[8]

The conference of Foreign Ministers (attended by Thailand's Thanat Khoman in the role of special envoy of a military government) endorsed a formula for regional order negotiated by a preceding meeting of senior officials. Lip service was paid to Malaysia's proposal by stating 'that the neutralisation of Southeast Asia is a desirable objective and that we should explore ways and means of bringing about its realisation'. A collective commitment was made, however, to an alternative formula which in nomenclature and legal quality constituted a much diluted version. Instead of upholding the legal precision of neutralisation, the Foreign Ministers indicated their countries' determination

> to exert initially necessary efforts to secure the recognition of, and respect for, South-East Asia as a Zone of Peace, Freedom and Neutrality, free from any form or manner of interference by outside Powers. ...that South-East Asian countries should

make concerted efforts to broaden the means of cooperation which would contribute to their strength, solidarity and closer co-operation.[9]

The alternative formulation was arrived at through pressure on Malaysia from regional partners which had mixed reasons for opposing neutralisation. For example, the military government in Thailand had publicly repudiated the proposal on the ground that it faced a continuing threat of aggression from the Communists. The Philippine government was not at all enthusiastic about any scheme which might prejudice its key security relationship with the United States, while Singapore was concerned that neutralisation might pave the way for a premature U.S. disengagement, giving rise in turn to an unacceptable local power dominance. The formula which prevailed was an expression of creative ambiguity which did not conspicuously appear to reject Malaysia's initiative. Despite an imprecise form, it acknowledged the kind of framework for regional order which Indonesia had long advocated and which had been reiterated by Adam Malik. In his statement in September 1971, he had urged that 'the nations of Southeast Asia should consciously work towards the day when security in their own region will be the primary responsibility of the Southeast Asian nations themselves'.[10] The Kuala Lumpur Declaration satisfied this objective but only in a declaratory sense. Regardless of the genuine consensus exhibited by the declaration, the ASEAN states were hardly in a position to ensure that South-East Asia would be 'free from any form or manner of interference by outside powers'. To that extent, the outcome of the meeting in Kuala Lumpur represented an intra-mural accommodation of views rather than any assertion of corporate will.

The most significant practical outcome of the *ad hoc* meeting of ASEAN Foreign Ministers was a separate agreement 'to continue to consult each other with a view to fostering an integrated approach on all matters and developments which affect the Southeast Asian region'. That statement in the context of uncertain change in regional environment indicated a formal acceleration in a process of bureaucratic and ministerial political consultation which became over time the distinguishing achievement of ASEAN. It indicated the semblance of a diplomatic community as it became increasingly necessary for regional partners to forge a common response to common regional problems. The limits to common action, however, were indicated also by the lack of any early sequel to a joint public recommendation that 'a Summit Meeting of the Heads of State or Government of the members of ASEAN be held in Manila at a date to be announced later'.

Whether as a result of Malaysian resistance because of the impediment of the Sabah claim or because of general misgivings that President Marcos intended to stage a spectacular political event primarily for domestic reasons, an ASEAN summit was delayed. The pace of 'recent developments in the international situation as they affect the region of Southeast Asia' (to employ the language of the joint communique) was also such as to make any summit a premature event unlikely to be able to do more than reiterate pious declarations. A first meeting of ASEAN's heads of government was only arranged after and because of the dramatic successes of revolutionary Communism in Phnom Penh and Saigon in April 1975. After careful planning, the five heads of government met for the first time in February 1976 – pointedly in Indonesia, not in the Philippines.

The Kuala Lumpur Declaration of November 1971 did not constitute a true meeting of ASEAN minds. It did indicate an approach to regional security complementary to that of development-induced political stability. Indeed, in general provision the Declaration stood in direct lineal descent to Indonesia's visionary approach to regional order which had been incorporated in the preamble to ASEAN's founding document. However, any proprietory claim to prescribe for regional order had arisen by default rather than by design. To the extent that a consensus was worked out in Kuala Lumpur, it was based on a refusal to lend corporate endorsement to a Malaysian-inspired regional accommodation to China. At that point, although an agreement was reached on a blueprint for a Zone of Peace, the formula was not employed as a symbol of the Association's common regional purpose. For example, it did not find a place in the joint communique of the next and fifth ASEAN ministerial meeting which convened in Singapore in April 1972. In other words, a consensus of aspiration by the foreign ministers of ASEAN meeting on an *ad hoc* basis did not constitute a commitment by ASEAN as a corporate entity. Moreover, by that time new differences had entered into the relationships between at least three regional partners which had their origins in attempts to provide safe navigation in the Straits of Malacca and Singapore.

From December 1957 Indonesia's government had asserted an archipelagic principle in a system of linked straight base-lines connecting the outermost points of the country's outermost islands. The object of the maritime initiative had been to establish a claim to the same quality of jurisdiction over waters surrounding and intersecting the island constituents of the Republic as applied to its fragmented territory. The archipelagic principle was an expression of a strategic perspective arising from the intrinsic vulnerability of Indonesia, which it sought to overcome by commanding its perimeter. The Straits of Malacca and Singapore fell within that strategic perspective because the linked waterway, which provides the shortest sea route between the Indian and Pacific Oceans, serves also as a point of entry to the maritime interstices of the distended archipelago. Indonesia shared jurisdiction in the Strait of Malacca with Malaysia and in the Strait of Singapore with both Malaysia and Singapore. All three states had responded with irritation to a Japanese attempt in 1971 to set up an international board to oversee safety of navigation to which the coastal states would be accountable. Their joint initiative on the basis of sovereign rights removed the issue from the agenda of the Inter-Governmental Maritime Consultative Organisation (now the International Maritime Organisation) and the three coastal states began consultations to overcome the problems of safety of navigation (especially those resulting from passage of deep-draught oil-tankers) on an exclusive basis.[11]

Public disagreement between coastal state regional partners became manifest in the middle of November 1971 shortly before the meeting of foreign ministers which produced the Kuala Lumpur Declaration. The three states agreed that safety of navigation in the linked straits was their sole collective responsibility but differed fundamentally about their legal status. Indonesia and Malaysia asserted that 'the Straits of Malacca and Singapore are not international straits, while fully recognising their use for international shipping in accordance with the principle [*sic*] of innocent passage'. This attempt to revise the customary legal status of straits long used for international navigation was resisted strongly by Singapore whose government interpreted the assertion as a fundamental threat to the island-state's economic *raison d'être*. It refused to endorse it, albeit without explicit rejection, by employing a formula which 'took note of the position' of its ASEAN partners.

The issue of the legal status of the Straits of Malacca and Singapore was settled by negotiations at the Third UN Conference on the Law of the Sea which concluded its deliberations in 1982.

The decisive factor was the solidarity of the maritime powers, including the United States and the Soviet Union, who insisted on a liberal regime of 'transit passage' for all straits used for international navigation. This powerful alignment served to safeguard Singapore's position making it possible for the island-state to avoid serious public contention with Indonesia and Malaysia. None the less, the episode did not assist the cohesion of ASEAN which was additionally divided by the mixed responses of the Philippines and Thailand to the maritime claim. The Philippines were sympathetic because of their own archipelagic condition, while Thailand indicated concern at the prospect of any impediment to freedom of navigation between its western and eastern coasts. For Singapore, the initiative by Indonesia and Malaysia revived fears of a local condominium undermining the independence of the Republic and reinforced apprehension of any scheme for regional neutralisation. A practical approach to the problem of safety of navigation was only adopted by the three coastal states after the success of revolutionary Communism in Indochina had concentrated the minds of regional partners. An agreement on establishing a traffic separation scheme in the linked Straits was reached at the end of 1976. It appeared to be more than a coincidence that its signature by the Foreign Ministers of Indonesia, Malaysia and Singapore occurred during a wider ASEAN meeting in Manila in February 1977. By that time, the Association had not only closed ranks but also had begun to conduct itself more like a diplomatic community.

Until the dramatic political transformation of Indochina, however, ASEAN had seemed unable to overcome a conspicuous sense of drift. Indeed, there was a pointed measure of reserve in the tone and content of remarks made by President Suharto in May 1974 in welcoming delegates to the Association's annual ministerial meeting in Jakarta. He admonished his fraternal partners, maintaining:

> The establishment of ASEAN has undoubtedly brought about a stronger regional unity, peace and stability, yet it will remain a very fragile reality unless we concentrate on our constant vigilance and our common noble dedication. Apart from the encouraging progress in certain areas, we have to admit that our collaboration in the economic, technical and administrative fields has remained largely at the study or preparatory stage of the projects.

During the course of that seventh annual meeting, the five Foreign Ministers reaffirmed a decision adopted in 1973 to set up an ASEAN Secretariat. Agreement was reached on locating it in Jakarta, with the Philippines withdrawing its offer of a site 'in the interests of regional unity and harmony'. It became evident, however, during the course of private discussions that a consensus did not exist for a strong centralised secretariat which would assume responsibility for co-ordinating the functions of the separate national secretariats that serviced the individual governments in regional co-operation. The initiative for an ASEAN Secretariat had come from Indonesia, whose government insisted on acting as host for its headquarters, consequently reviving apprehension about its regional ambition. It became apparent that support obtained only for a service organisation which would supplement, but in no way displace, the primary role of the national secretariats. The Foreign Ministers of Malaysia and the Philippines were vocal in objecting to the establishment of anything more than a secretariat symbolising the institutionalisation of the Association.

Symbolism had also been the only accomplishment of two intervening *ad hoc* meetings of Foreign Ministers which had convened in Manila in July 1972 and in Kuala Lumpur in February 1973. These meetings, arranged by the five Foreign Ministers when in Singapore in April 1972, presumed to address themselves to the future of Indochina which was well beyond the practical competence of ASEAN. The one in Manila sought to adopt an impartial pose in exploring a final settlement despite the common anti-Communism of all member governments and the invited presence at annual ministerial meetings of representatives from governments in Saigon, Phnom Penh and Vientiane in the role of observers. In Kuala Lumpur, apart from discussing the recent Paris Peace Agreements and the prospect of expanding ASEAN's membership, the issue of establishing diplomatic relations with the People's Republic of China was addressed. Plain talking followed as it became evident that the government of Malaysia was determined to proceed to this end. An agreement to disagree was reached which introduced an element of strain into relations between Malaysia and Indonesia. By contrast, a greater measure of rapport developed between Indonesia and Singapore. The latter made it known that it would contemplate establishing diplomatic relations with China only after Indonesia had done so. In practical terms, these ASEAN occasions had been concerned solely with intra-mural matters, with little or no impact made on wider regional issues. The government in Hanoi consistently refused to send an observer to ministerial meetings. For example, an invitation to a ministerial meeting in the Thai resort of Pattaya in April 1973 was refused because the U.S. bombing of Cambodia was being conducted from bases in Thailand. In the following year another invitation was declined because of the refusal of the Indonesian host government to entertain a representative from the Provisional Revolutionary Government of South Vietnam. Moreover, the government of Burma, long perceived as the most appropriate candidate for membership of the Association, never indicated any interest in sending an observer to one of its meetings.

The underlying sense of drift in ASEAN was confirmed at the end of May 1974 when Malaysia's Prime Minister, Tun Abdul Razak, began an official visit to the People's Republic of China. During the course of that visit diplomatic relations were established. Despite the formula of agreeing to disagree, there was little doubt that Malaysia had broken ranks, exposing the limits of political co-operation within ASEAN. Unable to make any notable impact on a turbulent region, ASEAN had also failed to demonstrate harmony in foreign policies. Hardly a diplomatic community, it was more an annual conference which shied away from taking decisions of substance. Indeed, the limited proprietary position of ASEAN was revealed in February 1973 when Australia's Prime Minister, Gough Whitlam, proposed that an Asia-wide regional organisation be established, including China, within which ASEAN would be subsumed as 'a subregional organisation'.

The sense of political torpor which surrounded the activities of ASEAN was rudely shattered by the dramatic successes of revolutionary Communism in Indochina during 1975, which came as a great shock to member governments. Apprehension over the outcome of the Vietnam Peace Agreements signed in Paris in January 1973 had been partially mitigated by the general expectation of a 'decent interval' before the eventual collapse of the Saigon regime. Indeed, Indonesia had been persuaded by the United States to participate in the International Commission for Supervision and Control, which was set up to monitor the Agreements on the basis of such an expectation. The fall of both Phnom Penh and Saigon in the second half of April 1975 destroyed any residual complacency within ASEAN capitals, obliging the member governments to come to terms with a fundamental change in the regional environment. A common view about how to cope with the new pattern of power in Indochina was not recorded in the joint communique published after ASEAN's eighth ministerial meeting, which took place in Kuala Lumpur in May 1975, only two weeks after the fall of Saigon. The word 'Indochina' did not merit a mention in that communique. The only reference by implication to revolutionary political change in that peninsula was the inclusion of a paraphrase from Prime Minister Tun Abdul Razak's opening address. In it, he suggested that never before in their history had the people of South-East Asia been given the opportunity to create and establish for themselves a new world of peace, free from foreign domination and influence, in which the countries of the region could co-operate with one another for the common good.[12] A common ASEAN position was not indicated, however. Most governments individually accorded recognition of the forcible transfers of power but the pattern was not uniform. A public blandness barely concealed a new sense of private urgency which introduced greater cohesion into the bureaucratic and ministerial deliberations of the Association. Public disarray, which had been a notable feature of corporate weakness was succeeded by a new commitment to political co-operation which expressed itself in the decision to hold the first meeting of ASEAN's heads of government.

The dramatic political transformation in Cambodia and South Vietnam during April 1975, which had direct consequences for the political identity of Laos by the end of the year, meant that the ASEAN states had to set aside any expectation of an expansion of the Association to include all the countries of the region. Any genuine expression of interest in membership by Communist governments in Indochina would have been a political embarrassment. Such membership would have been a mixed asset, imposing an intolerable strain on an embryonic sense of common identity. Accordingly, there is reason to believe that individual public statements about a wider membership from some ASEAN capitals did not represent a commonly agreed viewpoint. Moreover, if the government of a reunited Vietnam had then expressed an interest in regional co-operation it would certainly have required an institutional alternative to ASEAN in the way that Indonesia had insisted on such an alternative to ASA. Such a prospect did not present a desirable option to a group of regional partners who had worked together with a measure of harmony for nearly eight years.

Whatever ASEAN's limitations by way of practical accomplishment, the Association appeared to overcome the test of nerve imposed by the dramatic climax to the Second Indochina War. An evolving practice of consultation served to generate sufficient corporate confidence to withstand the possible application of the domino theory beyond the bounds of Indochina. Not even Thailand's government had expectations of an imminent military threat. Defence expenditure did not rise markedly as a direct consequence of revolutionary political change in Indochina.[13] Under the circumstances, it was deemed appropriate to convene the first meeting of ASEAN's heads of government not as an expression of collective panic but to invest the Association formally with a political identity. The feeble public pretense that ASEAN's main preoccupations were economic and social was set aside. Agreement to proceed on this basis, however, did not establish a full consensus on the conduct of a corporate foreign policy. ASEAN did not move as a single actor in response to political change in Indochina; individual governments adopted foreign policy initiatives at odds with those of regional partners. For example, the decisions by the Philippines and Thailand in close succession to establish diplomatic relations with the People's Republic of China in mid-1975 were not received with enthusiasm in Jakarta. In addition, at the end of 1975 Indonesia invaded and annexed the Portuguese colony of East Timor. That military action was subject to the passage of an adverse resolution in the United Nations, where Indonesia attracted full support from only three of its four regional partners. The government of Singapore abstained on a resolution critical of Indonesia in the General Assembly. It felt unable to endorse Indonesia's conduct without appearing to prejudice its own vulnerable independence. Correspondingly, and from the same motivation, Singapore also stood out in refusing to support the Malaysian-inspired challenge within the Fourth Committee of the General Assembly to the international status of the British-protected state of Brunei.

Despite persistent shortcomings in political co-operation, the five ASEAN heads of government agreed to meet on the Indonesian island of Bali in February 1976. Although the main purpose of the summit was to invest the Association with a more coherent political identity, it was concerned also with improving the quality of regional economic co-operation. Such co-operation had been conceived initially as having a bearing on regional security. But disagreement over the nature and pace of economic co-operation, particularly in trade liberalisation, almost brought the conference to grief before in convened, indicating how little progress had been made in realising ASEAN's principal declaratory goal. On the political side, prior disagreement arose also over an attempt to establish machinery for dispute settlement among member states. Resistance to a compulsory procedure was indicated by Malaysia because of apprehension that it might be invoked by the Philippines in pursuit of its claim on Sabah.

The Bali summit served to confirm the identity and viability of the Association. If the achievements of the agreements reached constituted more form than substance, the five heads of government asserted their commitment to membership on political grounds. They articulated publicly and plainly previously held private assumptions about the political role of ASEAN. To that end, the prime purpose of their meeting was to endorse two documents whose content had been worked out in prior meetings between senior officials. The first of these was a Declaration of ASEAN Concord which enunciated certain objectives and principles which the Association would take into account 'in the pursuit of political stability'. The significance of that Declaration was that a matter of secondary consideration in the original ASEAN Declaration had been elevated in priority, and the security goals of the Association, conceived as complementary, were reiterated. It was maintained that 'the stability of each member state and of the ASEAN region is an essential contribution to international peace and security. Each member state resolves to eliminate threats posed by subversion to its stability, thus strengthening national and ASEAN resilience.'[14] This statement, more than any other at the conference, set out the original and continuing consensus over security and highlighted its internal focus. It made also plain the connection between the internal dimension of national security and wider regional security by linking the Indonesian-inspired notions of national and regional or ASEAN resilience.

The immediate priority of ASEAN governments in August 1967 had been to promote regional reconciliation. At Bali the implicit collective internal security role of ASEAN was explicitly articulated. In its original usage by the League of Nations, collective security had been based on the idea of the indivisibility of peace, with an act of aggression by any state construed as a threat to all states. In a corresponding way, ASEAN imputed a positive connection between development and political stability not only in the case of individual member states but also throughout the

Association. In other words, the governments of ASEAN reiterated their common conviction that development-induced political stability was indivisible within the walls of the Association; that political stability attained in any one member state would contribute to the attainment of such a desirable condition in others. Moreover, it was understood and implied that the converse process would also apply; namely, that political instability in any one member state would not necessarily be self-contained but would affect regional partners. Such assumptions did not constitute a proven judgement. Resounding declaration did not indicate the operational application of the assumed positive connection as the later experience of the Philippines was to demonstrate to the acute concern of all of its regional partners. None the less, an explicit security priority had been articulated publicly on a corporate basis.

Second place in the objectives and principles which the Association would take into account in the pursuit of political stability was given to the Zone of Peace, Freedom and Neutrality which was brought formally under ASEAN's auspices. It was stated that 'Member states, individually and collectively shall take active steps' for its early establishment. As indicated above, the Zone of Peace formula had been a collective response to a Malaysian attempt to promote regional neutralisation. Although much less precise than neutralisation, the Zone of Peace formula then constituted the highest common denominator of declaratory prescription for regional order. But as set out within the Declaration of ASEAN Concord, it was represented as an ideal state of affairs to be approached through a consensus on internal security rather than through one on external security. If the general intention was to insulate South-East Asia from the rivalries of external powers, the Zone of Peace concept would find operational application as an expression and outcome of aggregate political stability. In other words, a Zone of Peace was not contemplated as a regional condition which ASEAN would be able to promote and establish through corporate measures. Rather, it was one which individual ASEAN states could work towards by pursuing a common approach whereby development-induced political stability would give rise to a regional effect. Such an approach was indicated by the terms of the third declared objective that 'the elimination of poverty, hunger, disease and illiteracy is a primary concern of member states'.

Within the Declaration of ASEAN Concord, one facet of the security role of ASEAN was articulated, albeit in ideal and other than conventional terms. Defence co-operation as such, however, did find specific mention in the Declaration but only a brief one. It endorsed 'continuation of co-operation on a non-ASEAN basis between the member states in security matters in accordance with their mutual needs and interest'.

A prior initiative from Indonesia's Defence Ministry had sought to make more explicit provision for such co-operation, but a consensus did not exist even for bringing existing bilateral defence collaboration under ASEAN auspices. A Malaysian objection was that such an arrangement would prejudice diplomatic overtures to Hanoi.[15] Accordingly in his opening address to his fellow heads of government President Suharto repudiated defence cooperation on an intra-ASEAN basis. He pointed out that

> it must be clear to us and to the world that we have no intention of establishing a military pact, as it was misinterpreted by some people. Cooperation among us in the realm of security is neither designed against other nor certain parties. We have neither the capability nor the intention to have it. *Our concept of security is inward looking* [emphasis added], namely to establish an orderly, peaceful and stable condition within each individual territory, free from any subversive elements and infiltrations, wherever from their origins might be [*sic*].[16]

President Suharto defined security primarily with reference to the concept of national resilience, 'which will in turn be conducive to the creation of a regional resilience'. This view was echoed by Malaysia's Prime Minister Datuk Hussein Onn, whose foreign ministry was then very keen to build a political bridge to Hanoi and therefore concerned to prevent any ASEAN initiative which might impede that exercise. He stressed that 'ASEAN is not, nor should be, a security organisation. In the final analysis, our security depends on our ability to provide the goods of life for our people and to build societies which are just and fair to all.'[17] An alliance role for ASEAN was also explicitly repudiated by Philippines President Marcos. No specific mention of conventional security cooperation was made in their opening addresses by either Prime Minister Lee Kuan Yew of Singapore or Prime Minister Kukrit Pramoj of Thailand.

Despite public protestations that ASEAN was not and should not become a security organisation, the second public document produced by the summit also embodied security connotations. That document was a Treaty of Amity and Cooperation in South-East Asia, intended to establish a code of conduct for regional inter-state relations and an institutional mechanism for peaceful settlement of disputes.[18] Its preamble made reference to regional peace and stability, while its first guiding principle was 'mutual respect for the independence, sovereignty, equality, territorial integrity and national identity of all nations'. Although the totality of guiding principles – including settlement of differences or disputes by peaceful means and the renunciation of the threat or use of force – were unexceptional and unexceptionable, being drawn from the UN Charter, the strong sense of self-denying ordinance expressed was contemplated as a basis for regional order. To this end, the provision that made for the treaty to be 'open for accession by other states in Southeast Asia' indicated an expectation that the Socialist states of Indochina might be prepared to endorse the guiding principles. The object was to encourage a *modus vivendi* as a practical alternative to expanding the membership of ASEAN. Accordingly, the Treaty of Amity and Cooperation was conceived as a way of promoting a greater common understanding both within and beyond the bounds of ASEAN, so serving general security interests. The essence of that common understanding was respect for national sovereignty.

At the conclusion of the Bali Summit, ASEAN as a corporate entity had gone as far as internal consensus would permit in approaching the issue of regional security. The obstacles to moving beyond that consensus to an alliance were formidable. They comprised individual limitations in military capability which in aggregate would in no way match the military strength of a united and triumphant Vietnam. Moreover such proven strength would be provoked by any pretensions to alliance on the part of ASEAN. ASEAN governments had begun to embark before 1975 on rearmament programmes which emphasised external defence, but it was well understood that it would be premature to gear them to a collective projection of power which would have required a degree of military co-operation likely to generate intra-mural tensions. Accordingly, military co-operation was restricted to bilateral border control operations begun before the advent of ASEAN as well as to mainly symbolic bilateral naval and air force exercises. The only significant exception was an increase in co-operation between intelligence communities which began to exchange information on a more regular basis. An underlying inhibition, however, to ASEAN moving from collective internal security to collective defence was the absence among member governments of a common strategic perspective. In the wake of dramatic political change in Indochina, those governments were joined by a common sense of apprehension and uncertainty but not by a common view of external threat. By the time of the Bali Summit, quite fundamental differences in external outlook had begun to crystallise. They expressed themselves, above all, in competing viewpoints held in Bangkok and Jakarta over whether Vietnam or China constituted the principal source of external threat.

Ironically, it had been Thailand and not Indonesia which had originally adopted a public position of antagonism towards the People's Republic of China and which had preferred to conduct diplomatic relations with Taiwan for a quarter of a century. In Thailand it had been the conventional wisdom (reflecting the U.S. view) that the principal security threat was posed by a monolithic international Communism whose vehicle for expansion in Asia was the People's Republic of China, serving as patron of the Vietnamese Communists. In other words, Thailand's historical enemy, Vietnam, was contemplated within a wider context of threat. In this context, Thailand had despatched troops to fight under UN command in Korea in 1950. Moreover, in September 1967 combat troops were sent to fight in South Vietnam as part of President Johnson's 'Many Flags Programme' of third-country support for the U.S. war effort. Although the prime object of the deployment had been to ensure continuing defence support from the United States, an underlying rationale was a perception of threat to the trans-Mekong region of Indochina traditionally viewed as Thailand's security zone.[19] None the less, the government of Thailand regarded the first two Indochina wars within the strategic context established by the Korean conflict and did not begin to draw any significant practical distinction between threats from Chinese and Vietnamese Communism until the mid-1970s when tensions between Beijing and Hanoi became manifest in the context of Sino-Soviet antagonism and Sino-U.S. rapprochement. At that time, the singular prospect emerged of China serving as an alternative source of external countervailing power against the more immediate external threat posed by a seemingly expansionist united Communist Vietnam.

By contrast, Indonesia had established diplomatic relations with Beijing soon after independence as part of a non-aligned foreign policy. During the Sukarno era, Indonesia's relationship with the

People's Republic had burgeoned into a close political alignment which was radically reversed in the wake of an abortive coup in October 1965 attributed to the local Communist Party. Diplomatic relations with China were suspended in October 1967 after its Communist Party had been accused of involvement in the coup attempt. The military establishment under General Suharto, who succeeded Sukarno became quite explicit in identifying China as the principal long-term source of external threat, governed in part by longstanding reservations about the loyalty of the resident ethnic-Chinese community. Even though the dramatic military victory of Vietnam's Communists came as a disagreeable surprise, a prevailing strategic perspective was not revised. Because of a conviction that Vietnam's Communists were primarily nationalists, arising from their challenge in 1945 to French colonialism concurrent with that of Indonesia's national revolution against the Dutch, Vietnam enjoyed a special position in regional outlook. That somewhat sentimental view was reinforced by the revival of historical antagonism between Vietnam and China. Thus Vietnam was perceived as a possible barrier and regional partner against any extension of Chinese influence in South-East Asia in the wake of America's apparent strategic decline.

If Thailand and Indonesia held conflicting views of external threat and of the appropriate regional balance of power, their three regional partners adopted strategic perspectives which either corresponded with or stood between these two alternatives. Malaysia had taken a unilateral initiative in May 1974 to establish diplomatic relations with China but that initiative had been based on the premiss that Chinese Communism constituted the principal source of external threat. One object of establishing diplomatic relations had been to secure public endorsement from the government in Beijing in order to demonstrate both to the Communist Party of Malaya and the resident ethnic-Chinese community that there was no point in looking to China for support. This object had been confirmed by the conspicuous use of photographs of Prime Minister Tun Razak in the company of Chairman Mao Zedong during general elections in Malaysia held in August 1974. This strategy was only a partial success, as the Chinese Communist Party refused to repudiate party-to-party relations, while the insurgent Communist Party of Malaya engaged in a campaign of armed action during 1975, evidently inspired by Vietnamese Communist success. Although disturbed by the political transformation of Indochina, fear of China loomed larger.

Indeed, Malaysia's Foreign Ministry sought to promote a special relationship with Vietnam in the expectation that it could secure the kind of political access which would enable the political distance between Indochina and ASEAN to be closed. For those reasons, in part, the government of Malaysia adopted a strategic perspective under Tun Razak and his successor Datuk Hussein Onn which corresponded closely with that of Indonesia, while not disregarding the buffer position of Thailand interposed between itself and a Communist Indochina.

By contrast, the government of Singapore gave higher priority to the likelihood of threat from Vietnam. Although wary of China and unwilling to establish diplomatic relations, the military success of Vietnam's Communists and their accumulation of a huge stockpile of U.S. arms gave rise to apprehension of support for regional insurgency. Moreover, given an abiding concern to encourage a continuing U.S. regional security role, there was little point in highlighting a Chinese threat in the context of Sino-U.S. rapprochement. Characteristically, the government of the island-state was the least inclined of any ASEAN member to appear politically accommodating to any of the revolutionary Communist regimes of Indochina in case such a stance gave the impression of appeasement or weakness. The view taken was that it was up to Vietnam, in particular, to demonstrate its regional *bona fides*. Accordingly, Singapore stood closest to Thailand in its assessment of external threat.

President Marcos had made a public statement during the Bali Summit that the Philippines did not envisage external aggression against any ASEAN state in the next decade, reaffirming that 'the principal danger against our respective countries is economic crisis and subversion'. In its maritime insulation, with a relatively small ethnic-Chinese community and protected by a mutual security treaty with the United States, the Philippines did not exhibit any pressing concern with an immediate threat from either Vietnam or China. Its security problems were primarily internal, with a Muslim rebellion in the southern islands of the archipelago and an insurgency mounted by a reconstituted Communist Party. The Philippines adopted a strategic perspective that did not reflect either the priorities of Thailand and Singapore or those of Indonesia and Malaysia.

Such divergence in strategic perspectives, however, did not place unacceptable strain on the relationships between regional partners. One reason which prevailed, at least until Vietnam's invasion of Kampuchea in December 1978, was that any potential for threat was not translated into actual form. The issue of which source of threat should be regarded as the more immediate did not assume practical proportions until the Vietnamese sought to assert political dominance over the whole of Indochina. In the meantime and in the absence of any acute necessity for choice, the ASEAN states could express their highest common denominator of interest in security through the assumed complementary policies of promoting development and prescribing in general terms for regional order. The former rested on individual state enterprise but was expected to realise itself in regional terms in a stable environment which would deny external powers the opportunity to indulge their rivalries at the expense of resident states. The latter involved such collective formulae as the Treaty of Amity and Cooperation and the Zone of Peace proposal.

With the Bali Summit, greater emphasis had been placed on a collective approach to regional order, but not to any practical avail. The success of such an approach depended, above all, on the response of Vietnam which had not displayed any political warmth towards the Association. On the contrary, ASEAN and its prescriptive formulae were regarded with intense suspicion. Moreover, the willingness of three of its member states to establish diplomatic relations with China did not help matters given the steady deterioration in Sino-Vietnamese relations. Vietnam steadfastly refused to acknowledge ASEAN as a corporate entity, indicating a willingness only to deal on a strictly bilateral basis with non-Communist regional states. In this respect, it pointedly included Burma in its bilateral dealings to avoid giving the impression that even an informal relationship with ASEAN existed.

At the time of the Bali Summit, Vietnam's position was not only hostile but also alarming because of open support proffered to revolutionary movements in the region. In February 1976 a joint statement by the Vietnamese and Laotian Communist Party leaders, Le Duan and Kaysone Phomvihan, proclaimed:

> The two sides fully support the just and victorious struggle of the peoples of this region for peace, national independence, democracy, and social progress and will actively contribute to helping the South-East Asian states become really independent, peaceful and neutral ones.[20]

At the end of the month, an article in the Vietnamese Communist

Party newspaper *Nhan Dan* affirmed:

> The struggle we have conducted at great costs for our own independence and freedom has also been intended for the support of the just struggle of our neighbours and for the building of this region into a zone of peace and friendly cooperation.[21]

The linking of support for 'just struggle' with a proposal for a 'zone of peace and friendly cooperation' was doubly disturbing in ASEAN capitals. It was construed as a missionary declaration of regional revolutionary intent framed in terms of a competing alternative to ASEAN's formulae for regional order.

The formal unification of Vietnam in July 1976 provided the occasion for a regional diplomatic opening by Deputy Foreign Minister Phan Hien. Assurances of good intent were joined, however, with a categorical refusal to acknowledge ASEAN as a corporate entity. Vietnam's refusal to countenance international endorsement either of ASEAN or its prescriptions for regional order was made explicit during the conference of non-aligned heads of government which convened in Sri Lanka during August 1976. At that gathering in Colombo, open exception was taken to the attempt by the three ASEAN governments participating (Indonesia, Malaysia, and Singapore) to include the Zone of Peace proposal in the final communique which had been done at the previous Non-Aligned Conference in Algeria in 1973. Joint Laotian and Vietnamese objections served to deny the Kuala Lumpur Declaration a place on the ground that a regional consensus did not exist for its inclusion.

Ngo Dien, the spokesperson for Vietnam's delegation commented, 'we decidedly do not tolerate any scheme to revive a none-too-bright past of ASEAN and to sell an outmoded and bankrupted policy of this organisation.'[22] It was made quite clear that ASEAN's prescriptions for regional order were not acceptable, even as a basis for negotiations. The Vietnamese, still flushed with their revolutionary success, regarded ASEAN governments with a mixture of contempt and suspicion. There were suspicions because of a continuing concern with the regional intent of the United States for which ASEAN was perceived as an insidious proxy. Ngo Dien had pointedly remarked of the ASEAN states that they had been 'directly serving or indirectly serving the U.S. aggressive war in Vietnam, Laos and Cambodia in complete contravention of the principles of the Non-Aligned Movement'.

Bilateral relationships with individual ASEAN states did not fare much better. For example, the rapprochement effected by the government of Kukrit Pramoj in Thailand reflected in an agreement to establish diplomatic relations in August 1976, was not sustained in the wake of a bloody coup in October which brought a close to three years of parliamentary democracy by reinstating a military-based government openly hostile to Vietnam. In Hanoi, exception was taken to joint Thai–Malaysian military operations conducted in January 1977 against Communist insurgents active along their common border. The operation was described as part of an anti-Communist scheme coordinated among the ASEAN countries and ordered by the United States.

ASEAN's formulae for regional order were unable to serve as a basis for widening a limited structure of regional relationships. They served primarily as a symbolic focus for solidarity among subregional partners. In the face of Vietnamese and Lao hostility and Kampuchean indifference, the governments of ASEAN closed ranks. The immediate post-summit annual ministerial meeting held in Manila in June 1976 had not indicated, however, any qualitative change in the nature or role of the Association, except for separate meetings of Economic Ministers. That gathering had expressed confidence that 'ASEAN would continue to progress through positive efforts towards the goal of regionalism through social, cultural and economic endeavours' and that

> the relaxation of tension in the prospect of increased regional peace and harmony, not withstanding the existence of difference economic and social systems within the region, would create favourable conditions for the establishment of the Zone [of Peace, Freedom and Neutrality].[23]

In effect, the existence and competing nature of different regional economic and social systems meant that ASEAN was incapable of either expansion in membership or of building a regionwide consensus around a code of inter-state conduct. Even Burma, whose government had evidently been disturbed by the nature of political change in Indochina, had not exhibited any interest in moving closer to the Association as a corporate entity. A year later, little of substance had appeared to have changed. The annual ministerial meeting which convened in Singapore in June 1977 did not have any tangible progress to record. Reaffirmation of commitment to declaratory principles contrasted with the absence of concrete achievement. In reviewing the situation in South-East Asia, the Foreign Ministers could only reiterate

> the desire for ASEAN countries to promote peaceful and mutually beneficial relations with all countries, including Kampuchea, Laos and Vietnam, on the basis of mutual respect for each other's sovereignty and territorial integrity, and of non-interference in each other's internal affairs.[24]

In the following month, a second meeting of ASEAN heads of government convened in Kuala Lumpur, primarily for the ceremonial purpose of marking the tenth anniversary of the Association's establishment. As a political occasion, it proved to be an anti-climax, in contrast to the first summit in 1976. Then a measure of political resolve had been displayed but the sense of achievement manifested at Bali proved to be ephemeral. Although expectations of economic co-operation had been generated, the meeting in Kuala Lumpur demonstrated that intra-ASEAN trade liberalisation had limited prospects. At Bali the five heads of government had appeared to assume a modest managerial role despite differences over strategic perspective. At Kuala Lumpur, platitudes were the order of the day. The only element of genuine optimism was indicated in the satisfaction expressed 'that exchanges of diplomatic and trade visits at high levels have enhanced the prospects of improved relations between ASEAN countries and the countries of Indochina'.[25]

ASEAN was in a condition of political stress rather than actual disarray. Its impotence arose from an inability to influence its wider regional environment, not from a particular failure in political co-operation. Between member states, genuine differences of interest were not permitted to stand in the way of a growing habit of private consultation and public solidarity. Moreover, the corporate sense of alarm which had obtained on the morrow of revolutionary success in Indochina had given way to a more self-assured view as it became evident before the end of 1975 that a monolithic Indochinese Communism was not in the making. The revolutionary movement which assumed power in Cambodia, and changed the country's name to Kampuchea, asserted a ferocious national independence defined very much with reference to its relationship with Vietnam, so denying political conformity in the peninsula. The advent of an obdurately independent Kampuchea interposed between Thailand and a unified Vietnam and which came to enjoy the benign political regard and active support of China, provided the basis for an inter-Communist balance of power of which the ASEAN states became a beneficiary *faute de mieux*. Moreover, the fact of that balance or distribution of power, which denied Vietnam's dominance, helped to accommodate differences of strategic perspective within ASEAN, expressed most strongly between Thailand and Indonesia. Vietnam's inability to assert full dominance in Indochina was welcomed in Bangkok and acceptable in Jakarta because a growing Sino-Vietnamese antagonism which served Kampuchea's and Thailand's interests had not subordinated Hanoi to Beijing. A Communist Indochina had represented a decided setback to ASEAN's regional aspirations, but the emergence of an inter-Communist balance of power constituted a structure of relations which did not pose an imminent challenge to either the collective or individual priorities of the ASEAN states. That balance of power made possible a tolerable *modus vivendi* which could be managed on a bilateral and multilateral basis.

By August 1977, however, concurrent with the second ASEAN summit, the inter-Communist balance of power in Indochina had become less than stable as the result of the accelerating antagonism between Phnom Penh and Hanoi.[26] This expressed itself in a major military confrontation in the following month and in a diplomatic rupture at the end of the year. Stimulated and reinforced by the involvement of external Communist patrons, it had the effect of bringing South-East Asia full circle to a pattern of conflict which had distinguished the two previous wars in Indochina.[27] ASEAN was not in any position to act as an arresting factor in checking that growing antagonism. Paradoxically, as a consequence of its growing intensity, the members of the Association found themselves the object of competing political attentions. At that time, the member governments had not worked out a viable collective approach to regional security because such a goal was beyond their will and capability. Intra-mural discussions between senior officials on how to proceed towards the declared common goal of a Zone of Peace, Freedom, and Neutrality had produced little of substance, and only accentuated divergent security perspectives.

Apart from a common rejection of the alliance option and an agreement on the common peril posed by domestic insurgencies, the governments of ASEAN had little of practical import to say to one another on regional security. Malaysia's proposal for regional neutralisation based on external power guarantees had been rejected. Indonesia had advocated concentration on an inner strength (national resilience) which would in aggregate form both encapsulate and insulate South-East Asia. The government of Singapore, however, was quite open in stating that ASEAN could not expect to decree a regional 'Monroe Doctrine' to exclude the great powers. The political leaders of the island-state contemplated security from the harsh political facts of life, arguing that while the great powers could not be excluded from the region, their balanced presence would prevent any unpalatable external dominance and would also impose restraint on any over-ambitious regional state.[28] The articulation of such individual positions did not constitute practical initiatives but were rather expressions of policy justification without positive effect on either regional co-operation or regional security.

For its part, Indonesia did provide some practical encouragement for greater bilateral military co-operation beyond ASEAN's auspices, as endorsed at Bali. For example, President Suharto and Prime Minister Datuk Hussein Onn met in Penang, in Malaysia, in April 1977 where they agreed to extend military co-operation from naval and air force exercises to joint army manoeuvres. Such an undertaking did not constitute the first step in a wider practice among regional partners, however. It was an *ad hoc* measure and as such an indication of the limits to defence cooperation among ASEAN states. Foreign Minister Adam Malik pointed these out shortly before the second meeting of ASEAN's heads of government. He indicated that his government did not object to military exercises between regional partners 'as long as these exercises are held on a bilateral or even trilateral basis but not in the framework of ASEAN'.[29] He then put forward a formula for defence co-operation which validated participation only when there was an identifiable defence interest which would exclude, for example, such co-operation between Singapore and the Philippines. He claimed that there was a stipulation in the original Bangkok Declaration that there can be 'continuation of co-operation on a non-ASEAN basis between the two member states in security in accordance with their mutual needs and interests'. This claim was a product of Mr Malik's fertile imagination and is not to be found in the text of the Bangkok Declaration. But his exegesis does indicate how his government contemplated defence co-operation.

The Association as a corporate entity did not take a public

position on defence co-operation beyond the brief statement at the Bali Summit. In January 1977 its Secretariat had begun functioning from a permanent headquarters in Jakarta. The first Secretary General (of the ASEAN Secretariat, *not* ASEAN) was an Indonesian, Major-General Hartono Rekso Dharsono, since incarcerated for political indiscretion. He claimed that ASEAN had achieved more since the Bali Summit than in the previous eight years of its existence. But when he was asked how seriously the ASEAN nations viewed insurgency in Thailand and how this problem impinged on ASEAN's relations with Vietnam, he replied, 'This is an internal problem of Thailand and ASEAN – up till now – as a regional organisation does not take a position in this matter.'[30] By this time, as indicated above, the governments of ASEAN had begun to enjoy a breathing space with respect to regional security. The five states were still adjusting to the impact of revolutionary Communist success in Indochina and reacting to the disposition of the new Carter administration in Washington which did not inspire great confidence, in particular because of an election campaign commitment to withdraw U.S. ground troops from South Korea. Yet, despite an underlying apprehension of the intentions of the Hanoi government, an initial fear of its active support for regional insurgencies had not been borne out. Direct security concerns had given way in some quarters to the more fanciful notion that Vietnam, by transferring national energies to peacetime economic pursuits, might even outpace the ASEAN states who were then displaying remarkable growth rates. In retrospect, such an anxiety would seem to have been quite bizarre and totally misplaced if stimulated by an interest in promoting greater economic co-operation between regional partners. It also reflected a concern that Vietnam might become the beneficiary of economic and technological assistance from Japan and the United States.

Such concern had been expressed most strongly in Jakarta but was never the subject of a collective ASEAN view. Moreover, individual governments were making attempts to build bilateral relationships with Indochina. For example, Malaysia's Foreign Minister, Tengku Ahmad Rithaudeen had visited Hanoi and Vientiane. In the Vietnamese capital he had discussed provision for assistance in rubber technology and palm oil production. Apart from the attempt by Malaysia to cultivate a cordial relationship, the government of the Philippines established diplomatic relations with Vietnam without U.S. military bases becoming a contentious issue in negotiations. Bilateralism was undoubtedly the most practical way of reducing regional tensions. They were mitigated in virtually every case, with the exception of Thailand for a year from October 1976 because of the open anti-Vietnamese disposition of the government led by Prime Minister Thanin Kravichien. Thanin, who enjoyed royal patronage, carried a fierce anti-Communism to diplomatic extremes going out of his way to arrest and reverse the process of rapprochement with Vietnam. Bilateralism, however, was the only way forward. Phan Hien, Vietnam's Deputy Foreign Minister, remarked during a visit to Kuala Lumpur in June 1977, 'Since the end of the war in Indochina, a new situation exists in Southeast Asia. Why should we be absorbed into an already existing organisation whose past is known?' During the course of the tenth annual meeting of ASEAN's Foreign Ministers held in Singapore in July 1977, Tengku Rithaudeen made it clear that there was no question of a joint approach to Indochina, by which he meant Vietnam and Laos in the light of the isolationist policy of Kampuchea. He was explicit in pointing out that the Indochinese states were not ready to enter into any kind of relationship with ASEAN on a regional basis.

In consequence, by the time that ASEAN's heads of government met in Kuala Lumpur to celebrate the tenth anniversary of its foundation, they were not more advanced in any joint endeavour to manage regional order than their respective Foreign Ministers had been when meeting at the same venue in 1971. The absence of any coherent intra-mural consensus was compounded by Vietnam's refusal to treat with the Association on its own terms. By contrast with the Chinese and Soviet ambassadors, the Vietnamese refused to attend the inaugural ceremony of the anniversary summit. During its course, it was reported that delegations had emphasised privately that security was not a topic of discussion, confirming a statement by the five Foreign Ministers at a press conference after a preparatory meeting that it had been decided that the time was not appropriate for realising the declared ASEAN resolve to make South-East Asia a zone of peace, freedom, and neutrality.[31] In actual fact, a measure of initiative did occur over security. Thailand had sought to encourage greater security co-operation, a viewpoint which attracted some support from Indonesia, which may have been influenced by the exposure of its military shortcomings during the invasion and annexation of East Timor in December 1975. An absence of consensus meant that the proposal, couched in general terms failed to make any headway. More striking by way of failure was an inability to establish a firm basis for significant trade liberalisation which had been held out as a practical means of stimulating the economies of regional partners. Singapore's Prime Minister, Lee Kuan Yew, was obliged to admit, 'We have to accept a pace of intra-ASEAN economic co-operation which is more congenial to all of us.' To abuse the jargon of ASEAN, individual concern with national resilience stood as an obstacle to the development of regional resilience. In practical terms a country such as Indonesia, which had pioneered the terms 'national' and 'regional resilience', was not prepared to risk the threat to its nascent industrialisation which might arise from a process of economic competition between regional partners which trade liberalisation would encourage. In this respect, a salutary lesson of the summit was that national resilience did not necessarily lead to regional resilience.

The most distinctive achievement by ASEAN at Kuala Lumpur was diplomatic. Its degree of progress as a regional institution was accorded recognition by the presence in the Malaysian capital of the Prime Ministers of Japan, Australia, and New Zealand, who took part in post-summit discussions with their regional counterparts. Of special significance was the presence of Takeo Fukuda marking a major Japanese reappraisal of the importance and role of the Association. At its establishment, Japan's Foreign Ministry had been sceptical of the political credentials and merits of ASEAN, while colleagues in the Ministry of Trade and Industry were concerned that the Association was intended to act as a producers' cartel. Reservations about ASEAN were sustained with the enunciation of the Kuala Lumpur Declaration of November 1971. 'Neutralisation' and a 'Zone of Peace, Freedom, and Neutrality' were regarded as ill-chosen terms which could serve to stimulate debate within Japan on the merits of the security relationship with the United States. Japanese attitudes began to change markedly with the success of revolutionary Communism in Indochina and the so-called ASEAN dominoes demonstrating their collective political nerve. Japan's longstanding preference for bilateral relationships was set aside when it was decided that the collegial character of ASEAN was of direct relevance to the protection of economic security interests in South-East Asia.[32] The Kuala Lumpur Summit provided the opportunity for Japan to communicate its approval in a most visible way. From the perspective of ASEAN's governments, the post-summit diplomatic exercise was a means of securing greater international recognition and of engaging Japan more constructively in the economic development of member states to prevent the balance of regional advantage shifting further in favour of a revolutionary Indochina. The presence of Malcolm Fraser from Australia and Robert Muldoon from New Zealand was encouraged to lend greater international legitimacy to ASEAN, and by a concern not to make Mr Fukuda's visit the prime object of the post-summit occasion.

Collective discussions with Japan's Prime Minister bore at least declaratory fruit in a speech which Mr Fukuda make in Manila on 18 August 1977, the last stop of his tour of all ASEAN states as well as Burma before returning to Tokyo. What became known as the Fukuda Doctrine set out the bases of Japan's intended 'heart-to-heart' relationship of equal partnership. Although this speech reflected a consensus about ASEAN within Japan's political establishment, from ASEAN's perspective it constituted less than a watershed in a relationship based on economic interdependence. An offer of extensive economic assistance to finance joint industrial projects was made conditional on feasibility studies which, when undertaken, exposed an inadequate facility for substantial economic co-operation. Despite the misplaced enthusiasm occasioned by Fukuda's offer, his presence in Kuala Lumpur together with that of antipodean counterparts inaugurated a wider process of dialogue and diplomatic practice which certainly served to enhance ASEAN's international standing. It also reinforced ASEAN's significance as a factor in the calculations of newly established regional Communist governments. The practice of dialogue was extended with a meeting in Manila in September 1977 between ASEAN ministers and a U.S. delegation led by an Under Secretary of State for Economic Affairs.

If the mainly ceremonial summit did possess a positive diplomatic dimension giving rise to the concept of extra-mural dialogue partners, it also displayed a measure of apparent progress in intra-mural conciliation. The utility of ASEAN as a framework for such conciliation seemed to be reinforced by a public remark by President Marcos that his country would be taking 'definite steps' to eliminate its claim to the east Malaysian state of Sabah. Irrespective of Malaysian reserve over a gesture that did not appear to possess tangible content, the statement helped to influence the political climate of the summit and to demonstrate the cohesion of ASEAN. That said, the second meeting of ASEAN heads of government was an anti-climax. It in no way fulfilled the promise generated by the political tone of the first such meeting in Bali in

February 1976. Moreover, although security concerns had become less acute since the fall of Indochina, an abiding common nervousness over the condition of regional security was not expressed in any tangible doctrine which might serve as the basis for practical collective measures. A common focus of security interest was not defined beyond a general concurrence about the dangers of internal subversion and insurgency. Apart from incidents along the border between Thailand and Kampuchea – to an extent provoked from the Thai side – external threat did not possess an immediacy for the five regional partners. Ironically, the prospect of assuming a security role beyond intra-mural bounds did not arise from the emergence of any direct threat to the territorial integrity of an ASEAN state. In the month after the second ASEAN summit, the testy relationship between the Communist parties of Vietnam and Kampuchea, which had been uneasy even before the attainment of revolutionary success in April 1975 expressed itself in a major military confrontation. The momentum of their conflict was accelerated from that point with a decisive effect on regional politics and in particular on the corporate life of the Association.

Military confrontation between Vietnam and Kampuchea reached a climax in December 1978. Vietnam's army invaded the neighbouring Communist state of Democratic Kampuchea, overthrowing its notorious government which was replaced with an administration established by Hanoi. In the intervening period of growing tension before ASEAN was obliged to adopt a common public position on this military intervention, the members of the Association found themselves increasingly the object of competing political attentions by those parties directly and indirectly engaged in the escalating conflict. Virtually concurrent with the development of a network of dialogue relationships with trading partners among the industrialised states, the governments of ASEAN become the diplomatic beneficiaries of initiatives by rival sets of Communist counterparts. Representatives from recently isolationist Kampuchea and once hostile Vietnam sought to put their relations with the ASEAN states in good order as they squared up against one another diplomatically and on the field of battle. Correspondingly, representatives of their external patrons, namely, the People's Republic of China and the Soviet Union, engaged in a similar exercise.

Although such competitive diplomacy was conducted on a strictly bilateral basis, its cumulative effect was to enhance the general standing of ASEAN as a diplomatic community. The

Association was invested with a regional significance which exaggerated its intrinsic importance as indicated by the measure of its corporate achievement. The experience of being subject to the competing attentions of rival Communist states obliged the member governments to improve their consultative practices. It became necessary to coordinate more closely the conduct of regional foreign policies, especially as ASEAN was being wooed politically in the pursuit of conflicting interests, not to expand a structure of genuine regional co-operation. For example, visits during 1977 to Indonesia, the Philippines, Malaysia and Thailand (Singapore was omitted because of continuing friction over the hijacking of a Vietnamese aircraft to the Republic) by Vietnam's Foreign Minister, Nguyen Duy Trinh, were interpreted not as a friendly gesture in their own right but as part of an attempt to break out of a perceived Chinese threat of encirclement. His visits did not reveal a willingness to accept ASEAN on its own terms. On the contrary, an accompanying Deputy Foreign Minister, Vo Dong Giang, had urged that the Association be disbanded because it was U.S.-backed and because troops from two of its member states had been fighting in South Vietnam when it was established in 1967. At the end of 1977, virtually concurrent with the breach in diplomatic relations between Kampuchea and Vietnam, the latter's Prime Minister Pham Van Dong was asked 'What kind of relations are you going to establish with ASEAN?' He replied,

> The policy of setting up such military blocs as ASEAN in Southeast Asia has failed and passed forever. The relationship of friendship and co-operation among countries of this region must be established on a new basis, in a new spirit.[33]

Correspondingly, during his visit to Malaysia in January 1978, Foreign Minister Vo Dong Giang indicated his government's interest in discussing a new form of regional co-operation with all of its South-East Asian neighbours.

For the governments of ASEAN, the evolving, if less than satisfactory, relationship with Vietnam was of considerable importance. In Indonesia, in particular, initial suspicions aroused by Hanoi's open espousal of a revolutionary cause for the whole of South-East Asia was compounded by a growing concern at the intensification of Sino-Soviet rivalry within the region. Although the government in Jakarta was prepared to endorse an inter-Communist balance of power in Indochina which pivoted on the bloodthirsty assertiveness of Pol Pot's Kampuchea, it had an interest also in attaching Vietnam to a structure of regional relations. This interest had a basis in a sentimental view of Vietnam as a fellow spirit in the struggle against colonialism and in a historical understanding of the nature of Sino-Vietnamese relations. If Vietnam could be encouraged to express its national independence through some form of association with regional states then the competitive engagement of Chinese and Soviet interests might be contained. Although the geopolitical perspective of Jakarta did not match that of Bangkok, an evolving sense of corporate solidarity within ASEAN was expressed in the management of diplomatic contact with Vietnam.

In retrospect, a softening in Vietnam's attitude towards ASEAN – manifested around the middle of 1978 and reflected also in Soviet outlook – was most probably the result of a Politburo decision to invade Kampuchea in order to overthrow and replace its objectionable government. At the time, although it was understood in ASEAN capitals that Vietnam's modification of attitude was directly connected to the stormy state of its relations with China, there is no evidence to suggest that an early outbreak of the Third Indochina War was anticipated. A major diplomatic opening by Vietnam to the ASEAN states by way of a tour of their capitals by Prime Minister Pham Van Dong during September and October 1978 was treated very much as an opportunity to accommodate competing formulae for regional order. Accordingly, the ASEAN governments receiving Pham Van Dong in turn took great pains to consult closely in advance in order to adopt a common position. Corporate ranks were held firm in response to attempts by Vietnam's Prime Minister to promote a structure of regional relations based on a set of bilateral treaties of friendship. There was a common insistence in every one of five joint communiques issued during his tour of the commitment by individual ASEAN governments to work towards the Association's declared goal of a Zone of Peace, Freedom, and Neutrality. For example, at the conclusion of Pham Van Dong's first call in Bangkok, the joint communique stated *inter alia:*

> The two Prime Ministers expressed their respective views on the desirability of Southeast Asia being an area of peace, independence, freedom and neutrality as well as of stability and prosperity. In this connection, the Thai Prime Minister

reiterated Thailand's commitment to work towards the realization of the ASEAN concept of the zone of peace, freedom and neutrality.[34]

The ASEAN states had engaged in symbolic politics in a corporate refusal to defer to Vietnam's formula. The expression of diplomatic solidarity constituted less than the assumption of a regional security role. Although a measure of satisfaction was exhibited at the assurances of non-interference in the internal affairs of regional states provided in every ASEAN capital by Vietnam's Prime Minister, such assurances did not constitute a major concession in the circumstances. None the less, there was some political significance in Pham Van Dong's regional tour, namely, the extent to which ASEAN as a corporate entity had become an important factor in the calculations of the government in Hanoi. From its perspective, there was no practical alternative to invading Kampuchea because of the threat posed by its relentless hostility, apparently encouraged and abetted by China. In contemplating such a military undertaking, ASEAN was of political account because its attitude would have a bearing on the international response to the intended *fait accompli*. In that respect, Pham Van Dong's tour of ASEAN capitals constituted an exercise in advance political damage limitation, albeit an abortive one.

The more that regional and external states brought ASEAN within the compass of their calculations, the more its member governments responded by conducting themselves as if they were part of a diplomatic community. The attendant enhancement of regional credentials, reinforced by an evolving network of dialogue partnerships with industrialised Western states, worked to the political advantage of the Association. Although in no sense a security manager in the manner of a dominant regional power, its collective diplomatic voice began to count for something on regional issues. This factor became evident immediately following Vietnam's invasion and occupation of Kampuchea at the end of 1978 when the member governments found themselves obliged to adopt a common public position. Indeed, not to have done so in the circumstances would have indicated a total abdication of responsibility for regional security in South-East Asia.

Notes

1. Chin Kin Wah, *The Defence of Malaysia and Singapore*, Cambridge University Press, Cambridge, 1983, Chapter 9.

2. *ASEAN Documents Series*, 1967–1985, ASEAN Secretariat, Jakarta, 1985.

3. For the voting break-down, see the *New York Times*, 27 October 1971.

4. Leszek Busznynski, *The Soviet Union in Southeast Asia*, Croom Helm, London 1986, Chapter 2.

5. For a discussion of Malaysia's motives, see Dick Wilson, *The Neutralization of Southeast Asia*, Praeger, New York, 1975, Chapter 5.

6. *Government Statement Before the Gotong-Royong House of Representatives, 16 August 1966*, Department of Information, Jakarta, 1966, p. 48.

7. Reprinted in the *Far Eastern Economic Review*, 25 September 1971.

8. Ibid.

9. *ASEAN Documents Series*, 1967–1985, op. cit., p. 21.

10. *Far Eastern Economic Review*, op. cit.

11. For a discussion of this episode, see Michael Leifer, *Malacca, Indonesia, and Singapore*, vol. 2 of *International Straits of the World*, Sijthoff and Noordhoff, Alphen aan den Rijn. 1978.

12. *ASEAN Documents Series*, 1967–1985, op. cit., p. 46.

13. Tim Huxley, *The ASEAN States Defence Policies, 1975–81: Military Responses to Indochina*, Strategic and Defence Studies Centre, Australian National University, Canberra, 1984.

14. *ASEAN Documents Series*, 1967–1985, op. cit., p. 23.

15. See David Irvine, 'Making Haste Less Slowly: ASEAN from 1975', in Alison Broinowski (ed.), *Understanding ASEAN*, St Martin's Press, New York, 1982, p. 45.

16. *Ten Years ASEAN*, ASEAN Secretariat, Jakarta, 1978, p. 88.

17. Ibid., p. 93.

18. Text in *ASEAN Documents Series*, 1967–1985, op. cit., pp. 26–8.

19. Charles E. Morrison and Astri Suhrke, *Strategies of Survival. The Foreign Policy Dilemmas of Small Asian States*, University of Queensland Press, St. Lucia, 1978, p. 119.

20. BBC, *Summary of World Broadcasts*, FE/5133/A3/2.

21. Ibid., FE/5147/A3/1

22. Ibid., FE/5298/A3/3

23. *ASEAN Documents Series*, 1967–1985, op. cit., p. 48.

24. Ibid., p. 51.

25. Ibid., p. 32.

26. For the origins of the Kampuchean conflict, see David W. P. Elliot (ed.), *The Third Indochina Conflict*, Westview Press, Boulder, CO, 1981; Nayan Chanda, *Brother Enemy*, Harcourt Brace, San Diego, CA, 1986; Chang Pao-min, *Kampuchea Between China and Vietnam*, Singapore University Press, Singapore, 1985; and Elizabeth Becker, *When the War Was Over*, Simon and Schuster, New York, 1986.

27. See the argument in Michael Leifer, *Conflict and Regional Order in South-East Asia,* International Institute of Strategic Studies, Adelphi Papers no. 162, London, 1980.

28. Quoted in Lee Khoon Choy, 'Foreign Policy', in C.V. Devan Nair (ed.), *Socialism That Works – The Singapore Way,* Federal Publishers, Singapore, 1976.

29. *Far Eastern Economic Review*, 10 June 1977.

30. Ibid., 24 June 1977.

31. Ibid., 12 August 1977.

32. For a discussion of Japanese attitudes to ASEAN, see Masahishi Shibusawa, *Japan and the Asia Pacific Region,* Croom Helm, London, 1984.

33. Interview with Nayan Chanda in *Far Eastern Economic Review*, 13 January 1978.

34. BBC, *Summary of World Broadcasts,* op. cit., FE/5914/A3/2.

4

ASEAN and the Invasion of Kampuchea

Any political optimism which had been generated among ASEAN governments by the tone of Prime Minister Pham Van Dong's visits during September and October 1978 was dissipated in early November. On 3 November, Vietnam concluded a treaty of friendship and co-operation with the Soviet Union. The full significance of that treaty became evident over a month later. None the less, it was noted at the time that its terms, including an article which had security implications, were similar to those of the Indian–Soviet treaty of August 1971 which had facilitated India's military intervention in east Pakistan in the face of China's hostility. The treaty of November 1978, which consolidated the bilateral relationship after Vietnam's membership of COMECON in the previous June, was intended to produce a corresponding deterrent effect. The object was to protect a vulnerable northern border with China, while the government in Phnom Penh was being despatched.

The actual invasion and occupation of Kampuchea which began on 25 December 1978 had a mixed impact on the ASEAN states. The event was disturbing for all, because it demonstrated that Vietnam, aided by the Soviet Union, was prepared to violate the cardinal rule of the society of states in pursuit of its interests. The sanctity of national sovereignty had been placed at the centre of collegial commitment in ASEAN's Treaty of Amity and Co-operation, designed to serve as a code of conduct for ordered regional relationships. The member governments were conscious, therefore, of the implications of endorsing, even by default, a precedent which might well be applied in the future to one of their number. Perhaps the governments of ASEAN should have been more hard-headed, but in some capitals Vietnam's invasion of

Kampuchea, coming shortly after Pham Van Dong's assurances of good intent, was regarded as an act of betrayal. It could not be left unremarked without the credibility of the Association being called into question.

Vietnam's invasion of Kampuchea constituted a blatant challenge to the public philosophy of ASEAN, but it had a differential impact on the actual security interests of its member states. That mixed impact has been indicated in alternative approaches to resolving the problem created by Vietnam's imposition of a client government in Phnom Penh. Those approaches will be discussed below. It is necessary to point out, however, that such underlying intra-mural differences have never been allowed to obstruct a public display of a corporate political consensus over Kampuchea. Despite the persistence of such differences, the ASEAN states have sustained a collegial solidarity which has had an important bearing on the diplomatic dimension of the Kampuchean conflict. That said, Vietnam's invasion and occupation of Kampuchea did have the paradoxical effect of dividing as well as of uniting ASEAN. The source of that division was unconnected with the moral issue of alignment with the bestial Khmer Rouge in challenging Vietnam. It arose from a natural divergence of strategic perspectives, which has been an important factor in denying the Association a conventional security role.

Without doubt, the greatest measure of concern was experienced and expressed in Bangkok by a military-led administration which had actually sought to promote an accommodation with the states of Indochina since it had assumed power in October 1977. Vietnam's expeditious overthrow of the notorious Khmer Rouge government and its replacement in early January 1979 by a compliant regime violated Thailand's strategic environment in an historically unprecedented manner.[1] Thailand and Vietnam had been rivals for dominant influence over the fertile valley of the River Mekong in the centuries before the establishment of French colonial rule throughout Indochina. French dominion had arrested a historical contention which was then resumed after France had been obliged to abdicate its colonial position in 1954. Vietnam's occupation of Kampuchea extended by force a structure of dominance already incorporating Laos. That extension assumed a political significance beyond any attendant military invasion of Thailand, which was not then anticipated. Vietnam's occupation foreshadowed the emergence of a historically unique centre of power in the mainland of South-East Asia besides which Thailand would almost certainly stand in a subordinate position. Such a prospect, permitting intervention in support of subversion, was viewed by the ruling military-bureaucratic establishment in Bangkok as posing a threat to the very independence of the Thai state. It was not assuaged by Vietnamese assurances of respect for Thai sovereignty. The only way to remove that threat was by challenging Vietnam's assertion of dominance.

In taking up that challenge, ASEAN occupied a significant but subordinate place in Thailand's strategic calculations. ASEAN could provide collective political defence but not countervailing power against Vietnam. The point has been well made that the major responses of the Thai government 'to the extension of the military power of its traditional rival Vietnam into Kampuchea involved large power diplomacy.'[2] Secret negotiations with Chinese representatives in Bangkok in January 1979 paved the way for material provision for a Khmer Rouge insurgency against Vietnam's occupation of Kampuchea and withdrawal of China's support for the Communist Party of Thailand. A visit to Washington in February by Prime Minister Kriangsak secured a public reinstatement of a U.S. security guarantee, while one to Moscow in the following month, if much less fruitful, indicated diplomatic access to Vietnam's patron. In this company, ASEAN constituted only a lesser complementary resource which Thailand's regional partners felt obliged to place at its service. That act of solidarity was accompanied by misgivings on the part of some of them, which were reinforced as a tacit alliance developed between Bangkok and Beijing.[3]

Within ASEAN, an alternative strategic perspective had been indicated by the government of Indonesia, in part because the insular location of the Republic made the expansion of Vietnamese territorial control less than an immediate threat. The government in Jakarta had exhibited a deep-seated hostility to Communism from its establishment in March 1966. It was also in dispute with Vietnam over maritime jurisdiction in the South China Sea, but there was a willingness to treat it as an exceptional Communist state. That willingness, alluded to above, was based in part on sentimental considerations arising from the perceived shared experiences of the Indonesian and Vietnamese nationalist movements in challenging colonial rule. All Indonesian governments have exhibited a special feeling for countries which have struggled to attain national independence. For that reason, for example, there has long been a sense of identification with Algeria.

Furthermore, in Vietnam's case there was a ready acceptance of a proprietary relationship to the whole of former French Indochina as a corresponding entitlement to that which Indonesia's nationalist movement, with a Javanese core, had exercised over the entire area of the former Netherlands East Indies. Beyond considerations arising from a projection of Indonesia's experience, its ruling military establishment held the view that the People's Republic of China, and not Vietnam, posed the most serious, if long term, threat to national security. Moreover, in the light of a historically rooted antagonism between China and Vietnam which had become so acute during 1978, the expectation was revived in Jakarta that Hanoi might be attracted to a structure of countervailing regional relationships. The prospect of Vietnam serving as an obstacle to the expansion of China's influence in South-East Asia had been encouraged by conversations with Vietnam's Prime Minister during his visit to Jakarta in September 1978.

The strategic perspectives of the other ASEAN states were located along a continuum whose extremes were marked by the positions of Thailand and Indonesia. In declaratory terms, Singapore appeared even more hostile to Vietnam than Thailand, a stand justified because of Soviet support for the invasion of Kampuchea. Singapore had been particularly concerned at the evident neglect of South-East Asia by the Carter administration. It held strongly to the view that a stable balance of power in the region required a U.S. military role. The public attention given to the part played by the Soviet Union in Vietnam's removal of an independent government in Kampuchea was intended to alert the United States to the expanding regional influence of its principal adversary. In addition Singapore had not relinquished the 'domino theory' perspective it had held during the course of the Second Indochina War. It regarded the non-Communist states to the north as protecting buffers whose integrity was threatened by the physical extension of Vietnamese political control. To that end, it was determined not to allow the issue of Kampuchea to escape persistent international attention. The international spotlight was deemed a practical weapon to arrest a presumed assertiveness by Vietnam, which posed a general threat to independent states in South-East Asia, of which Singapore was one of the most vulnerable.

Malaysia, at least during the incumbency of Prime Minister Datuk Hussein Onn, stood closer to the position of Indonesia even though it was more proximate to the locus of conflict and disputed sovereignty with Vietnam over islands in the Spratly Archipelago. Malaysia's outlook arose from a shared sense of external threat. China was identified as its principal source in the context of a residual insurgency which drew primary support from an ethnic-Chinese constituency. Malaysian political sensitivities had been sustained by the refusal of China's Communist Party to renounce support for the insurgent Communist Party of Malaya. They were reinforced by the flow of ethnic-Chinese refugees from Vietnam whose landfall on the east coast of peninsular Malaysia generated communal tensions. Malaysia's Foreign Ministry also regarded the condition of Sino-Vietnamese relations as encouraging Hanoi to consider itself as part of a regional constellation of states. That said, Vietnam's invasion had a disturbing effect, in part because of the prospect that Thailand might be obliged to neglect cross-border co-operation against the Malayan Communist Party.

The Philippines stood in an intermediate position in terms of its own security interests. Enjoying a maritime insulation from Indochina and China, while beset by serious internal challenges from Communist and Muslim insurrections, the alternatives of an immediate external threat from Vietnam and a longer-term threat from China did not seem to apply. On the other hand, it was also in dispute with Vietnam and China over some of the Spratly Islands. A long-established legalistic outlook in international relations made it difficult to accept any plea of mitigating circumstances for Vietnam's invasion of Kampuchea. Moreover, ASEAN had become an established point of reference in a foreign policy governed by the need to register a regional identity and to diversify external affiliations overshadowed by the U.S. connection. For those reasons, its government did not give the impression of dissenting from the ASEAN consensus.

In strategic perspective, the ASEAN states were not exactly bound by a shared central view which could serve as a firm common basis for responding to Vietnam's military initiative. Shared view or not, the five states were obliged to take a public position. ASEAN could not ignore Vietnam having conveyed a government into Kampuchea virtually in the saddle bags of its invading army without a serious loss of international credibility. The Association responded initially through a statement on 9 January 1979 made by Indonesia's Foreign Minister, Mochtar Kusumaatmadja in his capacity as chairman of its Standing Committee. That statement was less than direct and deliberately did not identify or denounce Vietnam. It merely deplored 'the current escalation and enlargement of the conflict between the two states in Indochina', also expressing 'grave concern over the implications of this development and its impact on the peace, security and stability in Southeast Asia'.[4] Three days later an emergency meeting of the Association's Foreign Ministers was held in Bangkok. A stronger stand was adopted, albeit still marked by restraint in choice of language, which reflected internal debate over the utility of trying to keep open lines of communication to Hanoi. That statement affirmed the five governments' determination 'to demonstrate the solidarity and cohesiveness of ASEAN in the face of the current threat to peace and stability in the Southeast Asian region' and recalled 'the Vietnamese pledge to ASEAN member countries to scrupulously respect each other's independence, sovereignty and territorial integrity'. It also 'strongly deplored the armed intervention against the independence, sovereignty and territorial integrity of Kampuchea' and 'called for the immediate and total withdrawal of the foreign forces from Kampuchean territory'.[5] A joint statement on January 13 addressed the issue of refugees from Indochina and stressed that Vietnam, which had pledged to promote regional peace and security, and other countries of origin should take appropriate measures to tackle the problem at its source.[6]

The choice of Bangkok for the emergency meeting was made deliberately, as the joint statement indicated, to demonstrate solidarity with a regional partner which had become the Association's front-line state. The Foreign Ministers did not specifically identify Vietnam as a transgressor of national sovereignty, but they made abundantly clear their refusal to recognize the transfer of political power within Kampuchea effected through Vietnamese force of arms. To that end, they invoked the regional credentials of the Association to set out requirements for regional security defined with reference to Kampuchea. At the centre of those requirements was an insistence on respect for national sovereignty and an adamant refusal to tolerate changes of government brought about by military intervention across internationally recognized boundaries. It was impossible for Indonesia, therefore, despite its own strategic perspective, to refuse to endorse such a common stand given the flagrant breach of a principle central to the cohesion and viability of ASEAN.

In truth, the credentials of some ASEAN members were not

unblemished in upholding respect for national sovereignty. In December 1975 Indonesian forces had annexed the Portuguese sovereign possession of East Timor in order to deny independence to a radical left-wing movement which had seized power there. During the mid-1970s Malaysia had inspired covert acts calculated to destabilise the British-protected Sultanate of Brunei. And during the late 1960s the Philippines had been implicated in a subversive exercise apparently designed to advance a territorial claim to the east Malaysian state of Sabah, which had provoked in turn Malaysian support for Muslim rebellion in the southern Philippines. By comparison, Vietnam's invasion of Kampuchea was a more blatant violation of national sovereignty, if also the result of considerable provocation. Regardless of the comparative demerits of the behaviour of Vietnam and some ASEAN states, the Association closed ranks to set the terms of public international debate over the Kampuchean issue and consequently assumed a security role of a kind. In this undertaking, an ability to influence international recognition was the major weapon in ASEAN's diplomatic armoury.

In embarking on this undertaking, ASEAN was in a sense swimming with the political tide. Vietnam's invasion of Kampuchea had its origins in more than just a bilateral conflict between ruling Communist parties in Hanoi and Phnom Penh. It also reflected a deep-rooted antagonism between Vietnam and China aggravated by Sino-Soviet tensions. In consequence, Thailand in particular and ASEAN in general received vigorous diplomatic support from the government of the People's Republic. Beijing became the principal source of military assistance for the retreating Khmer Rouge army. On regrouping, it established itself as an insurgent force in redoubts along the border between Kampuchea and Thailand with the active tolerance of the government in Bangkok.

Among some ASEAN governments, China's support was regarded as a mixed blessing. Among others it was viewed as a menacing involvement. When China assumed the role of regional gamekeeper by launching a punitive military intervention in northern Vietnam in February–March 1979 in an attempt to teach its neighbour a 'limited lesson',[7] mistrust of the People's Republic was confirmed in Jakarta and Kuala Lumpur. The fact that one apparent motive for China's intervention was the alleged persecution of the resident ethnic-Chinese community in Vietnam generated a wider apprehension over any future involvement on behalf of an economically powerful minority within the region. Some governments recalled the refusal by Vice-Premier Deng Xiaoping to renounce support by the Communist Party of China for revolutionary movements in South-East Asia during visits in November 1978 to Thailand, Malaysia, and Singapore. In addition, concern began to be expressed at the prospect of the ASEAN states becoming caught up in an entangling Sino-Soviet conflict being played out in Indochina. Such concern was indicated during a meeting in Medan in March 1979 between President Suharto and Prime Minister Kriangsak Chomanand of Thailand.

None the less, China's support, expressed in a willingness to embark on a military expedition against Vietnam despite its treaty of friendship with the Soviet Union, was a decisive factor in sustaining the momentum of ASEAN's initial stand. It was of signal relevance to the insistence by the Thai government that its regional partners stand up and be counted in a collective demonstration of ASEAN solidarity. If they had shown themselves to be unwilling in the circumstances to close ranks in confronting Thailand's historical enemy, then its future participation in ASEAN could well have been placed in jeopardy. Whether Thailand would have been disposed to confront Vietnam solely on the basis of diplomatic support from regional partners is an academic question. It would not seem to have been likely, however, in the light of its government's accommodating response after 1975 to the assumption of power in neighbouring Laos by the People's Revolutionary Party. In the case of Laos, viewed also as an interposing buffer between Vietnam and Thailand, Bangkok had no alternative but to accommodate to the change of regime in Vientiane, however unpalatable the elimination of monarchy in Luang Prabang. The relationship of political dominance and dependence between the ruling Communist parties in Hanoi and Vientiane was accepted grudgingly as inevitable in the absence of any credible internal opposition within Laos and of any significant external source of challenge to the new power structure.[8] In 1975 the change of government and political identity in Vientiane had been endorsed by the Chinese government. It had maintained a limited road-building presence in Laos, hoping to encourage a measure of local independence from the dominance of Hanoi and from the influence of the Soviet Union. Even the United States had retained its diplomatic mission in Vientiane. Accordingly, the political *fait accompli* was not susceptible to a Thai challenge in any serious sense. Correspondingly, neither was the situation in

Kampuchea from April 1975, which worked to Thai geopolitical advantage.

Self-styled Democratic Kampuchea, however, rejected Vietnam's offer of a special relationship. It became an aggressive buffer state, encouraged in this role by China. In consequence, an informal alignment between Thailand, Kampuchea and China was forged by the end of 1975, based on a common interest in containing the extension of Vietnamese influence within Indochina. That alignment was cemented by Vietnam's invasion of Kampuchea which constituted an affront to China's political standing as patron of the Khmer Rouge regime. An internal opposition of substance survived that invasion in the form of the military arm of the ousted Phnom Penh government. Its bestial record was of secondary consideration in Bangkok as long as its demonic energies could be directed against the Vietnamese in Kampuchea. The countervailing power possessed by China and the Khmer Rouge was a much more effective means by which to challenge Vietnam's hegemonic position than the diplomatic support of ASEAN. Without access to such power, especially from China, it is doubtful whether the Thai government would have adopted a policy of open confrontation as opposed to a characteristic posture of bending with the prevailing political wind. In other words, ASEAN may not necessarily have adopted, let alone sustained, the common position articulated in Bangkok in January 1979, in the absence of China's involvement in the conflict. Its engagement almost certainly made all the difference in Bangkok, where the political fortunes of ASEAN were made hostage to solidarity with Thailand.

ASEAN was also swimming with the political tide of Sino-U.S. rapprochement, which had its nexus in a common anti-Soviet position. Vietnam's invasion of Kampuchea under Soviet patronage gave the United States cause to suspend negotiations with the government in Hanoi over establishing diplomatic relations as well as to employ economic sanctions. Moreover, during a visit to Washington in February 1979 by Prime Minister General Kriangsak Chomanand, President Carter reaffirmed the validity of his country's commitment to Thailand under the terms of the Manila Pact. Although disturbed at the prospect of Vietnam becoming unduly dependent on the Soviet Union, the Japanese as well as European Community governments also entered the anti-Vietnamese alignment in a practical way by suspending economic aid allocations. Accordingly, ASEAN, which had begun to enjoy an increased international standing as a result of developing external dialogues and attracting competing political attentions, was far from alone in challenging Vietnam's dominance in Indochina. The Association was able to invoke regional credentials to underpin its case in taking the lead at the United Nations to mobilise international support against Vietnam, but it comprised only the diplomatic vanguard of an informal coalition of wider forces which also employed an armoury of military and economic sanctions. That coalition adopted a strategy of attrition designed to place breaking strain on Vietnam's society and government in order to coerce it into reversing its policy.

ASEAN's place in that informal coalition was an uneasy one. Swimming with the political tide was a mixed blessing. Some of its governments were less than happy with the implications of the strategy of attrition as well as with some of the political company which the Association had begun to keep. Its role in that strategy was not central but secondary. Vietnam was least affected by diplomatic pressure which was virtually all that ASEAN could employ. But its diplomatic initiatives did play an important part in defining the terms of international public debate over Kampuchea although the position adopted by the Association favoured China's interests, above all. For example, ASEAN's call for the withdrawal of all foreign forces from Indochina at the time of China's punitive expedition was received with satisfaction in Beijing. In Hanoi, that statement was not regarded as even-handed. Even less so was an ASEAN-sponsored draft resolution in March 1979 before the Security Council of the United Nations which requested that 'all foreign forces withdraw from the areas of conflict'. That initiative, which failed because of a Soviet veto, prompted a Vietnamese charge of collusion with 'Chinese reactionaries and other imperialist forces'.

ASEAN's response to Vietnam's invasion of Kampuchea was motivated by convergent considerations of principle, balance of power, and corporate solidarity. It was articulated also in the context of both regional and intra-mural tensions generated by a significant increase in the flow of refugees from Vietnam across the South China Sea to landfalls in ASEAN states which began in March 1978. A notable feature of that flow which reached a peak by the middle of 1979 was the conspicuously ethnic-Chinese identity of most of the boat people.[9] As such they were deemed to pose a threat to social and political order by disturbing the communal balance in Malaysia and by reviving fears of a subversive menace in Indonesia. Moreover, relations between Malaysia and Indonesia were strained by the practice adopted by the Federation's security forces of pushing back to sea boatloads of refugees who were then carried on by ocean currents to some of Indonesia's islands in the South China Sea. The government of Singapore adopted a rigid policy of refusing to take any refugees without a guarantee of asylum from a third country, on the ostensible ground of limited absorptive capacity but in reality this was from a deep-seated concern to discourage the idea that the island-state might serve as a regional refuge for persecuted overseas Chinese. Moreover, in all the agitation which arose over the boat people, the government of Thailand exhibited resentment that its regional partners in their individual preoccupations were disregarding the heavy burden imposed by the flow of land refugees from Laos and Kampuchea.[10] Intra-mural differences were accommodated as the member governments joined the issues of the boat people and the invasion of Kampuchea in their expression of common opposition to Vietnam's policies.

It is doubtful that the Vietnamese government sought deliberately to undermine the stability of any of the ASEAN states by encouraging a mass exodus of ethnic-Chinese residents during the first half of 1979. A more likely explanation was an interest in profiting financially from the sale of exit permits and an opportunity to reduce the size of an alien community regarded as socially and politically undesirable. Whatever the cause, the flow of refugees prompted a measure of disunity within ASEAN not only over burden sharing but also over whether a greater threat arose from the political impact of the ethnic-Chinese boat people than from the military action of Vietnam. Those governments holding the former view were more apprehensive of China's intentions and therefore inclined to be sympathetic to Vietnam's strategic predicament. However, as a result of its undisputed responsibility for the large flow of ethnic-Chinese refugees, the Vietnamese government actually alienated those regional counterparts which it had every reason to cultivate in order to divide ASEAN. The net result was a further closing of ASEAN ranks at its annual ministerial meeting held in Bali at the end of June 1979, expressed in the strongest condemnation thus far of Vietnam, which was held to be responsible for the 'unending exodus of illegal immigrants'.[11] At that meeting, Singapore's Foreign Minister, Sinnathamby Rajaratnam, depicted Vietnam as an expansionist power with ambitions to dominate South-East Asia and claimed that the refugees were being deployed as an instrument of political destabilisation. He advocated that ASEAN governments should actively take the side of the anti-Vietnamese resistance in Kampuchea by providing it with arms and material support. His strictures did not reflect the eventual consensus reached but the Association did not waver in reinforcing its firm stand on Kampuchea, despite some private misgivings that it had become entangled in a political web of Chinese manufacture. It has been pointed out that 'Less than six months after their special meeting in Bangkok which apportioned no public blame for the great exodus from Indochina, ASEAN foreign ministers had collectively placed Vietnam in the dock.'[12]

The Bali meeting drew international attention to the regional problem of refugees. A subsequent UN Conference in Geneva in July 1979 had the effect of persuading the Vietnamese government to control their flow. Complicity in such a flow had served to reinforce ASEAN solidarity over Kampuchea which Vietnam wished to undermine. The principal point of difference between ASEAN and the government in Hanoi remained unresolved, however. China's punitive military intervention had failed to overcome Vietnam's determination to consolidate a special relationship with Kampuchea, expressed formally in a treaty of friendship and co-operation concluded on 18 February 1979. ASEAN's initial diplomatic campaign had a lesser impact on the course of the conflict. Its object, however, was to keep the issue of Kampuchea in the forefront of international public attention in order to add to the more practical pressures being applied to the Vietnamese. To that end, its governments sought to establish the orthodoxy that the root of the conflict was Vietnam's invasion. A resolution could only follow its withdrawal. Their diplomacy was conducted with striking success in the debating chambers and lobbies of the United Nations, if less so within the Non-Aligned Movement. Moreover, ASEAN's role in helping to deny diplomatic recognition to the successor government in Phnom Penh had the effect of arresting its internal consolidation as well as denying it international status. ASEAN's ability to place Vietnam in the position of a pariah state and to depict the government of Kampuchea as an illegitimate proxy served to exclude them from eligibility for international economic assistance, other than relief aid. In that respect, it is interesting to note the conversation reported in January 1979 between Ha Van Lau, Vietnam's permanent representative to the United Nations and Singapore's counterpart Tommy Koh. Mr Lau informed his Singaporean colleague that the ASEAN states should not bother with the Kampuchea issue. 'In two weeks', he confidently said, 'the world would have forgotten the Kampuchea problem.'[13]

Six months later in Bali, ASEAN's Foreign Ministers affirmed their commitment to three goals over Kampuchea which have been upheld with consistency in public ever since. First, the solidarity of the Association was affirmed with reference to the security of Thailand and to the cardinal rule of the society of states. Accordingly, they 'reiterated their firm support [for] solidarity with the government and people of Thailand or any other country in the preservation of its independence'. Second, they called for 'the immediate and total withdrawal of the foreign forces from Kampuchean territory', referring directly to Vietnam by calling on its government 'to demonstrate its positive attitude towards Thailand and the other ASEAN member states by withdrawing its forces from the Thai–Kampuchean border'. Finally, support was reiterated for the right of the Kampuchean people 'to determine their future by themselves, free from interference or influence from outside powers in the exercise of self-determination'.[14] For the ASEAN states, issues of principle and security were logically joined over Kampuchea to the extent that respect for the former would provide for the latter, especially as far as Thailand was concerned. However, ASEAN was much more than Thailand, and consequently the strategic perspective held in Bangkok did not apply in a uniform manner among its regional partners.

Although ASEAN had been able to adopt a common stand on Kampuchea and on refugees from Vietnam, an underlying disagreement obtained over whose security interests were being truly served by the diplomatic stand of the Association. This problem of consensus has bedevilled its functioning ever since Vietnam's invasion of Kampuchea.[15] Indonesia's military establishment, in particular, was concerned from the outset that the common position adopted publicly would not cater for the Republic's interests. Related resentment arose from a shift in the political centre of gravity of the Association from Jakarta to Bangkok as a direct result of ASEAN's engagement in the Kampuchean conflict. That shift had the effect of diminishing Indonesia's assumed position of corporate leadership. Indonesia's view was shared initially by the government of Malaysia, which had engaged in a pioneering diplomatic exercise from 1975 to promote a *modus vivendi* with Vietnam so as to serve as a channel of political communication between Hanoi and its regional partners. The private dissenting view expressed in Jakarta and Kuala Lumpur was that despite the need to uphold the principle of national sovereignty, there were practical dangers involved in pursuing a policy of diplomatic confrontation of Vietnam. Of primary concern was the prospect of advancing the regional interests of the People's Republic of China. Furthermore, to the extent that Vietnam's invasion of Kampuchea constituted an expression of a deep-rooted antagonism between Vietnam and China, the more protracted the ensuing conflict, the greater the danger of encouraging the spread of Soviet influence with South-East Asia. Vietnam had not been willing to endorse the earlier Soviet proposal for an Asian collective security system. A Treaty of Friendship and Co-operation, as concluded between Vietnam and the Soviet Union in November 1978, had not been thought necessary by the Politburo in Hanoi during the entire course of the Second Indochina War when its adversary had been the United States. That treaty had been intended to deter any military riposte by China to Vietnam's invasion of Kampuchea. Although it had failed in that respect, China's willingness to undertake a punitive expedition served to ensure that the Soviet Union would be obliged to take measures to assist Vietnam in order to uphold its reputation as a credible ally and fraternal partner. Indeed, Vietnam's need to ensure access to reliable external countervailing power was expressed in a willingness from March 1979 to extend naval base facilities at Cam Ranh Bay to vessels of the Soviet Pacific fleet and aerial reconnaissance facilities at Da Nang for its air force.

Within ASEAN, therefore, there existed a dissenting position to the effect that the course of action adopted against Vietnam served only to compound regional security problems. By becoming involved in a coalition strategy directed at Vietnam, ASEAN had not only become a party to Sino-Soviet conflict but had also engaged itself in an exercise virtually certain to have the effect of opening South-East Asia to its wider expression. In the way that China's policy towards Vietnam had given rise to a self-fulfilling prophecy of a Soviet-Vietnamese alliance, there existed a corresponding concern that ASEAN's hardline policy towards Vietnam would help to bring about either one or the other of two objectionable outcomes: either a debilitated Vietnam subject to China's dominance or a debilitated Vietnam bound in a permanent client relationship to the Soviet Union which would in turn reinforce the Thai-Chinese relationship. In either case, the regional vision of a Zone of Peace, Freedom, and Neutrality held most strongly in Jakarta would be compromised and South-East Asia would be subject again to the affliction of external power rivalry and interference.

The measure of persisting dissent within ASEAN did not arrest the momentum of its diplomatic campaign during 1979. Although frustrated initially before the Security Council of the United Nations, ASEAN's cause was served by the treatment of the Kampuchean issue at the summit meeting of Non-Aligned States in Cuba in September.

In Havana, after an acrimonious debate it was decided not to seat a Kampuchean representative but to leave the place vacant. An important factor in this outcome was the role played by the host government which handled the administrative arrangements for the conference and presided over it. The Cuban government had issued visas to the two rival delegations claiming the Kampuchean seat: to that from the Phnom Penh Government ensconced by the Vietnamese and to another from its ousted predecessor, granted only at Yugoslavia's insistence. However, the head of the new Kampuchean government, Heng Samrin, had also been invited to pay a state visit timed to coincide with the Non-Aligned Conference. By contrast, diplomatic facilities and access to the conference hall were denied to the ousted government of Democratic Kampuchea headed by Khieu Samphan. Despite heated protest from representatives of participating ASEAN Governments, the Cuban chairman of the conference used his position to rule that there was a consensus in favour of keeping the Kampuchean seat vacant until the Coordinating Bureau of the movement could reach a clear decision.

This use or abuse of the chairman's prerogative proved to be a mixed blessing for ASEAN. On the one hand, it made the matter of Kampuchea's representation in the Non-Aligned Movement subject to an eventual resolution of the conflict over its political identity. On the other hand, it had the effect of aiding ASEAN's diplomatic cause within the United Nations. When the issue of the representation of Kampuchea came before the credentials committee of the General Assembly, a Congolese attempt to apply the precedent of the Non-Aligned Movement was rejected. A recommendation to accept the credentials of the Democratic Kampuchean delegation was then accepted with a clear vote in favour. This recommendation was endorsed by the General

Assembly despite an Indian move to revive the vacant seat formula. It was suggested that this outcome marked the reaction of some governments who 'were still smouldering over the high-handed behaviour of Fidel Castro in Havana'.[16] When the ASEAN states subsequently sponsored a resolution in the General Assembly in November calling for the immediate withdrawal of all foreign troops from Kampuchea, overwhelming support was forthcoming. Moreover, after the Soviet invasion of Afghanistan in the following month, that support was reinforced because of the identification of that military action with Vietnam's invasion and occupation of Kampuchea.

By the end of 1979 ASEAN had achieved a measure of diplomatic success over Kampuchea. Its member governments had displayed a facility for coordinating policies and exercising lobbying skills beyond expectation. The Association had never before projected itself as vigorously as a diplomatic community to such political effect. The net result was to confirm ASEAN in a distinctive role within the informal coalition ranged against Vietnam. That achievement and role, however significant, was also limited. Although enhancing the international standing of the Association and certainly confounding and annoying Vietnam and its supporters, ASEAN's diplomatic initiatives were not able to transform the political condition of Kampuchea.

ASEAN's limitations in this respect were put in context by the failings of more influential states. For example, after the meeting of ASEAN Foreign Ministers in Bali in June 1979, both Japan's Foreign Minister, Sunao Sonoda, and his U.S. counterpart, Cyrus Vance, who participated in post-conference dialogues, had indicated an interest in promoting a political settlement through an international conference. Such an initiative proved to be abortive then because the primary parties to the conflict were strongly opposed to such an initiative. Vietnam's government reinforced its commitment to Heng Samrin who was accorded honours due to a head of state when he passed through Hanoi en route to the Non-Aligned Conference in Cuba. Secretary of State for Foreign Affairs and acting Foreign Minister Nguyen Co Thach remarked in August, 'We don't consider such a conference necessary. The situation in Kampuchea is irreversible.'[17] He also dismissed the prospect of any contact with former head of state Prince Norodom Sihanouk, whom Cyrus Vance had suggested might be restored to office to preside over a neutral Kampuchea. The Chinese patrons of the insurgent Khmer Rouge displayed a correspondingly uncompromising mood. Their national news agency insisted that 'the urgent task with regard to Kampuchea is to force Vietnam to withdraw from that country'.[18]

The truth of the matter was that the ASEAN states as a collegial grouping were neither a direct nor an impartial party to the conflict over Kampuchea. Their collective standing arose from a subregional accomplishment heralded in Beijing but not acknowledged in Hanoi. ASEAN's governments were neither able nor willing to become involved in the military dimensions of the conflict, with the partial exception of Thailand, which offered cross border sanctuary to an insurgent challenge to Vietnam's occupation. The arguments as to why ASEAN had never entertained alliance pretensions have been rehearsed above. Diplomacy was the only weapon of substance at its disposal; it was not sufficient on its own. More coercive pressure on Vietnam could only come from other sources. It has also been suggested above that had China not made absolutely clear its unrelenting opposition to Vietnam's policy in Kampuchea, then Thailand would have almost certainly been obliged to accommodate itself to the political *fait accompli*. ASEAN's position adopted in Bangkok in January 1979 had been contingent on that adopted by Thailand. That position gave rise to a persisting predicament over the appropriateness, effectiveness and consequences of a corporate policy pursued in the name of regional security.

The Thai government, if not entirely of one mind, was content to sustain that policy because of a prevailing judgement that Vietnam had overreached itself by invading Kampuchea. Singapore, disturbed by the military assertion of Vietnam, saw advantage in highlighting a nefarious Soviet connection to stimulate a positive U.S. interest in South-East Asia. Such an interest had been absent from the initial priorities of the Carter administration. In Jakarta and Kuala Lumpur, however, the thrust of ASEAN's policy became a matter of growing concern, with private reservations giving rise to public disquiet. When Malaysia's Prime Minister Datuk Hussein Onn met with Indonesia's President Suharto in March 1980 in the east coast town of Kuantan in peninsular Malaysia, that disquiet was formally expressed, disturbing ASEAN's surface cohesion. Apart from an abiding anxiety over a burgeoning political relationship as well as military co-operation between Thailand and China, the circumstances of a recent change of government in Bangkok had reinforced a shared concern. The transfer of high office from Prime Minister General Kriangsak Chomanand to

General Prem Tinsulanond had been peaceful. But it had been engineered through factional conflict within Thailand's armed forces.[19] Apprehension at the prospect of internal political instability in Thailand being aggravated by involvement in the Kampuchean conflict encouraged a joint Indonesian-Malaysian initiative to find a format for resolving it. Moreover, Malaysia was still keen to explore a special relationship with Vietnam and had already indicated a willingness to receive Vietnam's Foreign Minister in the hope that political compromise based on a broadening of the Phnom Penh regime might be possible. As a result the two heads of government issued a statement in which they envisaged a Vietnam free of the influence of both China and the Soviet Union and pointedly took cognizance of Vietnam's security interests in Indochina. The point has been well made that 'In essence, the Kuantan principle was a reiteration of the 1971 Zopfan declaration but with direct applicability to the Kampuchean crisis.'[20]

The so-called Kuantan Declaration, by acknowledging a legitimate Vietnamese security interest in the political identity of Kampuchea, implied recognition of its hegemonial role. As such it proved to be totally unacceptable to Bangkok.[21] Indeed, General Prem, who undertook a tour of ASEAN's capitals in keeping with established practice for new heads of government, went out of his way in both Kuala Lumpur and Jakarta to indicate hostility to the Kuantan message insisting instead on the ASEAN position as expressed in the resolution endorsed by the General Assembly of the United Nations in the previous November. As a result, the joint statement was quietly discarded and omitted, significantly, from the series of public documents issued regularly by Malaysia's Ministry of Foreign Affairs.[22] The episode was important, however, because it marked a turning point in the public expression of internal debate within ASEAN. The Kuantan initiative had articulated Indonesia's and Malaysia's joint concern that the Association had become caught up in a policy that would not necessarily serve its corporate interests as defined in Jakarta and Kuala Lumpur and in its declaratory commitment. Serious consequences were deemed likely to flow from the untramelled play of Sino-Soviet rivalries within South-East Asia. The regional balance of power, viewed with reference to this daunting prospect, therefore assumed prior importance to the issue of principle which served as the public justification for ASEAN's position over Kampuchea.

For Thailand, however, different considerations of balance of power and principle coincided without any conflict of interests. Because the issue of Kampuchea was judged by Prem's government to be of acute security concern, the cohesion of ASEAN – hardly a source of countervailing power – constituted a lesser priority. Thailand's position and priority placed Indonesia in particular in a vulnerable situation. Its commitment to ASEAN was paramount. Its previous Foreign Minister, Adam Malik, had declared the Association to be the cornerstone of his country's foreign policy.[23] In the circumstances, President Suharto was not prepared to test the cohesion of the Association for the sake of a divisive joint formulation whose practical application was uncertain. For example, the Kuantan Declaration had not taken account of the asymmetry in Vietnam's relationships with the Soviet Union and China. As a consequence, Hanoi responded with more open hostility to the Kuantan initiative than Thailand.

The Kuantan Declaration was allowed to lapse because of the political embarrassment it had generated and because of its evident impracticability. And even though the governments in Jakarta and Kuala Lumpur did not relinquish the strategic perspective which had spawned the Declaration, they never again adopted a concerted public stand which exposed such a breaking of ranks within ASEAN. Moreover, circumstances conspired to oblige Thailand's regional partners to close ranks in a renewed show of corporate solidarity. In June 1980 the Thai government inaugurated a policy of 'voluntary repatriation' of Kampuchean refugees with the formal endorsement of the UN High Commission for Refugees. In the process, some 7,000 residents of Sa Kaeo refugee camp controlled by the Khmer Rouge were returned across the border to strengthen insurgent forces.[24] The government in Phnom Penh denounced this policy as 'a plot to enable the Pol Pot bandits and other reactionary gangs to harass the People's Republic of Kampuchea during the rainy season'. An artillery bombardment and then an armed incursion by Vietnamese troops at company strength were launched in retaliation against camps in Thailand holding non-Communist refugees. The object of the military exercise was to end the programme of 'voluntary repatriation' by posing a threat to cross-border international relief aid operations. An additional purpose was to try to revise the terms of international debate over Kampuchea against the orthodoxy established by ASEAN. The Vietnamese wished to vindicate their claim that the only conflict in Kampuchea was along the border with Thailand, one which could be contained and overcome through establishing a demilitarised zone and by Thailand's recognition of the Heng Samrin government in Phnom Penh.

Whatever the purpose of Vietnam's military action, its timing had the effect of obliging wavering members of ASEAN to close ranks once more in support of the Association's front-line state. The incursion took place just two days prior to the annual meeting of ASEAN's Foreign Ministers which convened in Kuala Lumpur. They were duty bound to take a public stand and accordingly 'expressed their serious concern over the act of aggression by Vietnam along the Thai-Kampuchean border and the intrusion of their troops into Thai territory'.[25] In addition, they maintained that 'any incursion of foreign forces into Thailand directly affects the security of the ASEAN member-states and endangers peace and security in the whole region'. This expression of collective political defence had the effect of diminishing the significance of the Kuantan episode. From that point, ASEAN became more explicit in its challenge to Vietnam. For example, at an informal meeting of its Foreign Ministers in Kuala Lumpur in August 1979, their initial statement of January that year strongly deploring the armed intervention in Kampuchea had been reiterated, but without specific mention of Vietnam. Now they were prepared to express 'their particular concern over the continued presence of Vietnamese troops in Kampuchea'. In addition they had even indicated the possibility of military support for Thailand, if attacked again by Vietnam.

That stand was significant as a change in declaratory position, but it did not have any visible effect on the problem at hand. Indeed, in their joint communique after their annual meeting in June 1980, the five foreign ministers 'noted with grave concern that despite the constructive efforts by ASEAN and the international community, the Kampuchean armed conflict remained unresolved'.[26] They also 'viewed with serious concern the increasing rivalry of outside powers in the Southeast Asian region which aggravates the existing tensions and undermines the earnest efforts of ASEAN member countries to seek a durable political solution to the conflict'. These unequivocal expressions of frustration on ASEAN's part were a true indication of the limits of its security role.

The ASEAN states were able to sustain their diplomatic success in mobilising international support. In the United Nations, a second challenge to the credentials of the Democratic Kampuchean delegation was easily fended off, while considerable support was attracted once more for a General Assembly resolution calling for the withdrawal of foreign forces from Kampuchea. As indicated above, ASEAN's cause had been served by the Soviet invasion of Afghanistan; the two issues of Kampuchea and Afghanistan were linked directly in a joint statement by ASEAN and European Community Ministers meeting in Kuala Lumpur in March 1980. Despite ASEAN attaining such diplomatic heights, Kampuchea remained beyond the Association's practical reach. The country itself appeared to be returning to a condition of normality; it had also become incorporated within a political structure of Indochinese states dominated by Vietnam. That structure was inaugurated in January 1980 when the Foreign Ministers of Vietnam, Laos and Kampuchea met in Phnom Penh during celebrations marking the first anniversary of the establishment of the People's Republic of Kampuchea. A pattern of biannual meetings was institutionalised when the three foreign ministers met again in July in Vientiane. On both occasions, there was no indication of any willingness to accommodate ASEAN's demands. All that was on offer was the prospect of non-aggression treaties with the government in Phnom Penh and direct negotiations between either government and non-government organisations in Kampuchea and Thailand. Moreover, there had not been any sign that the Soviet Union was disposed to withhold that economic and military assistance from Vietnam which made possible its continuing occupation of Kampuchea.

Within a year of the establishment of the Heng Samrin administration, ASEAN had reached an impasse over Kampuchea. It had become deeply involved in the conflict in part over a matter of principle but most practically over the issue of the balance of power – namely, the prospect of Vietnam consolidating its political dominance throughout Indochina. ASEAN had committed itself publicly to challenging that prospect with the intention of removing the government in Phnom Penh from a position subordinate to its counterpart in Hanoi and reinstating it as an independent international actor. Its regional credentials in that exercise were not matched by its corporate capability. Some stiffening of that capability through a greater compatability in arms employed and increased informal defence co-operation did not change ASEAN's role after Vietnam's invasion of Kampuchea. On the contrary, the effect of that invasion had been to reinforce its diplomatic expression. In order to give diplomacy a cutting edge, ASEAN was obliged to rely on the application of other pressures whose source did not encourage Vietnam to compromise. Compounding ASEAN's difficulty was the requirement to support the ousted government of Democratic Kampuchea as the legitimate alternative to the incumbent government of Heng Samrin. The irony of justifying its policy with reference to the sanctity of national sovereignty was to draw it into an unsavoury political relationship. The ASEAN states recognised the ousted Democratic Kampuchean government headed by Pol Pot and, at least implicitly, supported its claim to reinstatement.

The surviving military arm of the Pol Pot regime was the only significant source of internal challenge to Vietnam's client government. Its notorious reputation acquired between 1975 and 1978 meant that the Khmer Rouge resistance was regarded with dread by the surviving population of Kampuchea and with distaste by most governments. ASEAN was supporting indirectly an instrument of some military utility but of negative political appeal. Indeed, the spectre of a return to power by the Khmer Rouge made Vietnam's task of occupation of Kampuchea that much easier. Correspondingly, international support for ASEAN's diplomatic position was qualified and seemed likely to wane. That prospect was pointed up by withdrawal of recognition of Democratic Kampuchea by Britain in December 1979 and by Australia in the following year. Moreover, India's decision in July 1980 to establish diplomatic relations with the Heng Samrin government gave cause for alarm even if it did not produce any corresponding gesture among other non-aligned states. ASEAN was faced with the problem of how to sustain the momentum of its diplomatic undertaking, a course beset with additional difficulty because of misgivings by some regional partners.

ASEAN's recourse was to soldier on with its efforts to mobilise international pressure in the hope that some point of diplomatic junction over negotiations might be established with Vietnam. To this end, its governments had reiterated a request to the Secretary General of the United Nations to convene an international conference on Kampuchea under the auspices of the organisation. This initiative was purposely linked to establishing the Zone of Peace, Freedom, and Neutrality in an attempt to try to cater for Vietnamese security concerns. The government in Hanoi had previously accepted the Kuala Lumpur Declaration at least as a basis for discussions on the establishment of peace and stability in the region. Such reaffirmation did nothing to resolve the problem of overcoming Vietnam's objections to the United Nations as a vehicle for negotiations because a Democratic Kampuchean representative occupied the Kampuchean seat. For that reason, its government had proposed an alternative regional conference. The link with the Khmer Rouge posed a dilemma for ASEAN both in sustaining international support and in finding a diplomatic meeting point with Vietnam.

That dilemma had been recognised publicly by Tommy Koh, Singapore's ambassador to the United Nations, in a speech before the General Assembly in October 1980. In arguing that the credentials of Democratic Kampuchea should be endorsed despite the fact that its government had been a bloodthirsty despotism, he raised the issue of ASEAN's political intent. He remarked, 'I have been asked: "Do the ASEAN countries want to restore Pol Pot to power?" I answer categorically no. We do not want to restore Pol Pot to power.'[27] His attempt to explain away the apparent contradiction in ASEAN's position by seeking to persuade Vietnam's government to accept a political settlement incorporating free elections which Pol Pot and his minions would be unlikely to win was less than convincing. That rationale had failed to indicate who exactly ASEAN was for, if its members rejected both the Khmer Rouge and their Vietnamese-backed political successors.

In principle, a political alternative for ASEAN was not difficult to contemplate. Regardless of the military merits of the Khmer Rouge, the ASEAN governments shared a strong inhibition over supporting a Communist insurgent movement even if against a Communist administration. The practical problems of promoting a credible non-Communist political alternative to the Khmer Rouge were immense, however. Among the Khmer refugee encampments close to the Thai–Kampuchean border, the initial potential for such a prospect seemed limited as petty warlords contended for control over smuggling rights and international relief aid. At that point Prince Sihanouk, resident in North Korea, had not committed himself to leading a resistance movement because he retained expectations of being able to deal directly with the Vietnamese. The only other non-Communist candidate was the Khmer People's National Liberation Front, which had been set up under the leadership of a former Prime Minister and governor of the Central Bank, Son Sann, then already in his late sixties. It had held its first congress just across the border in Battambang Province in April 1980. Its attraction was its non-Communist credentials, but the KPNLF hardly constituted a fighting arm and the basis for an independent third force.

ASEAN's position expressed a clear contradiction between political and military purposes. In order to continue to deny legitimacy to the Heng Samrin government, it was necessary to promote a credible political alternative to the Khmer Rouge. Such an alternative had to possess both an internal political appeal within Kampuchea and an external one, especially within the General Assembly of the United Nations. To the extent that such an alternative detached from Chinese patronage could be promoted, it was believed to be possible to attract the Vietnamese to the negotiating table on the ground that their security would be safeguarded by restoring Kampuchea to an independent condition. Such a Kampuchea, envisaged as a genuine buffer state, would serve Vietnamese and well as Thai interests. But while such an alternative political format was no more than a matter of aspiration, sustained resistance to Vietnam's political design in Indochina required the bloody instrument of the Khmer Rouge, despite the political disadvantages arising.[28] A compromise in the form of a coalition incorporating the Khmer Rouge but which diluted its bestial identity seemed the only practical option. This judgement appeared to be the outcome of discussions conducted during a visit to China in October 1980 by Thailand's Prime Minister, General Prem Tinsulanond.

The ASEAN governments persisted with their attempt to promote a compromise alternative to the Khmer Rouge and to persuade their Chinese patron of the political urgency of such a policy. Singapore's Prime Minister Lee Kuan Yew followed his Thai counterpart in pursuing this objective during his visit to China in November 1980. He claimed to have received the impression that 'China is not seeking a reestablishment of China's influence in Kampuchea through the restoration of Pol Pot or the Khmer Rouge regime'.[29] He also pointed out:

> They agreed to the ASEAN stand that when the Vietnamese forces have withdrawn from Kampuchea, the people of Kampuchea should be free to decide their own future in a UN-supervised election without Vietnamese or Khmer Rouge or other armed resistance forces to intimidate the people from expressing their free choice.

Although Lee had indicated a Chinese preparedness to accept and support non-Communist Kampuchean patriots who wanted to be rid of and who would resist the Vietnamese, he could not confirm a willingness on the part of any well-known non-Communist Khmer figures to enter a coalition arrangement with the Khmer Rouge. Given the dominant role played by the Khmer Rouge in armed resistance to the Vietnamese, it was logical to try to promote a political alternative to them through a coalition arrangement. Such an arrangement was beset with major difficulties. The Khmer Rouge were certainly not prepared to entertain a coalition arrangement at the cost of their leading position and role; nor was China prepared to encourage such a self-denying initiative. At the time, the embryonic non-Communist resistance would not contemplate such an arrangement with the notorious company responsible for mass murder when in power in Phnom Penh. ASEAN appeared to have reached a point of impasse. The strength of the Khmer Rouge had created a point of fundamental political weakness in the conduct of the Association's policy which in turn reinforced Vietnam's determination not to compromise.

For ASEAN, however, there seemed little choice but to persist with a virtually impossible task. In February 1981, after talks in Washington with U.S. Secretary of State Alexander Haig, Singapore's Second Deputy Prime Minister Sinnathamby Rajaratnam announced that ASEAN's immediate objective was to create a third force consisting of a united front of all anti-Vietnamese and anti-Heng Samrin resistance groups with the object of making clear to the government in Hanoi that opposition to its occupation of Kampuchea would continue. By this time, ASEAN governments had begun to place strong pressure on Son Sann and Prince Norodom Sihanouk to overcome their objections to joining a united front with the Khmer Rouge. Of interest in this exercise was the role played by Indonesia's Foreign Ministry, which employed a French-speaking retired diplomat, Anwar Sani, to persuade Prince Sihanouk to participate despite Jakarta's reservations about the general direction of the Association's policy.

ASEAN's persistence in looking for a political opening to resolve the Kampuchean conflict was indicated at its ministerial meeting which convened in Manila in June 1981. Singapore's Foreign Minister Suppiah Dhanabalan set out the basis of a revised corporate position which was partly endorsed in the final communique. His remarks merit extensive reproduction. He pointed out:

There can be no solution to the Kampuchean problem without

the following elements: Withdrawal of Vietnamese forces, a UN force to maintain law and order, disarming of all Kampuchean factions and a free UN-supervised election in which all Kampuchean factions, including the Heng Samrin faction, can participate. There can also be no solution to the Kampuchean problem if the legitimate security interests of ASEAN and Vietnam are not safeguarded. A solution must, therefore, incorporate a guarantee that Kampuchea will not pose a threat to its neighbours as well as the external powers who are indirect parties to the present conflict. The elements which I have enumerated provide the basis for a realistic solution to the Kampuchean problem.[30]

This formulation suggested a measure of change in ASEAN's thinking, without a repudiation of its basic position on the nature of the Kampuchean conflict. It indicated an attempt to reconcile differences within the Association reflected by the Kuantan statement and the Thai response as well as those between ASEAN and Vietnam. The final communique failed to spell out the Singapore Foreign Minister's understanding of the legitimate security interests of Vietnam or the entitlement of the Heng Samrin faction to participate in United Nations supervised elections. None the less it urged, as initial steps to a comprehensive political settlement, the despatch of UN peace-keeping forces to Kampuchea, the withdrawal of all foreign armed forces in the shortest possible time under UN supervision, and the disarming of all Khmer factions immediately after the completion of the withdrawal of foreign forces from Kampuchea. The foreign ministers also defended their right to continue to recognise the government of Democratic Kampuchea and to extend their support for its continued representation at the UN. They stressed that their grounds for support were based 'on the fundamental principles that foreign intervention must be opposed and that any change in the recognition of Democratic Kampuchea's credentials would be tantamount to condoning Vietnamese military invasion and occupation of Kampuchea'.[31]

In the communique there was an evident effort to reconcile defence of principle with some signalled understanding of Vietnam's security interests. This attempt to square the circle gave rise to a paradox. ASEAN's Foreign Ministers reaffirmed their recognition of Democratic Kampuchea but called at the same time for disarmament of its military wing within Kampuchea by a UN force despatched to supervise Vietnam's withdrawal from the country. It merits recalling in this context, the response of Singapore's Prime Minister in November 1980 to the question whether he had received any indication that the Chinese were prepared either in the short or long term to withdraw their support from the Khmer Rouge. Lee had responded:

> The Chinese position is consistent, that they must support the Khmer Rouge. The Khmer Rouge has been and is the main anti-Vietnamese resistance force. They will not withdraw their support. But they are prepared to accept and also to support non-Communist Kampuchean patriots who want to be rid of and will resist the Vietnamese.

It was evident from Lee's remarks that the Khmer Rouge and their Chinese patronage constituted a very mixed blessing. They served to underpin the diplomatic challenge to Vietnam's political design in Indochina but they also tied ASEAN to an unpopular political relationship which both tarnished its cause and made Vietnam unwilling to negotiate on other than its own terms. One way in which ASEAN might hope to overcome Vietnam's obduracy, so it was calculated, would be to hold out the prospect of a credible non-Communist alternative to the Khmer Rouge which would attract popular support without posing a threat to the security of Vietnam. A necessary step to this end, given the fact of political life of the Khmer Rouge, would be to make practical provision for disarming all Khmer factions immediately after the withdrawal of all foreign forces from Kampuchea. The fact of life of the Khmer Rouge, including their tenure in a United Nations seat, also meant that a political alternative to them initially required some form of coalition arrangement. The ASEAN Foreign Ministers therefore 'welcomed the current consultations among the Kampuchean nationalists with a view to the early setting up of a coalition government of Democratic Kampuchea in pursuit of their inalienable right to liberate their country from foreign occupation and domination'.[32]

ASEAN had demonstrated a measure of flexibility and ingenuity designed to reconcile the complex internal and external interests engaged in the conflict over Kampuchea. That conflict had placed a strain on intra-mural relationships and had served also to polarise South-East Asia into contending camps whose opposed positions were reinforced by competing external patrons. At issue was whether the Association could find an appropriate formula which would both encompass and satisfy the divergent interests at the roots of conflict over Kampuchea which, in effect, meant reconciling Vietnam and China.

A major test of ASEAN's ability to shape the course of conflict over Kampuchea took place during July 1981 in New York when an international conference was convened under the auspices of the Secretary General of the United Nations. Holding such a conference was a diplomatic success of a kind. A UN conference had been a persistent demand of the Association in the year following Vietnam's invasion. The diplomatic success was one of form rather than of substance, however. The conference was distinguished by the absence of Vietnamese and Laotian as well as Soviet representation. An ASEAN initiative to show even-handedness by soliciting non-government representation from Heng Samrin's Kampuchea in the form of a delegation from the ruling People's Revolutionary Party was blocked by China. The Conference began its deliberations as a gathering of states opposed to Vietnam's position which partly defeated ASEAN's purpose. It also became a forum for contention within the anti-Vietnamese alignment.

The International Conference on Kampuchea exposed major differences of interest between members of ASEAN and China over the terms of any settlement. The differences which emerged served also to reinforce apprehensions among some member governments over the Chinese-inspired strategy of attrition designed to impose a breaking strain on the society and government of Vietnam. None of the ASEAN governments – including that of Thailand, whose interests were most directly at risk – had any wish to see the dominance of Vietnam in Indochina replaced by that of China. They shared a common interest that China should not become the political beneficiary in Indochina of Vietnam's failure to impose its will in Kampuchea.

Sharp differences in priorities between the ASEAN states and China arose when the former sought to secure endorsement for the terms of settlement advocated by its five Foreign Ministers at Manila in the previous month. An attempt was made to carry the proposal that all Khmer factions be disarmed immediately after the withdrawal of all foreign (i.e. Vietnamese) forces from Kampuchea. Complementary to this proposal was another that an interim administration be set up in advance of free elections to be conducted under UN supervision. The practical point of the diplomatic exercise was to offer a measure of asssurance to the Vietnamese government that participation in a UN-sponsored political settlement in Kampuchea would not involve the resumption of power there by the Khmer Rouge and correspondingly the resumption of a threat to Vietnam's security.

This attempt to test Vietnam's willingness to engage in political compromise foundered on the rock of Chinese opposition assisted by tacit U.S. support. Its delegation rejected ASEAN's intended gesture of conciliation ostensibly on the ground that the proposal constituted an unwarranted interference in Kampuchea's internal affairs. It was argued in addition that 'the approach also confounds the forces of justice and those of reaction, putting on a par the resistance forces against Vietnamese aggression and the forces of the Heng Samrin regime, the pawn of that aggression'.[33] More to the point, it was maintained that

> the Democratic Kampuchean government has expressed in its political program willingness to hold a free election 'without threat from any armed forces or other forces'. This means that if there's no threat from any other armed forces than that led by the Kampuchean government, the proposed election will be a free one.

Such logic, if familiar to the Politburo in Hanoi, was not reassuring to the governments of ASEAN. In some respects even more disturbing was the willingness of the United States to tolerate China's obstruction of ASEAN's diplomatic purpose apparently in the interest of managing its adversary relationship with the Soviet Union.

ASEAN's proposals did not find a place in the final declaration of the conference, which reiterated previous General Assembly resolutions on Kampuchea. Instead, a bland provision was made for 'appropriate arrangements to ensure that armed Kampuchean factions will not be able to prevent or disrupt the holding of free elections, or intimidate or coerce the populations in the electoral process'.[34] ASEAN sources confirmed to one writer that 'American influence on ASEAN to accept ultimately a vaguely worded French compromise formula probably saved the conference from ending in an embarrassing failure'.[35] If not exactly an embarrassing failure, the outcome of the conference was nothing less than a diplomatic defeat for ASEAN, whose collective efforts had been frustrated. The occasion served to expose the limitations of the Association as an aspiring manager of regional order. In practical terms, it meant that ASEAN's attempt to offer an alternative political format for a Kampuchean settlement excluding both Vietnamese dominance and a resumption of Khmer Rouge rule had been denied.

The only consolation for ASEAN was a willingness on China's part to accept a broadening of the political base of resistance within Kampuchea. Its government was certainly opposed to any initiative which might blunt the edge of Khmer Rouge power, but it was also cognisant of the danger of losing international support for the anti-Vietnamese cause by not acting to dilute the bestial identity of so-called Democratic Kampuchea. Attempts to promote a united Khmer front quickened after the failure of the International Conference on Kampuchea to do more than issue a declaration which was denounced immediately by Vietnam and its supporters. The ability of the Heng Samrin government to conduct elections in Kampuchea between March and May 1981 endorsing the leading role of the People's Revolutionary Party provided an additional incentive.

A united Khmer front was intended to serve a number of functions. Dilution of the bestial reputation of the Khmer Rouge was paramount. A more acceptable format for resistance was intended to influence popular loyalties within Kampuchea by indicating the practical prospect of an alternative to both the Khmer Rouge and Heng Samrin. Such a prospect might dispose the Vietnamese ultimately to political compromise because of a lessening popular acceptance of Vietnam's occupation. Dilution of bestial reputation within a Khmer resistance coalition was intended also to enable ASEAN's governments to adopt a more consistent position on international representation and importantly to ensure the continued retention of the Kampuchean seat in the United Nations. Moreover, the manufacture of a politically more wholesome resistance movement would enable governmental provision of material support to sustain the challenge to Vietnam's occupation from donors other than the People's Republic of China which had acted as quartermaster for the Khmer Rouge. It was impossible for any Western government and for those of ASEAN to be seen to be providing material and military support for the Khmer Rouge. Support for non-Communist factions in a broad-front resistance movement would be another matter.

ASEAN-inspired and supported negotiations to create a united front proved to be a chequered process. It had not materialised by the time of the International Conference on Kampuchea in July

1981. An initial measure of success was attained, however, in September 1981 when Prince Sihanouk (heading a separate organisation loyal to his person), Son Sann (of the KPNLF) and Khieu Samphan (who had nominally succeeded Pol Pot as head of the Khmer Rouge) met in Singapore. There they expressed 'the desire to form a coalition government of Democratic Kampuchea with a view to continuing the struggle in all forms for the liberation of Cambodia from the Vietnamese aggression'.[36] But that agreement in principle was concluded to the sound of public discord between the parties to it, which indicated the fragility of the embryonic united front which was, in effect, a format for eventual civil war. Indeed, the meeting held in Singapore marked a false start in coalition-building. A further combination of pressure and compromise was required before a final accord was reached in June 1982 in Kuala Lumpur on the terms of a coalition government. That accord constituted a diplomatic achievement of a kind and served ASEAN's purpose within the United Nations, where it was made easier to hold the Kampuchean seat. However, its main effect was to safeguard a diplomatic position rather than to advance the prospect for a political settlement. Vietnam's response was to denounce the accord as a vehicle for the Khmer Rouge and to reiterate the irreversibility of the situation in Kampuchea.

To its credit, ASEAN had made its mark over Kampuchea as a diplomatic community. Despite intra-mural discordance, it had been possible to sustain a common opposition to Vietnam's occupation with some effect. The need to concert such a position had improved the practice of intra-mural consultation making ASEAN a more efficient diplomatic instrument. But if ASEAN had withstood the test of intra-mural discordance and its governments had learned how to accommodate the interests of regional partners, only limited impact had been made in South-East Asia beyond the bounds of the Association. The Kampuchean conflict, which served as the tangible basis of corporate solidarity was still effectively beyond its practical grasp. It had become a diplomatic party to a conflict whose military momentum it could not control. That aligned as well as dependent position gave its diplomatic endeavours an ambivalant quality. On the one hand, its governments had demanded that Vietnam abdicate from a forward policy lauched from a sense of strategic imperative. On the other, they were engaged in an attempt to reconcile a defence of principle, defined with reference to Vietnam's violation, with provision for those Vietnamese interests which had prompted that violation.

Alignment partners had obstructed an attempt to square the circle of conflict, giving Vietnam no reason to talk on ASEAN's terms. The Association could not afford to retreat politically, but its members were also unable to advance.

Notes

1. For appreciations of Thai strategic perspective, see Muthiah Alagappa, *The National Security of Developing States: Lessons from Thailand*, Auburn House Publishing, Dover, MA, 1987, Chapter 3; Sarasin Viraphol, 'Thailand's Perspective on Its Rivalry with Vietnam', in William S. Turley (ed.), *Confrontation or Coexistence. The Future of ASEAN–Vietnam Relations*, Institute of Security and International Studies, Bangkok, 1985.

2. Charles Morrison and Astri Suhrke 'ASEAN in Regional Defence and Development', in S. Chawla and D.R. Sardesai (eds), *Changing Patterns of Security and Stability in Asia*, Praeger, New York, 1980, p. 205.

3. See Sukhumbhand Paribatra, *From Enmity to Alignment. Thailand's Evolving Relationship with China*, Institute of Security and International Studies, Bangkok, 1987.

4. *Documents on the Kampuchean Problem 1979–1985*, Ministry of Foreign Affairs, Bangkok, 1985, p. 73.

5. Ibid., p. 74.

6. Ibid., p. 75.

7. During his visit to the United States in February 1979, Deng Xiaoping informed President Carter: 'We consider it necessary to put a restraint on the wild ambitions of the Vietnamese and to give them an appropriate limited lesson.' Zbigniew Brzezinski, *Power and Principle*, Farrar, Straus & Giroux, New York, 1983, p. 409.

8. For an account of the subordinate relationship between Lao and Vietnamese Communists, see MacAlister Brown and Joseph J. Zasloff, *Apprentice Revolutionaries: The Communist Movement in Laos, 1930–1985*, Hoover Institution Press, Stanford University, Stanford, CA, 1986.

9. Bruce Grant et al. *The Boat People*, Penguin Books, Harmondsworth, Middlesex, 1979; Barry Wain, *The Refused*, Dow Jones Publishing (Asia), Hong Kong, 1981; Michael Richardson in Alison Broinowski (ed.), *Understanding ASEAN*, St Martin's Press, New York, 1982, Chapter 5.

10. The initial callousness of Thai refugee policy is recorded in William Shawcross, *The Quality of Mercy*, Andre Deutsch, London, 1984, Chapter 4.

11. *ASEAN Documents Series*, 1967–1985, ASEAN Secretariat, Jakarta, 1985, p. 56.

12. Richardson in Broinowski, *Understanding ASEAN*, op. cit., p. 107.

13. Kishore Mahbubani, 'The Kampuchean Problem: A Southeast

Asian Perception', *Foreign Affairs* (Winter 1983/84): 409–10.

14. *ASEAN Documents Series*, 1967–1985, op. cit., pp. 55–6.

15. Michael Leifer, 'ASEAN under stress over Cambodia', *Far Eastern Economic Review*, 14 June 1984.

16. *The Guardian*, London, 24 September 1979. See also Michael Leifer, 'The International Representation of Kampuchea', *Southeast Asian Affairs 1982*, Heinemann Asia, Singapore, 1982.

17. BBC, *Summary of World Broadcasts*, FE/6193/A3/4.

18. Ibid., FE/6243/A3/1.

19. Chai-anan Samudavanija, *The Thai Young Turks*, Institute of Southeast Asian Studies, Singapore, 1982.

20. Donald Weatherbee, 'The Diplomacy of Stalemate' in Donald Weatherbee (ed.), *Southeast Asia Divided. The ASEAN–Indochina Crisis*, Westview Press, Boulder, CO, 1985, p. 12.

21. Sheldon Simon, *The ASEAN States and Regional Security*, Hoover Institution Press, Stanford University, Stanford, CA, 1982, p. 69.

22. The only implicit public acknowledgement was by Prime Minister Datuk Hussein Onn in answer to a parliamentary question. See *Foreign Affairs Malaysia* (Kuala Lumpur) 13, no. 2 (June 1980):213.

23. Adam Malik, 'Indonesia's Foreign Policy', *The Indonesian Quarterly* (October 1972):28.

24. The seamier side of Thai policy is discussed by Shawcross, *The Quality of Mercy*, op. cit., Chapter 16.

25. *Documents on the Kampuchean Problem*, op. cit., p. 81.

26. *ASEAN Documents Series*, 1967–1985, op. cit., p. 60.

27. Full speech in United Nations, General Assembly 35th Session. *General Assembly Provisional Verbatim Record of the 34th Meeting*, New York, 13 October 1980, 9A/35/PR 34), pp. 27–36.

28. Weatherbee, 'Diplomacy of Stalemate', op. cit., p. 4 points out that 'The problem for ASEAN from the very beginning of its campaign to alter the situation in Kampuchea was to disengage from direct political and diplomatic support of the Khmer Rouge but at the same time keeping them in the field against the Vietnamese.'

29. *Singapore Government Press Release*, 02-1/80/11/14.

30. *Singapore Government Press Release*, 09-1/81/06/17.

31. *ASEAN Documents Series*, 1967–1985, op. cit., p. 68.

32. Ibid.

33. *New China News Agency*, 16 July 1981.

34. *Documents on the Kampuchean Conflict*, op. cit., p. 123.

35. Justus M. Van der Kroef, *Kampuchea – The Endless Tug of War*, University of Maryland, Baltimore, MD, 1982, p. 26.

36. *Agence France Presse*, 4 September 1981.

5

The Elusiveness of Regional Security

When the Foreign Ministers of ASEAN met in Singapore in June 1982, they had little of substance to show for their collective endeavours over Kampuchea. The UN Conference had exposed the limits of ASEAN's diplomatic strength. An attempt to promote a coalition of a kind between the Communist and non-Communist factions of the Khmer resistance had revealed the likely frailty of any such arrangement. The Kampuchean seat had been held in the United Nations, but this registration of international legitimacy had minimal impact beyond New York. Success at the General Assembly was also symptomatic of a basic inability to resolve a conflict whose momentum and course were not subject to ASEAN's control. A statement of self-congratulations by Singapore's Foreign Minister at the opening session of the annual ministerial meeting conspicuously omitted the role of other parties to the conflict in challenging Vietnam's continuing occupation of Kampuchea. ASEAN could justifiably congratulate itself up to a point, but Dhanabalan's statement exaggerated its influence:

We have successfully denied Vietnam legitimacy to its action in Cambodia and enjoyment of the fruits of its military occupation. We have been able to mobilise support to maintain the diplomatic, political and economic isolation of Vietnam. We shall continue in our principled stand until a political solution is found for Cambodia. We continue to hold the door open for Vietnam to come to the conference table and until Vietnam agrees to a political solution and to withdraw its troops from Cambodia, we shall continue to apply 'all-round' pressure on Vietnam.[1]

ASEAN's capability and will to apply so-called all round pressure off its own bat was limited. Because of such limitations it was obliged to deal in the symbolism of conflict. It could deal only marginally with its substance; especially over the central issue of the regional balance of power. In that respect, the communique of the 1982 ministerial meeting had virtually nothing to offer. It reiterated previous expressions of grave concern and deplored non-compliance with resolutions of the UN General Assembly and the Declaration of the International Conference on Kampuchea. Incorporated in the communique, however, was a statement expressing continued support for the formation of a Kampuchean coalition government. At the final press conference Thailand's Foreign Minister, Siddhi Savetsila was able to announce that an agreement had finally been reached on establishing such a government.

Four days later, the leaders of the two non-Communist Khmer factions met in Kuala Lumpur with Khieu Samphan, the nominal head of the Khmer Rouge. They concluded an agreement setting up a formal Coalition Government of Democratic Kampuchea. Under the terms of that agreement, former head of state Prince Norodom Sihanouk became its President, Son Sann its Prime Minister with Khieu Samphan as Vice-President responsible for foreign affairs. The agreement was not a commitment to a political merger, however. On the contrary, it stipulated that the coalition partners would retain their separate organisational and political identities as well as freedom of operational action. Moreover, the Khmer Rouge insisted on having written into the agreement their proprietory right to the political trademark 'Democratic Kampuchea' and to the UN seat should the coalition break up.[2] The accord was a crude expression of tactical political convenience cobbled together without needing to persuade either the Chinese or the Khmer Rouge of the political utility of the arrangement. It was the non-Communist factions who required cajoling into participation. They complied from necessity, not from any expection of political reconciliation; too much blood had flowed too recently for such a prospect. Prince Sihanouk consoled himself with the rationalisation 'We have no choice. It is lesser evil. To be with the Khmer Rouge is not to support the Khmer Rouge.'[3]

The establishment of the coalition represented a political advance of a kind for ASEAN. It made it easier to refute charges of engaging in an immoral political relationship with the murderous Khmer Rouge. It made it easier, therefore, to solicit voting support in the United Nations because of the more acceptable credentials of the non-Communist components of the coalition. More optimistically, there was an expectation that by entering the coalition, the non-Communist factions would not only lend it political respectability but would also establish an entitlement to receive international support in challenging Vietnam's occupation. Although ASEAN's governments could not agree on corporate provision of military assistance, implicit in their calculations was the expectation that over time it might be possible to revise the balance of military advantage among the Khmer resistance groups at the expense of the Khmer Rouge. If so, apart from presenting a credible alternative to the Heng Samrin government, those non-Communist factions would not pose a security threat to Vietnam of the kind which had provoked the invasion of December 1978. The Vietnamese might come to realise the utility of non-Communist dominance within the coalition leading to their tolerance of an independent buffer state to the southwest.

At the formation of the coalition, this aspiration was no more than an idle dream. It was idle in any assumption that the Khmer Rouge and their Chinese patron would be willing parties to revising the balance of military advantage at their expense. Indeed, a recurrent source of tension within the coalition has been unprovoked military attacks by the Khmer Rouge on coalition partners, designed to demonstrate their military superiority and to keep their political rivals off balance. Correspondingly, it was idle also to entertain the prospect that the non-communist factions in terms of military capability and resolve would be able in good time to match the military role of the Khmer Rouge in harassing Vietnam's occupation. The record of those factions has not been at all promising; their military performance has suffered because of failings of leadership and discipline. The most that can be said for the coalition arrangement is that it has helped to sustain the charge that Vietnam had implanted a politically illegitimate government in Kampuchea. It has never given a practical impression of being an alternative administration in the making. Indeed, ASEAN has never acknowledged it as the rightful successor to the Heng Samrin regime, preferring an electoral determination as part of a political settlement. More realistically, the coalition has constituted a recipe for civil war should the Vietnamese ever be brought to the point of major political concession as a result of sustained external pressures on their society and government.

With the formation of the coalition, the ASEAN states could argue with greater conviction that their goal was the establishment of a neutral and independent Kampuchea which would not pose a threat to any of its neighbours. Vietnam's government was not at all impressed with such an argument, primarily because of the patron role of China in servicing its client Khmer Rouge which dominated the military activities of the coalition. In its view, the formation of the coalition had not changed anything. Its leaders have shared a private consensus that a truly neutral Kampuchea is not a practical prospect because of its condition of human and physical debilitation. Kampuchea did not possess those autonomous resources required of an independent buffer state. It could only be the satellite of a stronger neighbour, and Vietnam's government was determined to consolidate that role in its own security interests. It has proved impossible for ASEAN to disabuse Vietnam of this unstated conviction. And although the advent of the coalition was a disturbing event for Vietnam, reflected in the torrent of abuse in its media, such abuse was not an indication of any loss of political will. ASEAN's achievement was one of political damage limitation. Faced with obduracy from Hanoi, the ASEAN states had little alternative other than to continue on in the hope that some way might be found of revising Vietnam's position. With the possible exception of Indonesia, the ASEAN states were not confronted with any pressing requirement to come to terms. The political and economic costs of prosecuting their primarily diplomatic challenge to Vietnam were easily acceptable, especially for Thailand. It had been well compensated by international agencies for harbouring refugee recruits for cross-border insurgency, while Vietnam's military ripostes helped to ensure corporate solidarity and to draw international attention to its occupation of Kampuchea.

ASEAN's diplomatic position drew strength from success in securing overwhelming endorsement at the United Nations for the international representation of Kampuchea by its nominee. It sought to capitalise on that endorsement by insisting on a UN role in a political settlement of the Kampuchean conflict which meant, in effect, a settlement on ASEAN's terms. The Vietnamese refused to countenance such a role as long as Democratic Kampuchea in one form or another was represented at the UN. The UN was seen as having been manipulated to serve ASEAN's political purpose which ran counter to that of Vietnam. Accordingly, Vietnam looked for an alternative regional vehicle for diplomatic dialogue with ASEAN in terms of reference extending beyond the Kampuchean conflict. ASEAN refused to accept such a forum because it appeared to involve conceding Vietnam's position over Kampuchea, which was that the situation there was irreversible. The difficulty over alternative diplomatic means was, in effect, only symptomatic of the entrenched obstacles to conflict resolution. In such circumstances of political impasse the only way to appear to go forward was to tinker incrementally with the procedure and general terms of negotiation in the hope that other pressures over time might make the Vietnamese see reason.

Prior to the ministerial meeting in Singapore in June 1982, Dhanabalan, speaking on behalf of ASEAN had warned Vietnam, 'We can afford to wait'.[4] If expressing public confidence that Vietnam had overreached itself, the ASEAN governments were obliged to search for diplomatic initiatives. Above all, they were concerned not to permit the impasse over Kampuchea with Vietnam in possession and its client government in place to become generally accepted as the political *status quo*. They were obliged to sustain the momentum of their diplomatic attack in order to keep the issue alive and not to let their position go by default. In this respect, it was necessary also to give a public impression of reasonableness in seeking a settlement as a way of retaining their supporting international constituency. In consequence, there followed a series of abortive initiatives, some corporate some more unilateral, which served also to expose intra-mural tensions over the management of the Kampuchean issue reinforced by clashes of personality among some foreign ministers.

The emergence of such tensions, which have been present in the corporate relationship from the outset, has cast doubts on the merits of the Kampuchean issue as a basis for ASEAN political co-operation. ASEAN has exercised a security role over Kampuchea, primarily as a diplomatic gamekeeper posting warning signs but without wielding a shotgun. In the most practical sense, security has been promoted through reinforcing a habit of subregional consultation. Vietnam's invasion of Kampuchea required the governments of the Association to develop a collegial working style and practice. But to the extent that their corporate endeavours resulted in frustration and pointed to the subordinate role of ASEAN in the conflict, reservations were revived of the kind that had been initially expressed by Indonesia's and Malaysia's heads of government at Kuantan in March 1980. These reservations strongly sustained in Indonesia's case, have had the effect of testing the cohesion of the Association and of reinforcing Vietnam's conviction that, despite Dhanabalan's expression of optimism, time was on its side – not on ASEAN's.

Symptomatic of the element of frustration within ASEAN's ranks was an initiative taken in March 1983 during the meeting of non-aligned states which convened in New Delhi. At that meeting, the ASEAN representatives present failed to revise the vacant seat arrangement in favour of the Coalition Government of Democratic Kampuchea. Malaysia's Foreign Minister, Tan Sri Ghazali Shafie, in private discussions with his Vietnamese counterpart Nguyen Co Thach then suggested a formula for diplomatic dialogue which might overcome the issue and obstacle of Kampuchean representation by excluding it altogether. He proposed a meeting between ASEAN and Indochinese governments minus that in Phnom Penh to which Nguyen Co Thach agreed in what seemed to be a significant concession, at least in procedural terms. It implied that the composition of the government in Kampuchea was a matter for negotiation and not an irreversible fact. Premature public disclosure of this tentative agreement gave rise to a display of diplomatic confusion, with both Vietnam and the ASEAN states retreating from dialogue. On ASEAN's side, it would appear that the Malaysian initiative had not followed standard consultation procedure. Public revelation by Singapore's Second Deputy Prime Minister and former Foreign Minister Sinnathamby Rajaratnam served to alert the Thai chairman of the Standing Committee to the danger of ASEAN being drawn into a process of negotiation which might compromise its own established position based on the recommendations of the International Conference on Kampuchea. An indication of the ability of the Thai government to exercise a veto over ASEAN's diplomacy was demonstrated at an *ad hoc* meeting of Foreign Ministers in Bangkok at the end of March 1983, which reiterated that a political solution to the Kampuchean problem had to be pursued within the framework of the UN Conference. The hardening of the Thai position was reaffirmed in May when its government made a Vietnamese withdrawal of 30 kilometres from the Kampuchean border a precondition for Foreign Minister Siddhi Savetsila to visit Hanoi for talks with Nguyen Co Thach. Vietnam's anticipated negative response was followed in June in Bangkok by ASEAN's Foreign Ministers at their annual meeting holding to an endorsement of the recommendations of the International Conference on Kampuchea. They also reiterated their conviction that 'the formation of the Coalition government of

Democratic Kampuchea constituted a significant step towards a comprehensive political settlement of the Kampuchean problem'.[5]

That position was modified in a so-called Joint Appeal by ASEAN's Foreign Ministers on 21 September 1983, which appeared to be directed primarily at the forthcoming session of the UN General Assembly. It avoided reference to the UN Conference in calling for self-determination and national reconciliation with an implied political role for the followers of Heng Samrin. It restated established demands for a Vietnamese military withdrawal but no mention was made of the United Nations in the role of peacekeeping forces or observer groups both to verify withdrawal and to monitor the attendant cease-fire. This would be a preliminary to an act of self-determination through internationally supervised elections. A novel element in the appeal, which represented an attempt to test the credibility of Vietnam's commitment in February 1982 to begin partial troop withdrawals from Kampuchea, was a proposal that further withdrawals should take place on a phased territorial basis beginning from the western-most territory of Kampuchea along the Thai–Kampuchea border.[6]

Whatever utility this 'appeal' may have possessed as a means of sustaining UN endorsement of ASEAN's established position, it fell on deaf ears in Vietnam. Moreover, the ability of ASEAN to mobilise international support against Vietnam began to show signs of weakening. For example, the government of France indicated its reserve over the status of the Coalition Government of Democratic Kampuchea because of the dominant role within it of the Khmer Rouge. Correspondingly, the Labour government in Australia, keen to explore alternative options for Vietnam to an undue dependence on the Soviet Union, refused to sponsor the annual resolution on Kampuchea in the General Assembly of the United Nations. Moreover, China, which was an alignment partner in the diplomatic confrontation with Vietnam, was not as willing as the United States to follow ASEAN's lead over Kampuchea. For example, in March 1983 its government had unilaterally put forward a five-point proposal incorporating a demand for a declaration of unconditional withdrawal of troops as a precondition for bilateral talks with Vietnam. Diplomatically, ASEAN seemed to be treading water, which had the effect of reviving intra-mural tensions. In Jakarta the view began to be even more strongly held that the Association's corporate policy was pointless.

Indonesia's frustration was caused by a belief that ASEAN was holding back the Republic's resumption of an independent and active foreign policy justified by its achievement in economic development. That frustration may have been compounded by the attitude of Dr Mahathir Mohamad who on becoming Prime Minister in July 1981 sought to differentiate Malaysia's foreign policy from that of Indonesia's. His outlook reflected personal ambition but also a revised awareness of the geostrategic importance of Thailand for Malaysia. Interest in greater solidarity with Thailand was linked to securing more effective cross-border co-operation against the insurgent wing of the Malayan Communist Party. Whatever the motivation, Indonesia could no longer count to the same extent on Malaysia's backing within ASEAN in registering its reservations at the direction of corporate policy over Kampuchea. Indeed, at a later stage, Malaysia violated corporate consensus over an Indonesian scheme to promote the development of human resources in co-operation with ASEAN's dialogue partners from the Pacific region. One expression of Indonesia's frustration was the convening in January 1984 in Hanoi of a seminar between the Institute of International Relations, attached to the Foreign Ministry, and Jakarta's influential Centre for Strategic and International Studies. Terms for a settlement of the Kampuchean conflict were discussed.[7] In February in a visit that was perceived as more than coincidental, Armed Forces Commander General Benny Moerdani met with Vietnamese officials. During a tour of military installations near the border with China, he remarked that 'The Indonesian armed forces and people do not believe that danger to Southeast Asia comes from Vietnam'.[8] His statement delighted his hosts and caused consternation in some ASEAN capitals.

General Moerdani's statement implicitly identified China as the principal source of external threat to the region. It suggested also that Vietnam might be drawn into a regional structure of security co-operation against China and accordingly loosened from its relationship with the Soviet Union. Such reasoning assumed also that the political identity and prevailing external relations of the People's Republic of Kampuchea were beyond revision. In spite of a subsequent qualification explicitly objecting to Vietnam's presence in Kampuchea,[9] damage was done to the public cohesion of ASEAN. General Moerdani's visit, which had followed others by him in a covert intelligence role, was an exploratory one. It was also a signal to regional partners of the limits to Indonesia's patience over Kampuchea. Its effect was to strain relations between Jakarta and Bangkok in particular, and it became necessary for

General Moerdani to engage in a series of conciliatory meetings in Bandar Seri Begawan later in February during official celebrations to mark Brunei's assumption of full independence.

Indonesia sought to employ its dissenting position to sustain the momentum of diplomatic exploration with Vietnam. To this end, President Suharto, attended by Foreign Minister Mochtar Kusumaatmadja, received Vietnamese Foreign Minister Nguyen Co Thach in Jakarta in March 1984. At the meeting President Suharto proposed a formula for negotiations over Kampuchea which excluded a direct representative role for the Phnom Penh government but with a peace-keeping one for Vietnam in any settlement. Nguyen Co Thach's apparent repudiation of this formula provoked Suharto's personal annoyance, because it had been made without consultation with ASEAN counterparts. The meeting exposed the limits of understanding between Indonesia and Vietnam and once again underlying tensions within the Association. In May it was found necessary to convene a special meeting of ASEAN Foreign Ministers in Jakarta, who were briefed by President Suharto on his encounter with Nguyen Co Thach. A statement was issued that 'The President welcomed the convening of the meeting of ASEAN foreign ministers as an opportunity to show the world the complete unity of ASEAN on the Kampuchean problem'.[10] For their part, the six Foreign Ministers (including Prince Mohamad Bolkiah representing Brunei which had joined the Association in January 1984) engaged in a public closing of ranks. They sustained their common position of placing the onus on Vietnam over measures required to resolve the Kampuchean conflict and reiterated the validity of the Association's joint appeal of September 1983. That restatement served to provide the core of the communique issued after the annual ministerial meeting held in July 1984 also in Jakarta. Indonesia's diplomatic opening to Vietnam had failed to have any impact on the political impasse. Its return to ASEAN ranks restored a formal unity but not a common purpose.

The theme of national reconciliation, interpreted quite differently between the ASEAN and Indochinese states, provided the common idiom in a continuing diplomatic dialogue of the deaf. Vietnam's indifference to ASEAN's entreaties was displayed blatantly in early 1985 when its forces launched a military offensive which overran the encampments of the disparate Khmer resistance movement located along the Thai–Kampuchean border. That offensive provoked a corporate statement in Bangkok in

February in which it was maintained that Vietnam's actions contradicted its professions for a negotiated solution. ASEAN's basic position was reiterated yet again: 'National Unity can be achieved only through the participation of all Kampucheans in the act of self-determination to be held under international supervision.'[11] A change of emphasis was indicated, however, in the appeal of the Foreign Ministers to 'the international community to increase support and assistance to the Kampuchean people in their political and *military* [emphasis added] struggle to liberate their homeland from foreign occupation'. The governments of ASEAN had all provided some material support to the non-Communist resistance, but only Singapore and Malaysia had given limited military aid and training, respectively. The appeal indicated a willingness to become collectively identified with, if not engaged in, military support for the insurgent challenge to Vietnam. It bore minor fruit through a U.S. congressional initiative to extend token aid to the non-Communist factions. Apart from that appeal, there was nothing novel in the communique, which called on Vietnam to engage in a direct dialogue with the Coalition Government of Democratic Kampuchea.

At this point, Malaysia was occupying the position of chairman of ASEAN's Standing Committee. A cabinet reshuffle had returned Tengku Rithaudeen to the office of Foreign Minister. By then Indonesia's Foreign Minister, Mochtar Kusumaatmadja, had been accorded the role of 'designated interlocutor of ASEAN' in diplomatic explorations with Vietnam. In that role, he had sought to promote an improvement in U.S.-Vietnamese relations in the expectation that Hanoi would become more amenable to compromise as it became less isolated diplomatically. He claimed later to have identified a twelve point process of settlement, which could lead to a government of national reconciliation headed by Prince Sihanouk.[12] In any event, Malaysia's Foreign Minister undertook a separate initiative. He proposed proximity talks on the Afghanistan model between the Heng Samrin government and the Coalition Government of Democratic Kampuchea. This initiative provoked dissension within the Coalition and a rebuke from China, to which Thailand did not object. At issue was the representation of the conflict. Malaysia's proposal suggested that it had its source in civil war, while the longstanding ASEAN position had been that the conflict was a direct consequence of Vietnam's invasion. The proximity talks proposal was modified on the ground that it would serve to lend legitimacy to the Heng Samrin government. As an alternative, the ASEAN Foreign Ministers in a joint statement in Kuala Lumpur in July 1985 proposed proximity talks, but between the Coalition Government of Democratic Kampuchea and Vietnam, with representation from the Phnom Penh government only as part of the Vietnamese delegation and with the agenda restricted to ASEAN's formulation for a comprehensive settlement.[13] To make the point, at their annual meeting in the same month held also in Kuala Lumpur, the Foreign Ministers reiterated their commitment to the ASEAN appeal of September 1983.[14]

The proximity talks proposal never got off the ground. Vietnam derived a measure of satisfaction from the evident differences displayed within ASEAN ranks, including the delight of Indonesia's Foreign Minister at the discomfiture of his presumptuous Malaysian counterpart. It was left to the Thai Foreign Ministry to reassert the conventional ASEAN stand in explaining the declared common position over the proximity talks. It pointed out, 'The reason why ASEAN made the proposal is logical. As Vietnam is the aggressor and Kampuchea is the victim, the two sides should meet because they are directly involved in the conflict.'[15] That statement did not represent a negotiable position. Indeed, it represented a non-negotiable one, symptomatic of the strategy of attrition designed to secure a political solution through Vietnam abdicating its position from weakness.

Despite its tenacity, ASEAN had more or less run out of ideas. The strength of its corporate position rested on an ability to deny international recognition to the Heng Samrin government. Any concession over negotiating procedure which indicated lack of consistency and resolve over recognition could not be countenanced by Thailand and Singapore in particular. Correspondingly, the Vietnamese, while interested in giving the impression of dialogue, had no reason to accommodate ASEAN over the format of so-called talks about talks if that meant appearing to repudiate the government in Phnom Penh. An entrenched military stalemate was well matched by diplomatic stalemate, which meant that ASEAN could not build on its initial diplomatic accomplishment. Indeed, initiative was taken away from ASEAN by the disparate leadership of the Coalition Government of Democratic Kampuchea at a meeting in Beijing in March 1986. It put forward an eight point proposal calling for negotiations for a timetable for Vietnam's withdrawal and the establishment of a quadrapartite coalition government, including the Heng Samrin faction, to be headed by Prince Sihanouk as

President and Son Sann as Prime Minister. Such a government would hold free elections under the supervision of a UN observer group. Despite the controversial venue for that initiative, it attracted ASEAN's support at a special meeting of its Foreign Ministers in Bali in April 1986, held during a visit to Indonesia by President Reagan.

Singapore's Foreign Minister, Suppiah Dhanabalan made reference to this eight-point proposal at the annual ministerial meeting in Manila in June 1986, pointing out that certain longstanding ASEAN requirements, such as the disarming of all factions and free elections supervised by an international group, were missing. He claimed, however, that the proposal did have enough important elements to form part of the framework for a political settlement, remarking:

> We remain committed to a political solution that will guarantee withdrawal of Vietnamese occupation troops, provide self-determination to Cambodians and deny Pol Pot and his henchmen an opportunity to come back to power. This has been ASEAN's position for some time.... I do not therefore see any need for ASEAN to make new proposals at this ministerial meeting.[16]

The final communique sought to have the best of all worlds by reiterating an established stand over Kampuchea which reaffirmed the validity of the Joint Appeal of September 1983 and the proposal of July 1985 for indirect or proximity talks between the CGDK and Vietnam. In addition, it reaffirmed support for the CGDK proposals, which it represented as able 'to serve as a constructive framework for negotiations', despite an awareness that it was construed in Hanoi as an attempt at *diktat*. Finally,

> The Foreign Ministers reviewed the diplomatic effort of ASEAN in its search for a comprehensive and durable political solution to the Kampuchean problem. They reaffirmed their determination to continue their efforts in seeking such a solution to the Kampuchean problem as envisaged in the UNGA Resolution on the situation in Kampuchea.[17]

These efforts failed to bring any immediate change to the condition of political and military stalemate over Kampuchea. The ministerial meeting in Manila in 1986 had convened just prior to the death of Vietnam's leader, Le Duan who had himself succeeded Ho Chi Minh. He was replaced ultimately in December 1986 by Nguyen Van Linh. His assumption of stewardship of Vietnam's Communist Party had been preceded by authorised public debate on the gross shortcomings of Vietnam's economy. Nguyen Van Linh encouraged attempts to grasp the nettle of economic reform. That exercise in so-called renovation, reflecting Soviet interests, was not matched, however, by any public indication of significant change in foreign policy. Accommodation to ASEAN's position over Kampuchea did not follow acknowledgement of economic weakness. Moreover, expectations that Soviet interest in rapprochement with China might lead to visible pressure on Vietnam to compromise over Kampuchea were not realised. Speaking at the Congress of Vietnam's Communist Party in December 1986, Soviet Politburo member Yegor Ligachev encouraged normalisation of Vietnam's relations with China on the basis of dialogue but then assured his hosts that Soviet aid for the period 1986–90 would be doubled. When Soviet Foreign Minister Eduard Shevardnadze visited Vietnam in March 1987, after stopping off in Bangkok and then spending time in Jakarta, he failed to indicate any intent to apply pressure on Vietnam over Kampuchea. On the contrary, he made quite explicit his support for the common position of the three Indochinese states. The Soviet Union had an undoubted interest in a settlement over Kampuchea but could not compromise the security of a fraternal partner in any crude abdication of support.

When ASEAN's Foreign Ministers met in annual session in Singapore in June 1987, they were obliged to record that 'Vietnam's basic position on Kampuchea has not changed despite the recent attempts to give the impression of flexibility'. Their final communique did not reflect the optimism of Prime Minister Lee Kuan Yew's opening address, in which he suggested that the chances of a negotiated settlement had increased because both the Soviet Union and Vietnam had put the revival of their economies at the top of their priorities. They merely went over old ground in expressing deep concern over Vietnam's illegal occupation of Kampuchea, said to pose a grave threat to peace and stability in South-East Asia. The Foreign Ministers reaffirmed the validity of their joint appeal of September 1983 and reiterated support for the Coalition Government of Democratic Kampuchea's eight-point proposal of March 1986 'as a constructive framework for negotiations'.

In light of Vietnam's insistence on the dismantling 'of the infrastructure of Pol Pot' (i.e. the liquidation of the Khmer Rouge as a political and military organisation) as the precondition for a Kampuchean settlement, ASEAN's diplomatic position did not seem a basis for constructive dialogue. Moreover, that position had weakened because of open disunity within the Khmer coalition. Shortly before the ministerial meeting had convened, Prince Norodom Sihanouk announced his intention of taking at least a year's leave of absence as President of the Coalition Government of Democratic Kampuchea ostensibly because of armed attacks on forces loyal to him by both the Khmer Rouge and the KPNLF. Sihanouk had been treated by all ASEAN governments as a symbol of Kampuchean legitimacy and as central to their diplomatic undertaking. His half-defection raised the prospect of a separate deal with the Vietnamese behind the backs of both ASEAN and China.

The sense of drift in ASEAN's Kampuchean policy encouraged Indonesia's Foreign Minister to press ahead with a much postponed visit to Hanoi in July 1987. Two years previously, Dr Mochtar had been critical of Malaysia's proximity talks proposal because their likely effect would be to accord recognition to the government in Phnom Penh. He had held to the position that the main protagonists were the CGDK and Vietnam. In a speech at Columbia University in New York in October 1985, he had maintained that direct talks between the CGDK and the Heng Samrin government should not be countenanced, since they would confirm the legitimacy of the latter. Despite this fundamental reservation, he affirmed support for the idea of national reconciliation which he advocated 'should include all factions'. The problem was how to begin such a process without cutting the ground from under ASEAN's position. Its main impact had been made by charging that the conflict over Kampuchea had arisen from external invasion and not civil war, therefore requiring Vietnam to be a prime party to any negotiations.

During his visit to Vietnam in July 1987, Dr Mochtar took up the idea of an informal meeting or 'cocktail party' between the Kampuchean parties to the conflict. He reached an understanding with his counterpart, Nguyen Co Thach, that an informal meeting of the two Kampuchean sides be convened 'on the basis of equal footing, without preconditions and with no political labels', to which at a latter stage Indonesia would invite other concerned countries, including Vietnam, to participate. Any optimism in

Hanoi and Jakarta at an apparent diplomatic breakthrough was short-lived as other ASEAN governments – especially Thailand and Singapore – made clear politely but firmly that Dr Mochtar had conceded too much in his attempt to promote a settlement. At a special meeting held in Bangkok in mid-August, while not repudiating the idea of an informal gathering among Khmer parties, Foreign Ministers collectively insisted on tying it to Vietnam's virtually immediate participation because it was the invading and occupying power. They insisted also that the CGDK's eight point proposal, endorsed previously by ASEAN, should serve as the basis for discussions. These revised conditions were then denounced by Vietnam, which reiterated its support for the willingness of the Phnom Penh government 'to discuss national reconciliation on the basis of the elimination of Pol Pot'. Significantly, on the very day in late July when Dr Mochtar had travelled to Vietnam, the Communist Party's daily newspaper *Nhan Dan* affirmed that 'The PRK's international prestige has not ceased to grow. The fact is that nobody can reverse the situation in Kampuchea.'[18]

Dr Mochtar's abortive initiative was almost certainly the product of a mixture of motives, including an interest in bolstering his domestic political position. He was moved also by a longstanding concern that the Kampuchean conflict, if not settled, would entrench Sino-Soviet rivalry and influence in South-East Asia. His peacekeeping effort ran into a persistent obstacle. Because the costs of continuing the conflict were acceptable to some parties – certainly to Thailand and Singapore as well as to China – there was not felt to be any strong reason to accommodate Vietnam gratuitously. The net effect of attendant intra-mural discordance was to convey an impression of political impotence on the part of the Association as a corporate entity.

That impression of political impotence was reinforced when the diplomatic initiative was then seized by Prince Sihanouk in the wake of his taking leave of absence as President of the Coalition Government of Democratic Kampuchea. This breaking of coalition ranks paved the way for informal talks near Paris in early December 1987 between Prince Sihanouk and Hun Sen, the Prime Minister of the People's Republic of Kampuchea, encouraged by the Soviet Union, whose domestic priorities were reflected in the changed tone of its relationship with the United States. The motives for the meeting were mixed, although both principals had a strong interest in eliminating the Khmer Rouge from any role in government. A skeletal agreement on procedure and political aims between Prince

Sihanouk and Hun Sen marked the onset of protracted negotiations over a political settlement in Kampuchea, to which ASEAN was not a party but which it felt obliged to endorse, despite the fact that they represented the conflict as a civil war and not as the product of Vietnamese invasion. Significantly, neither China nor the Khmer Rouge expressed any enthusiasm over the negotiations, which took on an artificial political quality in the absence of Vietnamese participation.

The course of events over Kampuchea since the formation of the coalition government has served to expose the limits to ASEAN's attempts to employ diplomacy in a security role beyond its regional bounds.

When the heads of government of ASEAN met in Manila in December 1987, they could congratulate themselves on having hung together up to a point over Kampuchea. The outbreak of the Kampuchean conflict in the wake of radical political change throughout the whole of Indochina had given the Association a new lease of corporate life. The need to engage in intensive political co-operation in order to confront that change and then the invasion of Kampuchea had produced a regenerating political effect. But the actual threat posed to the ASEAN states by that invasion was not uniform. Thailand was most directly menaced, if not by military invasion. It is of interest to record that some eight years after Vietnam's invasion of Kampuchea, the Commander-in-Chief of Thailand's Army, General Chaovalit Yongchaiyudh could remark that while his country's security was threatened, there was no danger of full-scale aggression 'at least within the next five years'.[20] In Bangkok, deeper concern arose over the prospect of a historically unprecedented concentration of power in Indochina, against which the Thai state would come to occupy a subordinate position. That threat was met primarily through recourse to external countervailing power. By the end of 1987, however, mixed views were being expressed in Bangkok over that threat in the light of Vietnam's economic distress. Political co-operation within ASEAN had played only a supplementary part in creating a climate of security for Thailand, valued none the less because of the international support obtained for its corporate cause. Indeed, over Kampuchea, ASEAN has been drawn primarily into the service of Thai interests. Thailand has been in a position to determine the direction of corporate policy by conveying an implicit threat that undue resistance by its regional partners could provoke an even closer association with the People's Republic of China. That position has provoked corresponding resentment and frustration in Jakarta finding expression in recurrent misgivings over the allegedly misguided way in which Indonesia has been led by the regional partners.

The net effect has been for the Kampuchean issue to become a mixed blessing for ASEAN. It has provided a basis for corporate solidarity as well as for enhancing the international standing of the Association. As a consequence ASEAN has become an important factor in the diplomatic calculations of Vietnam, as indicated by an unprecedented act of recognition in the form of congratulations at the convening of the Manila Summit in December 1987. At the same time, the Association has found its internal cohesion tested while the centrality of its diplomatic role has diminished. Paradoxically, the basis for political solidarity has served also as the source of intra-mural dissension because strategic perspective and therefore security interests have been divisible between member states. Mixed feelings have been aroused by the policy of diplomatic confrontation of Vietnam, even though an important measure of common interest has been served by upholding the principle of respect for national sovereignty. In the absence of a common definition of external threat, alignment with China and the United States in a regional expression of their global competition with the Soviet Union has been in direct contradiction to the Association's declaratory vision of South-East Asia as a Zone of Peace, Freedom, and Neutrality. Such a visionary undertaking, reaffirmed at the third meeting of heads of government in Manila in December 1987, has remained beyond the competence of ASEAN. Since its diplomatic engagement in the Kampuchean conflict, the problem of regional security has assumed an intractable quality.

There have been a number of reasons for that continuing state of affairs.

First, the question of an appropriate format for regional order among the resident states of South-East Asia has become subordinate to the prior immediate but also symptomatic issue of which government should rule in Phnom Penh and on what terms. Contending formulae for regional order have in effect expressed fundamental differences over terms of settlement in Kampuchea which would have a direct bearing on the regional balance of power.

Second, the issue of the appropriate political identity of Kampuchea has brought into confrontation adverse geostrategic interests held by Thailand and Vietnam which cannot be reconciled.[21] Those interests have been sustained in competition with one another through external power support which has reinforced political polarisation in South-East Asia.

Third, the underlying and fundamental issue of the Kampuchean conflict – whether or not Vietnam will be confirmed as the dominant state in Indochina – has been from the outset more than a matter of regional significance, as indicated above. It has attracted competitive external intervention in a manner characteristic of regional conflicts since the onset of the transfers of sovereignty from colonial domination. The net effect has been to demonstrate that in the absence of regional concord, regional order is well beyond the ministrations of a small set of local states capable of only a limited measure of political co-operation.

Fourth, in challenging Vietnam's assertion of dominance, the ASEAN states have engaged in a classical practice of balance of power but without employing the traditional requisite of collective military capability. They have only been able to engage in a diplomatic undertaking. In that undertaking, ASEAN has become a party to a wider coalition whose capability for coercing Vietnam arises primarily from China's military involvement. The dependent quality of ASEAN's own security role, diplomatically expressed, has been evident all along.

Finally, the dependent quality of that diplomatic role points to the conspicuous limitations of its declaratory regional aspirations. The Zopfan formula, for example, envisages regional insulation from intruding external quarrels. ASEAN's policy over Kampuchea has not only been symptomatic of Zopfan's elusiveness but also has been in direct contradiction to it. As indicated above, this contradiction between declared aspiration and an operational corporate foreign policy has had the effect of setting up tensions within the Association which have been accommodated but not reconciled.

One consequence of its deep diplomatic engagement in the Kampuchean conflict has been to demonstrate conclusively that regional order in a grand sense is well beyond the corporate capacity of the Association. Paradoxically and in part because of the requirement of political co-operation over Kampuchea, some order has been realised but on an intra-mural scale. The established if imperfect habit of co-operation has helped to contain a number of intra-mural differences, giving rise to an embryonic security community. Certainly, the degree of corporate attachment to principle over Vietnam's invasion and occupation of Kampuchea has served to increase the confidence of more vulnerable ASEAN states in the *bona fides* of regional partners. One minor fruit of this process of confidence-building was Brunei's membership in ASEAN immediately after it resumed sovereignty in January 1984.

Brunei had sought to perpetuate its quasi-colonial status because of its fear of Indonesia and Malaysia, both of whom had once threatened its integrity. A change of attitude both to assuming full independence and joining ASEAN occurred concurrently with the corporate evolution of the Association in the wake of revolutionary change in Indochina. The special emphasis given to national sovereignty was also of importance. Attachment to that principle implied a self-denying ordinance on the part of member governments. In this context, an attempt by any member state to interfere in the internal affairs of another would be certain to discredit the Association to the point of damaging its cohesion and viability. The evident link between public philosophy and corporate viability as well as a proven record of political co-operation encouraged membership in ASEAN, tested by a prior period of observer status. By joining ASEAN, Brunei made its independence a hostage to the political fortunes of the Association. Put less dramatically, membership in ASEAN was undertaken as a way of ensuring a more secure local environment.

A further expansion of ASEAN's structure of special relations for a corresponding reason is not likely. An obvious candidate is Burma, but its sense of non-alignment expressed in resignation from the Non-Aligned Movement in 1979 rules out membership in any grouping which is a party to regional conflict. Papua New Guinea has long enjoyed observer status at ASEAN ministerial meetings, but its membership of the South Pacific Forum has been regarded as an obstacle to membership in an exclusive association.[22] Accordingly, its special relationship to ASEAN has been expressed only in interest in accession to the dormant Treaty of Amity and Co-operation. The political bounds of the Association and therefore its scope for promoting regional order would seem to be more or less fixed for the time being.

ASEAN has a fair record as a working diplomatic community. It has become a factor of some significance in the calculations of both regional and extra-regional states. It has been able to assume a prerogative role in intermittent negotiations about establishing regional rules of the game. That role, however, is subject to tremendous limitations. First, the condition of the balance or distribution of power within South-East Asia is such that ASEAN even if in complete internal accord, would not be in any position to act corporately and autonomously to revise it to reflect its declaratory version of regional order. Second, the overall interests of the ASEAN and Indochinese states and their external patrons are so adversely entrenched that a settlement over Kampuchea would seem unlikely without one side or the other making unacceptable concessions, or in ASEAN's case being obliged to accept a *fait accompli* from a diplomatic initiative which had by-passed it. Such a prospect arose when ASEAN was by-passed in December 1987, when preliminary negotiations to settle the Kampuchean conflict began between Prince Sihanouk and Prime Minister Hun Sen.

ASEAN as a corporate entity has sought to secure practical endorsement of the cardinal rule of the society of states as it applied regionally before 25 December 1978, which is when Vietnam invaded Kampuchea. The opposing Indochinese constellation led by Vietnam has sought to apply that rule in a more discriminate manner from 8 January 1979, when the People's Republic of Kampuchea was established. Until it is agreed finally on what basis the line should be drawn across the page of South-East Asian history, regional order in a full sense cannot be addressed. For ASEAN, order can only be an intra-mural undertaking until this issue is fully resolved.

Such an intra-mural undertaking has evident utility for individual governments. They benefit from being part of a structure of special relationships which enables accommodation and management of subregional tensions and disputes. The measure of corporate solidarity and identity demonstrated in the process has attracted interest beyond South-East Asia, bearing fruit, for example, in the form of so-called dialogue relationships with Western industrialised states. Japan, in particular, reaffirmed interest in ASEAN as a zone of economic opportunity when Prime Minister Noburo Takeshita attended the second day of the ASEAN summit in Manila in December 1987. An ability to sustain viable working relationships within ASEAN reinforced by a display of external confidence has served to promote a subregional climate of security. Co-operation within ASEAN, however, has tended to be primarily one-dimensional. Economic co-operation has been limited and disappointing in terms of expectations. Trade liberalisation in the corporate interest has not been possible on any significant scale because such an interest does not exist. The legacy of colonial economies reinforced by the mutually exclusive priorities of national economic development policies has stood in the way of any flowering in economic co-operation. For example, meetings of ASEAN Economic Ministers in July and October 1987 preliminary to the summit in December were restricted to tinkering with preferential trading arrangements. A proposed free trade area was too controversial for serious consideration. Just as the strategic perspective has been divisible among member governments, so economic co-operation has been obstructed by structural conflicts of interest.[23]

An additional weakness in the structure of special regional relations has been the underdeveloped institutional basis of ASEAN. Such underdevelopment has been the result of considered neglect. For example, the High Council provided for in the Treaty of Amity and Co-operation as a mechanism for peaceful settlement of disputes has never been constituted. The machinery of ASEAN is distinguished by the primacy of the national foreign ministries. That primacy reflects the national governments' determination to prevent centrist tendencies from developing in the form of corporate institutions with more than a minimal service function. The ASEAN Secretariat does not have any significant policy-initiating role. That responsibility has remained with the ASEAN National Secretariats of the respective foreign ministries. Corporate institutionalisation obtains primarily at the level of meetings of senior officials whose role is critical to the annual and *ad hoc* meetings of Foreign Ministers. Because of the annual switching of the chairmanship and personnel of the key Standing Committee, there is a built-in discontinuity in formal provision for institutional continuity.

Institutionalisation at the level of top decision-makers has been more embryonic. Heads of government, who occupy so central a position in all ASEAN states, have met on only three occasions collectively and with limited frequency on a bilateral basis, and then unevenly. At the conclusion of the Manila summit in December 1987, it was agreed that heads of government would meet 'every three to five years, if necessary'.

The corporate structure of ASEAN is less than tight, but it has been held together by some accomplishment in political co-operation. For the better part of a decade that co-operation has focused on the Kampuchean issue, which has been a mixed blessing. It was not the kind of issue or involvement contemplated in Bangkok in August 1967. At the outset, a climate of reconciliation and a corresponding commitment to regional co-operation was expected to counter threats between member governments. An attendant ability to address problems of domestic political stability through the mechanisms of economic development was viewed as equally important for security. Ideally, it would prevent the contagion of internal subversion from spreading to infect the body politic of regional partners. The rationale employed was the indivisibility of security among member states, with linkages expressing themselves both positively and negatively. That rationale can be overstated. For example, the Philippines was set in a state of political decay from at least August 1983 with the assassination of opposition leader Benigno Aquino at Manila airport. Membership of ASEAN did not have any apparent effect in countering its political condition. Moreover, preoccupation with internal politics, however, certainly weakened the practical participation of the Philippines in the Association. During the dying throes of the Marcos regime, the other five ASEAN governments broke with precedent in commenting collectively on the political crisis in the Philippines. It had been an established tenet of the Association that interference in the internal affairs of a regional partner is prohibited. On this occasion, five governments issued a statement widely interpreted as a tactful call to President Marcos to relinquish office in the interest of national unity. But that appeal was of marginal significance compared with domestic political challenge and the withdrawal of U.S. support. It was with a collective sense of relief that the five ASEAN governments greeted the virtually bloodless transfer of power to Mrs Aquino in February 1986. It indicated concern over the likely impact of a more radical political change in the Philippines, which could dispossess the United States of its military bases, valued among all ASEAN governments as a counter to the Soviet military presence in Vietnam. In the case of the Philippines, the indivisibility of security in a positive sense had not been demonstrated; its negative dimension was of common concern but beyond common action.

Regional order in a full sense has always been beyond the corporate capacity of ASEAN. The experience of the Philippines under both Presidents Marcos and Aquino has demonstrated also the limitations of the implied theory of collective internal security. Yet membership of ASEAN has evident practical utility by comparison with the problems which could arise in its absence.[24] The signal accomplishment of the Association has been to demonstrate that it is possible to accommodate intra-mural differences while sustaining working relationships which are relevant to subregional security. In practising intra-mural accommodation and political co-operation, ASEAN has proceeded by consensus. That practice of consensus has never entailed full uniformity in foreign policy. For example, the ASEAN states divided at the United Nations over Britain's military recovery of the Falkland/Malvinas Islands in 1982. Political co-operation has been confined in the main to regional issues, without any strong suggestion before 1986 that a veto should be applied to the foreign policy of any member government. Even on regional issues, consensus has been interpreted at times to mean an agreement to disagree, which was the case when Malaysia broke ranks with its partners and established diplomatic relations with the People's Republic of China in 1974.

The issue of a veto being applied to a member state's foreign policy arose in concrete form in November 1986. Objections were lodged by the governments of Brunei, Indonesia and Malaysia to an official visit to Singapore by President Chaim Herzog of Israel. Protests by Brunei and Indonesia were perfunctory. In the case of Malaysia, however, they were vehemently raised by senior cabinet ministers, two former prime ministers, and by an *ad hoc* action committee dominated by political opponents of Prime Minister Dr Mahathir Mohamad. The Malaysian government had initially adopted the standard ASEAN position that it did not have the right to protest at the visit because the matter was an internal affair of another country. That principle has been central to state practice within the Association. It was set aside in the face of agitation begun ostensibly by a local branch of the youth wing of the United Malays National Organisation (UMNO), the dominant party within the ruling National Front coalition. In the process, an established practice of intra-ASEAN constraint was overridden as Malaysia's domestic politics determined the tone and priorities of its foreign policy.

The furore aroused by President Herzog's visit to Singapore was partly a product of domestic political circumstances within Malaysia. The visit occurred concurrently with intense competition for political leadership within UMNO, which reached a peak in April 1987 in party elections in which Dr Mahathir only narrrowly retained presidential office. It occurred also at a time of communal tension between Malay and Chinese parties within the ruling coalition, from which Singapore has never been insulated completely because of its physical proximity, its prevailing ethnic-Chinese identity, and the legacy of its brief but stormy experience as a constituent state of the Federation. It is important also to take into account the extent to which Islamic credentials had become the central factor in the identity of the politically dominant Malay community as well as the focal point in Malay politics.[25] In consequence, the cause of Palestinian nationalism had come to be viewed as a co-religionist issue given special content because of Israel's jurisdiction over Islamic holy places in Jerusalem.

Prime Minister Mahathir had been consistently firm in his vocal support for the Palestinian cause as well as expressing publicly from mid-1986 the conviction that Zionism was a pernicious influence which threatened the well-being of Malaysia through its control of international media.[26] One of a number of such statements had been made by him less than two weeks before it was made known publicly that Israel's President would be visiting Singapore. In consequence, the visit to Singapore by the head of the Zionist state came to be viewed by Dr Mahathir as a personal insult. In the context of Malaysian politics, it was interpreted as a public flaunting of a politically disagreeable relationship. Inspired agitation by UMNO youth then provided a heaven-sent opportunity for opposition elements to mobilise support over an issue which was beyond government reproach. The Herzog visit attracted formal diplomatic protests from Malaysia, Indonesia, and Brunei; the former two states also temporarily withdrew the heads of their diplomatic missions from Singapore. Wild talk was then succeeded by calmer counsels as governments in Malaysia and Singapore engaged in political damage limitation.

The Herzog episode was an exceptional one in intra-ASEAN relations. It was the product of special circumstances which have not obtained between any ASEAN states other than Singapore and Malaysia. Indeed, it may be represented as a worst possible case which is, therefore, not fully representative of ASEAN's condition.

The Herzog visit to Singapore has also pointed to a paradoxical feature of ASEAN present at its creation which has not changed out of recognition during more than two decades of its existence. ASEAN was established between adversaries of different kinds in an attempt to promote a structure of reconciliation through which it was hoped that regional security might be promoted. The regional enterprise was embarked upon in the full knowledge that certain underlying facts of political life could not be changed at will, including the mixed sense of vulnerability of member states. Foreign policy would, therefore, always be a problem among member states; some partners in reconciliation would be likely to remain potential enemies. The Herzog affair exposed this reality and indicated the danger of taking the cohesion and viability of ASEAN for granted. Indeed, there would seem to be a problem of corporate regeneration.

That problem has been compounded because of the Herzog affair and attendant controversy in which the suggestion of a veto by one government over the foreign policy of a regional partner was raised. The argument was advanced in Malaysia that, because of the offence to Muslim feelings, second thoughts over Herzog's visit were required of Singapore in the interests of ASEAN solidarity. Indeed, Malaysia's attitude made explicit that in certain instances, independence in foreign policy should assume a conditional quality. Put in extreme form, that attitude may be compared to the idea of limited sovereignty employed by the late Leonid Brezhnev to justify the invasion of Czechoslovakia by the Soviet Union. Certainly, this is how Malaysia's position was interpreted and represented in Singapore. The charge was levelled of unwarranted interference in the island-state's internal affairs, which had violated the established practice of ASEAN. This charge was reiterated when a subsquent controversy within Singapore over the role of the Malays in its armed forces also precipitated a Malaysian diplomatic intervention coincident with an unprecedented leadership struggle within UMNO. That intervention occurred after an evident attempt by President Suharto to repair relationships by visiting both Malaysia and Singapore.

The issue arising for ASEAN from the Herzog visit may be posed in less extreme form by taking into account that membership of any club, whether of individuals or states, will require some limitation on freedom of action. It could be argued that, without compromising sovereignty, ASEAN governments ought to be sufficiently sensitive to the special interests and feelings of regional partners not to engage in foreign policy initiatives likely to be viewed as gratuitously provocative. It was on this ground that the wisdom rather than the right of Singapore's government to invite the President of Israel was questioned.

This general maxim, if unexceptional, may not account for specific circumstances especially if a member government is disposed to display sovereignty in order to overcome an abiding sense of vulnerability which in turn violates the sensibilities of a regional partner. The furore aroused in Malaysia by President Herzog's visit to Singapore was exceptional because of domestic circumstances in Malaysia, including the personal offence taken by Dr Mahathir. It was also symptomatic in pointing to the problem of conserving the system of subregional order attained by ASEAN. The structure of special relationships established over more than two decades enjoys a mixed quality in terms of bilateral linkages. Their value may be measured with reference to conditions likely to obtain in their absence. But such conditions highlighted in the early 1960s are a matter of fading memory at a time of transfer of political generations without any guarantee of continuity of the commitment to ASEAN which was displayed by its founding fathers. Accordingly, the view that 'the ASEAN process has created a sturdy structure of trust, confidence and goodwill between the member states' cannot be taken at face value.[27]

By the beginning of its third decade, ASEAN had become well established as a regional actor enjoying a widespread international standing. Its evolution had proceeded in the absence of frequent multilateral contact between heads of government. When the Association's Foreign Ministers met in Bali in April 1986, shortly after the political downfall of President Marcos, they agreed to recommend to their respective heads of government that a third summit be convened in Manila in the latter half of 1987. That agreement was recalled and reaffirmed at the annual ministerial meeting held in Manila in June 1986. By the following year in Singapore, preparations for a third summit in mid-December 1987 were well in hand under the guidance of a steering committee comprising senior officials. The priority for that summit was identified as providing 'new impetus towards qualitative improvements in intra-Asean economic co-operation.'

When the six heads of government gathered in Manila in December 1987 they were not able to transform intra-mural economic relationships so that the volume of intra-ASEAN trade could be increased dramatically. Nor were they able to exercise any new influence on the course of the Kampuchean conflict, having been by-passed in negotiations between Kampuchean parties. Their presence constituted a collective act of faith in the Association as a going concern and in the government of President Corazon Aquino, which had been buffeted by a series of abortive coups. Indeed, given the violent abortive coup in Manila in the preceding August as well as continuing acts of urban terror by Communist insurgents, at issue at the summit was the requirement of security for the principal participants. In other words, convening and conducting the conference was an achievement in itself, made necessary by

Mrs Aquino's refusal to contemplate an alternative venue. The governments concerned were only too well aware of the danger of sliding backwards, but they did not possess a clear view of how to proceed forwards. Regeneration was on their minds but not well articulated in the Manila Declaration, which expressed aspirations but no new achievement.[28]

The ASEAN states have recorded practical achievement as a diplomatic community even if the implied model of collective internal security has enjoyed mixed application. That achievement has had practical expression in transforming the tone of bilateral and multilateral relationships over more than two decades. The exceptional Herzog episode, lingering territorial differences between Malaysia and the Philippines, as well as fundamental differences of strategic perspective between Indonesia and Thailand suggest that such achievement cannot be taken for granted. At the same time, there is no ready practical alternative basis on which to renew the fabric of regional co-operation. Economic co-operation offers limited promise. Formal defence co-operation is out of the question.

Part of the problem is that the actual attainment of ASEAN is somewhat mundane and even politically uninspiring. The task confronting regional partners in their third decade of association is how to invest a commonplace but fruitful habit of consultation and mutual consideration with critical significance. Conservation rather than innovation would seem to be the pressing priority. It is self-evident that conservation is not readily obtained by standing still and that the symbolism of institutional progress is important. Regional order in any minimal and practical sense for ASEAN governments will depend first of all on appropriate attention being paid to the commonplace, which requires special collective attention because it is commonplace and therefore in danger of being taken for granted. Whatever success ASEAN has enjoyed has been the product of its collegial identity. That identity has emerged because of the hard-headed recognition by member governments that sufficient interests are shared to merit sustained political investment in a multilateral working relationship. That relationship remains in essence intergovernmental which means that while interests may be shared they are rarely held truly in common. ASEAN's predicament is hardly unique but is none the less of practical relevance to its viability during its third decade. An obvious question for that decade is what will serve to hold ASEAN together if and when some solution is found to the protracted conflict in Kampuchea, which has occupied so much of its energies and attention with mixed results in solidarity and strain.

Notes

1. *Singapore Press Release*, 03-1/82/06/14.
2. *Documents on the Kampuchean Problem, 1979–1985*, Ministry of Foreign Affairs, Bangkok, 1985, pp. 119–20.
3. *The Times*, 23 June 1982.
4. *Straits Times*, 13 June 1982.
5. *ASEAN Documents Series*, 1967–1985, ASEAN Secretariat, Jakarta, 1985, p. 79.
6. *Documents on the Kampuchean Problem*, op. cit., p. 104.
7. The papers presented at this conference have been reprinted in *The Indonesian Quarterly* 12, no. 2 (1984).
8. *Straits Times*, 22 February 1984.
9. Ibid., 24 February 1984.
10. *Documents on the Kampuchean Problem*, op. cit., p. 105.
11. Ibid., p. 111.
12. See his interview with *Asiaweek*, 26 July 1985.
13. *Documents on the Kampuchean Problem*, op. cit., p. 112.
14. Ibid., pp. 113–16.
15. Ibid., p. 117.
16. *Singapore Government Press Release*, Amm 1/19 Amm (2).
17. *Joint Communique of the Nineteenth ASEAN Ministerial Meeting*, Manila, 23–24 June 1986.
18. BBC, *Summary of World Broadcasts*, F/E 8633/A3/4.
19. *International Herald Tribune*, 2 December 1987.
20. *The Nation*, Bangkok, 28 November 1986.
21. See Michael Leifer, 'Obstacles to a Political Settlement in Indochina', *Pacific Affairs* (Winter 1985–86).
22. Note Dhanabalan's comment, *Straits Times*, 13 April 1987.
23. An attempt by the private sector to overcome such conflicts to common advantage may be found in proposals intended for the third ASEAN summit. See *ASEAN: The Way Forward. The Report of the Group of Fourteen on ASEAN Economic Co-operation and Integration*, Institute of Strategic and International Studies, Kuala Lumpur, 1982.
24. See the argument in Noordin Sopiee 'ASEAN and Regional Security', in Mohamad Ayoob (ed.), op. cit.
25. Chandra Muzaffar, *Islamic Resurgence in Malaysia*, Penerbit Fajar Bakta SDN, BHD, Petaling Jaya, 1987.
26. See the *International Herald Tribune*, 9 October 1986.
27. See Sopiee in Mohammed Ayoob (ed.), *Regional Security in the Third World*, Croom Helm, London, 1986, p. 227.
28. *The Manila Declaration of 1987*. See documentary appendices.

6

ASEAN in Retrospect and Prospect

ASEAN began its corporate life as a diplomatic device for subregional reconciliation. Represented initially as an undertaking in economic co-operation, its governments have displayed a primary concern with politically expressed security co-operation. ASEAN's performance in such co-operation, which lacks a military dimension, may be assessed with reference to two interrelated domains: the intra-mural, comprising its subregional membership and the extra-mural, extending within and beyond South-East Asia.

The membership of ASEAN has expanded only marginally since its formation, when it aspired to a full regional structure of relationships. The Association has not been able to transcend its political limitations to match the conventional bounds of South-East Asia. Within its restricted intra-mural domain, however, ASEAN has provided a stable structure of relations for managing and containing tensions among governments of a corresponding political disposition. Its record in this endeavour has been far from perfect. Some bilateral relationships have been stormy at times, while institutional provision for dispute settlement has not yet been put into effect. None the less, a collective ability to sustain a working association among five and then six governments over more than two decades is a testament to the value placed on continued membership. In that period, membership has only been in question with reference to its expansion. No member government has found its interests so imperiled by corporate priorities that it has contemplated withdrawal. Correspondingly, nor has any member government been found guilty of so transgressing corporate rules that expulsion has been considered.

ASEAN has functioned through an adherence to a collegial style which avoids confrontation. Proceeding by consensus on the basis of a common denominator has obvious drawbacks. Yet the Association provides for common security in a practical respect. It serves as an institutional point of reference against which the political opportunity costs of clashing with a regional partner may be measured. The cohesion and viability of ASEAN have come to constitute a hostage to worst case predatory intent. The structure of common constraint arising from the evolution of ASEAN has an evident utility in an uncertain regional environment. An established practice of political co-operation induces confidence among regional partners, which has been matched in the regard indicated by extra-regional governments and private economic interests.

The working ties established and sustained among ASEAN's governments provide for common security. They stand in the way of unrestrained intra-mural conflict and, in principle, permit fuller deployment of national energies for politically related economic development. The benefits from membership for promoting political stability have been mixed and have depended on qualities of political leadership displayed unevenly within the Association. With one exception, member governments have not taken collective action in response to political instability in a regional partner. For example, the other governments of ASEAN were obliged to observe impotently from a distance when accelerated political decay attacked the personal rule of President Marcos. They shared a sense of collective relief when political disintegration gave way to political redemption and Mrs Aquino succeeded as Philippine President. Within a relatively short time, the other governments of ASEAN were faced with a corresponding concern as the political promise of President Aquino's restoration of constitutional democracy turned sour. Apprehension over risks to personal security in a terror-ridden Manila was set aside, however, in a necessary show of solidarity by fellow heads of government intended to bolster the domestic political standing of the Philippine President. The decision to proceed as planned with the third meeting of heads of government in Manila in December 1987 was taken in the belief that any postponement or change of venue would encourage her adversaries from right and left to reinforce their challenge. Accordingly, a form of collective political defence was undertaken in order to uphold the position of a regional partner. In effect, such an exercise was directly relevant to the overall cohesion, viability, and credibility of ASEAN because Mrs Aquino had made the presence of her fellow heads of government in Manila for a summit meeting a test of confidence both in her leadership and in the solidarity of the Association. The convening according to schedule of the third ASEAN summit provides an exceptional example of political co-operation serving the security interest of a regional partner as well as the standing of the Association.

ASEAN's performance in security co-operation has had its most visible impact beyond its walls in collective dealings with regional and extra-regional states. Through an evolving practice of political co-operation whereby five and then six governments have spoken most of the time with one voice on regional issues, ASEAN has established itself as a recognised international actor.

In a diplomatic role, ASEAN has assumed a corporate identity as more than just the sum of its political parts. That identity was recognized and confirmed as a consequence of the corporate challenge posed to Vietnam's invasion and occupation of Kampuchea. That challenge took the form of collective political defence. The term, employed first by a former foreign minister of Thailand, acknowledges that the Association is not a defence community in the conventional sense. Collective political defence with an extra-mural point of reference has been expressed through diplomatic solidarity in the face of a threat to the premisses of regional order and more specifically to the security of a member state. By employing regional credentials, ASEAN has been successful in keeping the Kampuchean issue in the international limelight thereby contributing to Vietnam's difficulty in consolidating a political relationship asserted by force of arms. In October 1987, 117 votes were cast in the General Assembly of the United Nations in support of its annual resolution on Kampuchea; the widest margin attained since such a resolution was first introduced in 1979.

Collective political defence has been employed to uphold the principle of national sovereignty. It has also been utilized to serve the particular interests of Thailand which have been most at risk as a consequence of Vietnam's occupation of Kampuchea. A direct threat to the territorial integrity or political identity of Thailand has not been at issue. The problem has not been how to respond to aggression against a member of ASEAN but how to prevent Vietnam from consolidating a position of dominance throughout Indochina which would have the effect of placing Thailand at a permanent geopolitical disadvantage.

ASEAN's conduct in its operational experience of collective political defence has been expressed totally in diplomatic terms, which has limited ASEAN's role as a party to the Kampuchean conflict. Individual governments have provided some arms, military training, and material supplies to the non-Communist factions within the Khmer resistance movement. Thailand, through its control of access to the border with Kampuchea has provided territorial sanctuary as well as transfer of arms and supplies to all insurgent factions. ASEAN as a corporate entity has restricted its efforts to the diplomatic struggle including the promotion of the Coalition Government of Democratic Kampuchea. These collective efforts have been effective in themselves to a limited extent only. While capable of helping to keep alive the issue of Kampuchea, the employment of collective political defence has not in itself persuaded Vietnam to revise a course of action governed by strategic perspective. ASEAN's expression of diplomatic solidarity has been made more effective, albeit not decisively so, by being linked to a wider coalition which has employed more coercive methods against Vietnam and its client government in Phnom Penh. Correspondingly, ASEAN's diplomatic challenge has served the security interests of members of that wider coalition, which has generated tensions within the walls of the Association.

The dependent nature of the practice of collective political defence over Kampuchea points to a notable deficiency in ASEAN as a security organisation. Moreover, the employment of collective political defence to the seeming advantage of non-ASEAN states raises the obvious question: Whose security has been catered for? ASEAN has never been more than an intergovernmental entity. The nature of its institutional structure has faithfully reflected a strong disposition against any supranational tendency. Member governments have viewed their participation in terms of how their separate interests might best be served. Indeed, a persisting inability to overcome structural obstacles in the way of fuller economic co-operation has demonstrated a conventional reluctance to sacrifice particular for so-called corporate interests. For those governments at the receiving end of Indonesia's Confrontation, ASEAN was intended to provide a framework within which the restless energies and ambitions of the Republic might be constructively channelled. That intention was well understood by President Suharto's government in Jakarta from the outset. The constraining framework of ASEAN was acceptable partly as a way of re-establishing international credentials which would serve the course of economic recovery. As indicated in the preamble to the Association's founding declaration, however, the government of

Indonesia did not give up well-established ideas about the management of regional order.

ASEAN was contemplated by Indonesia as a vehicle through which a structure of willing co-operation might be expanded over time to encompass all of South-East Asia. Because of the legacy of Confrontation and the priority of economic reconstruction and development, Indonesia's government, skilfully advised by Foreign Minister Adam Malik, was most careful to avoid conveying an impression of assertiveness towards its regional partners. Indeed, it adopted a restrained stance which went against a natural inclination to play a leading role. Such self-restraint within the context of ASEAN was tolerable in Jakarta as long as the direction of corporate policy was not in contradiction to Indonesia's interests. Such was the case for more than the first decade of ASEAN's existence. The convening of the first summit in Bali and the location of ASEAN's Secretariat in Jakarta confirmed the understanding that Indonesia was the natural political centre of gravity of the Association.

The question of whose security interests were being served by ASEAN first became an issue as a result of an initiative taken outside of its institutional framework. Malaysia pursued an independent path seeking political accommodation with China through a proposal for the neutralisation of South-East Asia. The terms of that proposal were in direct contradiction to long-held Indonesian views about the management of regional order. With the willing co-operation of other regional partners, the Indonesian government was able to modify Malaysia's proposal to make it consistent with its own strategic perspective. That diplomatic exercise conducted in November 1971, albeit of declaratory significance, indicated the extent of Indonesia's influence aided by the reservations of other regional partners. That influence has been less evident over the issue of Kampuchea, which has been at the centre of ASEAN's security concerns since Vietnam's invasion and occupation at the end of 1978.

ASEAN's response to that invasion was determined partly by the requirement to display solidarity with Thailand whose strategic environment had been violated. An act of collective political defence was undertaken to enable Thailand to cope with a threatening predicament. To that extent, the diplomatic voice of ASEAN was placed at Thailand's service, with the effect of shifting corporate initiative from Jakarta to Bangkok. Such a shift did more than displace Indonesia from an assumed pivotal position to one of shared centrality. ASEAN's commitment to diplomatic confrontation with Vietnam within a wider coalition, including China, came to be viewed in Indonesia as working against priorities for regional order endorsed by ASEAN from 1971 in the form of the Zone of Peace formula. Thus, while committed to ASEAN as a structure of special relationships, Indonesia's government has indicated resentment and frustration at a policy encouraging the entrenched involvement of China as well as that of the Soviet Union in the political fortunes of South-east Asia.

Resentment has been expressed at advantage being taken of Indonesia's evident stake in the Association to entrap it in a corporate policy of doubtful utility. Frustration has taken the recurrent form of unilateral initiatives towards Vietnam with the object of settling the Kampuchean conflict and so reversing a relationship between Thailand and China deemed to be politically undesirable. It has also been expressed in successful insistence on ASEAN's commitment to a regional nuclear-weapons free zone incorporated in the Manila Declaration of 1987. That proposal, represented by Indonesia's President Suharto as an important component of the Zopfan concept, was conceded, despite misgivings by most regional partners, in the interest of corporate harmony.

The problem of forging a consensus over common external security has been pointed up more dramatically over Kampuchea. The general problem may be expected to remain if and when a solution is arrived at for that particular protracted conflict, regardless of ASEAN's role in conflict resolution, which has been shown to be limited. The persistence of the problem has been indicated over an issue on which the public positions of ASEAN governments have also been at odds with their private ones. It arises from anxiety over the balance of external interests bearing on South-East Asia. The regional environment within which the states of ASEAN reside has changed since the Association was first established. An imminent prospect of external threat is not anticipated, but common concern is held at the regional impact of a modernising China as well as at the continuing military presence of the Soviet Union in Vietnam. Whether or not formally non-aligned, all ASEAN governments look to the United States as a guarantor of stability in the regional balance of power.

Expectations of the United States in this role are predicated on its continued operational control of military bases in the Philippines held under a lease which expires in 1991. The five regional partners of the Philippines share the view, some only privately, that the lease should be extended for fear of the strategic uncertainty which would ensue should it lapse. Indeed, Prime Minister Lee Kuan Yew of Singapore has remarked publicly that in such circumstances, the region would have to 'start a new way of life'. The government in Manila, committed to renegotiating U.S. base rights, has to cope with a Communist insurgent movement set to exploit a rising Filipino nationalism defined with reference to the United States. It has indicated its preference for an open endorsement of the U.S. military presence as a contribution to regional security by its ASEAN partners and as a way of managing domestic dissent. Foreign Secretary Raul Manglapus suggested in November 1987 that all ASEAN states should assume a joint political responsibility for the U.S. military presence in the Philippines. That suggestion met with a very mixed response including a statement of reserve from Singapore's Foreign Minister, Suppiah Dhanabalan, who was fully conscious of the reluctance of Indonesia, in particular, to compromise its non-aligned status, as well as of the declaratory prescription in ASEAN's founding document against the regional presence of foreign military bases. Accordingly, Mr Manglapus was obliged to backtrack to the extent of denying he had been insisting on a joint statement which would have been made public at the third ASEAN summit in Manila. A second best call by President Aquino for recognition by regional partners of her country's role in upholding regional security in her address to the ASEAN summit fell on deaf ears, without mention in the attendant Manila Declaration.

This discordant episode pointed to persistent differences over provision for regional security among ASEAN's governments. At issue and unresolved is whether such an undertaking can be managed on an exclusively regional basis. The longstanding declaratory position of ASEAN is that it can; the practical experience of its governments is that it cannot. Indonesia, however, with support from Malaysia, refuses to compromise publicly that declaratory stand. The problem for the Association is that discordance over appropriate provision for regional security has a direct bearing on the quality of intra-mural political co-operation and confidence which has been ASEAN's principal achievement.

ASEAN is not different in kind from any other intergovernmental institutional arrangement established for a common purpose. That common purpose expressed in general terms co-exists with a central tension which is characteristic of such institutions. That tension arises from the conflict between such an institution conceived as a political marketplace in which individual states' interests are advanced and accommodated and one conceived more ideally as a purposive corporate body with an identity and life above and beyond the mere sum of its membership. The latter conception is one to which intergovernmental arrangements do not normally approximate. If any did so, then they would be institutional contradictions in terms. Given the prevailing reality of the model of the political marketplace, then the success of any venture in regional co-operation for security will depend on the ability of member governments to forge an integral view of common purpose. But such an integral view cannot be taken for granted or automatically assumed, because there is nothing naturally determined in political terms about either regions or regional associations.

A common sense of even subregional identity is no easier to promote because what may be viewed as central by one partner to an association may be of only peripheral concern to another. In the case of ASEAN, its intergovernmental structure encompassing a mixed range of experience and perspectives ensures that common security interests cannot be taken for granted. Corresponding political dispositions and external affiliations have given rise to a measure of common outlook expressed primarily with reference to domestic political orders. A contribution to upholding such orders has been made by managing and overcoming and containing intra-mural differences. The habit of co-operation serving that end has been promoted by taking the opportunity of negotiating collectively with industrialised states to secure better terms of economic advantage. An evolving practice of political co-operation expressed in bureaucratic and ministerial consultation has served also in ASEAN's case to create a subregional security community. The sense of community is still embryonic, however, exemplified in recurrent expressions of bilateral tension which place a strain on intra-mural relations. Such tensions have always been accommodated, so far, because of the common recognition of the utility of membership, including the greater international influence which comes from corporate association.

The security interests served through ordered intra-mural association have a practical external dimension. ASEAN has not been able to promote security to the extent of forging a regionwide structure of relations based on common values and interests. None the less, the diplomatic solidarity of the six states can be mobilised to act as a deterrent of a limited kind in the face of an external security threat to any of their number. It can only be of a limited kind because diplomatic solidarity is hardly a sufficient instrument on its own with which to respond to political change imposed by force of arms. For reasons indicated above ASEAN is not expected to overcome that deficiency which means that it can never aspire to act as a guarantor of security in the conventional sense. As a consequence, where a member state faces a perceived external threat, it may be expected to seek recourse to more efficacious forms of countervailing power than an ASEAN-based diplomacy. In such a circumstance (which has obtained for Thailand over Kampuchea) the cohesion and viability of ASEAN will depend on regional partners' willingness to display diplomatic solidarity in the special interest of the most exposed and seemingly vulnerable member. A logical problem arises in theory and practice where such a display may be deemed to work not only to the special advantage of one member state but also against the advantage of others. Such a problem is not unique to ASEAN as a regional body, but it is one which has entered the institutional life of the Association ever since it became necessary to adopt a common position in response to Vietnam's invasion of Kampuchea. It is not the kind of problem which lends itself to ready solution. It is one, however, which the governments of ASEAN have so far learned to live with, without placing breaking strain on its cohesion and viability.

ASEAN's record is one of mixed achievement. It has displayed a facility to sustain quasi-friendships which serve common security interests but not always in a symmetrical sense. That consideration informed the meeting of ASEAN's heads of government in Manila in December 1987 as they deliberated, conscious of the need to count political blessings and not to prejudice modest attainment by rhetorical overindulgence. The problem remains, however, that in the realm of security co-operation, progress can only be limited. Apart from deficiences in capability, there is an absence of interest in transforming ASEAN into a different kind of corporate entity. Political metamorphosis is out of the question, which means that the member governments will be obliged to continue working within a structure of relations governed by a common denominator and not by a truly integral purpose. ASEAN has the natural defects of its inherent qualities, which cannot be overcome by any indulgence in symbolic forms of achievement. Provision for security through political co-operation is the most that can be expected, but that collective enterprise cannot be taken for granted as the protracted experience over Kampuchea has demonstrated. If the habit of that co-operation is sustained in the full understanding of its limited but practical merits by succeeding generations of political leadership, then the Association should pass its third decade as a going concern. Its record over more than two decades lends itself to the same judgement and qualified praise as that once offered by E. M. Forster about democracy; namely, two cheers.

Documentary Appendices:

The ASEAN Declaration (Bangkok Declaration)

The Presidium Minister for Political Affairs / Minister for Foreign Affairs of Indonesia, the Deputy Prime Minister of Malaysia, the Secretary of Foreign Affairs of the Philippines, the Minister for Foreign Affairs of Singapore and the Minister of Foreign Affairs of Thailand:

Mindful of the existence of mutual interests and common problems among countries of South-East Asia and convinced of the need to strengthen further the existing bonds of regional solidarity and co-operation;

Desiring to establish a firm foundation for common action to promote regional co-operation in South-East Asia to the spirit of equality and partnership and thereby contribute towards the peace, progress and prosperity in the region;

Conscious that in an increasingly interdependent world, the cherished ideals of peace, freedom, social justice and economic well-being are best attained by fostering good understanding, good neighbourliness and meaningful co-operation among the countries of the region already bound together by ties of history and culture;

Considering that the countries of South-East Asia share a primary responsibility for strengthening the economic and social stability of the region and ensuring their peaceful and progressive national development, and that they are determined to ensure their stability and security from external interference in any form or manifestation in order to preserve their national identities in accordance with the ideals and aspirations of their peoples;

Affirming that all foreign bases are temporary and remain only with the expressed concurrence of the countries concerned and are not intended to be used directly or indirectly to subvert the national independence and freedom of States in the area or prejudice the orderly processes of their national development;

Do Hereby Declare:

First, the establishment of an Association for Regional Co-operation among the countries of South-East Asia to be known as the Association of South-East Asian Nations (ASEAN).

Second, that the aims and purposes of the Association shall be:

1. To accelerate the economic growth, social progress and cultural development in the region through joint endeavours in the spirit of equality and partnership in order to strengthen the foundation for a prosperous and peaceful community of South-East Asian Nations;

2. To promote regional peace and stability through abiding respect for justice and the rule of law in the relationship among countries of the region and adherence to the principles of the United Nations Charter;

3. To promote active collaboration and mutual assistance on matters of common interest in the economic, social, cultural, technical, scientific and administrative fields;

4. To provide assistance to each other in the form of training and research facilities in the educational, professional, technical and administrative spheres;

5. To collaborate more effectively for the greater utilization of their agriculture and industries, the expansion of their trade, including the study of the problems of international commodity trade, the improvement of their transportation and communications facilities and the raising of the living standards of their peoples;

6. To promote South-East Asian studies;

7. To maintain close and beneficial co-operation with existing international and regional organisations with similar aims and purposes, and explore all avenues for even closer co-operation among themselves.

Third, that to carry out these aims and purposes, the following machinery shall be established:

(a) Annual Meeting of Foreign Ministers, which shall be by rotation and referred to as ASEAN Ministerial Meeting. Special Meetings of Foreign Ministers may be convened as required.

(b) A Standing Committee, under the chairmanship of the Foreign Minister of the host country or his representative and having as its members the accredited Ambassadors of the other member countries, to carry on the work of the Association in between Meetings of Foreign Ministers.

(c) Ad-Hoc Committees and Permanent Committees of specialists and officials on specific subjects.

(d) A National Secretariat in each member country to carry out the work of the Association on behalf of that country and to service the Annual or Special Meetings of Foreign Ministers, the Standing Committee and such other committees as may hereafter be established.

Fourth, that the Association is open for participation to all States in the South-East Asian Region subscribing to the aforementioned aims, principles and purposes.

Fifth, that the Association represents the collective will of the nations of South-East Asia to bind themselves together in friendship and co-operation and, through joint efforts and sacrifices, secure for their peoples and for posterity the blessings of peace, freedom and prosperity.

Done in Bangkok on the Eighth Day of August in the Year One Thousand Nine Hundred and Sixty-Seven.

Zone of Peace, Freedom and Neutrality Declaration

We the Foreign Ministers of Indonesia, Malaysia, the Philippines, Singapore and the Special Envoy of the National Executive Council of Thailand:

Firmly believing in the merits of regional co-operation which has drawn our countries to co-operate together in the economic, social and cultural fields in the Association of South East Asian Nations;

Desirous of bringing about a relaxation of international tension and of achieving a lasting peace in South East Asia;

Inspired by the worthy aims and objectives of the United Nations, in particular by the principles of respect for the sovereignty and territorial integrity of all states, abstention from threat or use of force, peaceful settlement of international disputes, equal rights and self-determination and non-interference in the affairs of States;

Believing in the continuing validity of the Declaration on the Promotion of World Peace and Co-operation of the Bandung Conference of 1955 which, among others, enunciates the principles by which states may coexist peacefully;

Recognising the right of every state, large or small, to lead its national existence free from outside interference in its internal affairs as this interference will adversely affect its freedom, independence and integrity;

Dedicated to the maintenance of peace, freedom and independence unimpaired;

Believing in the need to meet present challenges and new developments by co-operating with all peace and freedom loving nations, both within and outside the region, in the furtherance of world peace, stability and harmony;

Cognizant of the significant trend towards establishing nuclear-free zones, as in the Treaty for the Prohibition of Nuclear Weapons in Latin America and the Lusaka Declaration proclaiming Africa as a nuclear-free zone, for the purpose of promoting world peace and security by reducing the areas of international conflicts and tension;

Reiterating our commitment to the principle in the *Bangkok Declaration* which established ASEAN in 1967, that the countries of South East Asia share a primary responsibility for strengthening the economic and social stability of the region and ensuring their peaceful and progressive national development and that they are

163

determined to ensure stability and security from external interference in any form or manifestation in order to preserve their national identities in accordance with the ideals and aspirations of their peoples;

Agreeing that the neutralization of South East Asia is a desirable objective and that we should explore ways and means of bringing about its realization; and

Convinced that the time is propitious for joint action to give effective expression to the deeply felt desire of the peoples of South East Asia to ensure the conditions of peace and stability indispensable to their independence and their economic social well-being;

Do Hereby State:

1. that Indonesia, Malaysia, the Philippines, Singapore and Thailand are determined to exert initially necessary efforts to secure the recognition of, and respect for, South East Asia as a Zone of Peace, Freedom and Neutrality, free from any form or manner of interference by outside Powers;
2. that South East Asian countries should make concerted efforts to broaden the areas of co-operation which would contribute to their strength, solidarity and closer relationship.

Done at Kuala Lumpur on Saturday, the 27th of November 1971.

Declaration of ASEAN Concord

The President of the Republic of Indonesia, the Prime Minister of Malaysia, the President of the Republic of The Philippines, the Prime Minister of the Republic of Singapore and the Prime Minister of the Kingdom of Thailand:

Reaffirm their commitment to the Declarations of Bandung, Bangkok and Kuala Lumpur, and the Charter of the United Nations;

Endeavour to promote peace, progress, prosperity and the welfare of the peoples of member states;

Undertake to consolidate the achievements of ASEAN and expand ASEAN co-operation in the economic, social, cultural and political fields;

Do Hereby Declare:

ASEAN co-operation shall take into account, among others, the following objectives and principles in the pursuit of political stability:

1. The stability of each member state and of the ASEAN region is an essential contribution to international peace and security. Each member state resolves to eliminate threats posed by subversion to its stability, thus strengthening national and ASEAN resilience.
2. Member states, individually and collectively, shall take active steps for the early establishment of the Zone of Peace, Freedom and Neutrality.
3. The elimination of poverty, hunger, disease and illiteracy is a primary concern of member states. They shall therefore intensify co-operation in economic and social development, with particular emphasis on the promotion of social justice and on the improvement of the living standards of their peoples.
4. Natural disasters and other major calamities can retard the pace of development of member states. They shall extend, within their capabilities, assistance for relief of member states in distress.
5. Member states shall take co-operative action in their national and regional development programmes, utilizing as far as possible the resources available in the ASEAN region to broaden the complementarity of their respective economies.
6. Member states, in the spirit of ASEAN solidarity, shall rely

exclusively on peaceful processes in the settlement of intra-regional differences.

7. Member states shall strive, individually and collectively, to create conditions conducive to the promotion of peaceful co-operation among the nations of South East Asia on the basis of mutual respect and mutual benefit.

8. Member states shall vigorously develop an awareness of regional identity and exert all efforts to create a strong ASEAN community, respected by all and respecting all nations on the basis of mutually advantageous relationships, and in accordance with the principles of self-determination, sovereign equality and non-interference in the internal affairs of nations.

And Do Hereby Adopt

The following programme of action as a framework for ASEAN co-operation:

A. Political

1. Meeting of the Heads of Government of the member states as and when necessary.
2. Signing of the Treaty of Amity and Co-operation in South East Asia.
3. Settlement of intra-regional disputes by peaceful means as soon as possible.
4. Immediate consideration of initial steps towards recognition of and respect for the Zone of Peace, Freedom and Neutrality wherever possible.
5. Improvement of ASEAN machinery to strengthen political co-operation.
6. Study on how to develop judicial co-operation including the possibility of an ASEAN Extradition Treaty.
7. Strengthening of political solidarity by promoting the harmonization of views, co-ordinating position and, where possible and desirable, taking common actions.

B. Economic

1. Co-operation on Basic Commodities, particularly Food and Energy
   (i) Member states shall assist each other by according priority to the supply of the individual country's needs in critical

circumstances, and priority to the acquisition of exports from member states, in respect of basic commodities, particularly food and energy.

(ii) Member states shall also intensify co-operation in the production of basic commodities particularly food and energy in the individual member states of the region.

2. Industrial Co-operation

(i) Member states shall co-operate to establish large-scale ASEAN industrial plants, particularly to meet regional requirements of essential commodities.

(ii) Priority shall be given to projects which utilize the available materials in the member states, contribute to the increase of food production, increase foreign exchange earnings or save foreign exchange and create employment.

3. Co-operation in Trade

(i) Member states shall co-operate in the fields of trade in order to promote development and growth of new production and trade and to improve the trade structures of individual states and among countries of ASEAN conducive to further development and to safeguard and increase their foreign exchange earnings and reserves.

(ii) Member states shall progress towards the establishment of preferential trading arrangements as a long term objective on a basis deemed to be any particular time appropriate through rounds of negotiations subject to the unanimous agreement of member states.

(iii) The expansion of trade among member states shall be facilitated through co-operation on bias commodities, particularly in food and energy and through co-operation in ASEAN industrial projects.

(iv) Member states shall accelerate joint efforts to improve access to markets outside ASEAN for their raw material and finished products by seeking the elimination of all trade barriers in those markets, developing new usage for these products and in adopting common approaches and actions in dealing with regional groupings and individual economic powers.

(v) Such efforts shall also lead to co-operation in the field of technology and production methods in order to increase the production and to improve the quality of export products, as well as to develop new export products with a view to diversifying exports.

4. Joint Approach to International Commodity Problems and Other World Economic Problems.

    (i) The principle of ASEAN co-operation on trade shall also be reflected on a priority basis in joint approaches to international commodity problems and other world economic problems such as the reform of international trading system, the reform of international monetary system and transfer of real resources, in the United Nations and other relevant multilateral fora, with a view to contributing to the establishment of the New International Economic Order.

    (ii) Member states shall give priority to the stabilisation and increase of export earnings of those commodities produced and exported by them through commodity agreements including buffer-stock schemes and other means.

5. Machinery for Economic Co-operation

Ministerial meetings on economic matters shall be held regularly or as deemed necessary in order to:

    (i) formulate recommendations for the consideration of Governments of member states for the strengthening of ASEAN economic co-operation;

    (ii) review the co-ordination and implementation of agreed ASEAN programmes and projects on economic co-operation;

    (iii) exchange views and consult on national development plans and policies as a step towards harmonizing regional development; and

    (iv) perform such other relevant functions as agreed upon by the member Governments.

C. Social

1. Co-operation in the field of social development, with emphasis on the well being of the low income group and of the rural population, through the expansion of opportunities for productive employment with fair remuneration.

2. Support for the active involvement of all sectors and levels of the ASEAN communities, particularly the women and youth, in development efforts.

3. Intensification and expansion of existing co-operation in meeting the problems of population growth in the ASEAN region, and where possible, formulation of new strategies in collaboration with appropriate international agencies.

4. Intensification of co-operation among members states as well as with the relevant international bodies in the prevention and eradication of the abuse of narcotics and the illegal trafficking of drugs.

D. Cultural and Information

1. Introduction of the study of ASEAN, its member states and their national languages as part of the curricula of schools and other institutions of learning in the member states.
2. Support of ASEAN scholars, writers, artists and mass media representatives to enable them to play an active role in fostering a sense of regional identity and fellowship.
3. Promotion of South East Asian studies through closer collaboration among national institutes.

E. Security

Continuation of co-operation of a non-ASEAN basis between the member states in security matters in accordance with their mutual needs and interests.

F. Improvement of ASEAN machinery

1. Signing of the *Agreement on the Establishment of the ASEAN Secretariat*
2. Regular review of the ASEAN organizational structure with a view to improving its effectiveness.
3. Study of the desirability of a new constitutional framework for ASEAN.

Done at Denpasar, Bali, this Twenty-Fourth Day of February in the year One Thousand Nine Hundred and Seventy-Six.

Treaty of Amity and Co-operation in Southeast Asia: Bali, 24 February 1976

Preamble

The High Contracting Parties:

Conscious of the existing ties of history, geography and culture, which have bound their peoples together;

Anxious to promote regional peace and stability through abiding respect for justice and the rule or law and enhancing regional resilience in their relations;

Desiring to enhance peace, friendship and mutual co-operation on matters affecting Southeast Asia consistent with the spirit and principles of the Charter of the United Nations, the Ten Principles adopted by the Asian-African Conference in Bandung on 25 April 1955, the Declaration of the Association of Southeast Asian Nations signed in Bangkok on 8 August 1967, and the Declaration signed in Kuala Lumpur on 27 November 1971;

Convinced that the settlement of differences or disputes between their countries should be regulated by rational, effective and sufficiently flexible procedures, avoiding negative attitudes which might endanger or hinder co-operation;

Believing in the need for co-operation with all peace-loving nations, both within and outside Southeast Asia in the furtherance of world peace, stability and harmony;

Solemnly Agree to enter into a Treaty of Amity and Co-operation as follows:

Chapter I: Purpose and Principles

Article 1

The purpose of this Treaty is to promote perpetual peace, everlasting amity and co-operation among their peoples which would contribute to their strength, solidarity and closer relationship.

Article 2

In their relations with one another, the High Contracting Parties shall be guided by the following fundamental principles:

a. Mutual respect for the independence, sovereignty, equality, territorial integrity and national identity of all nations;
b. The right of every State to lead its national existence free from external interference, subversion or coersion;
c. Non-Interference in the internal affairs of one another,
d. Settlement of differences or disputes by peaceful means;
e. Renunciation of the threat or use of force;
f. Effective co-operation among themselves.

Chapter II: Amity

Article 3

In pursuance of the purpose of this Treaty the High Contracting Parties shall endeavour to develop and strengthen the traditional, cultural and historical ties of friendship, good neighbourliness and co-operation which bind them together and shall fulfill in good faith the obligations assumed under this Treaty. In order to promote closer understanding among them, the High Contracting Parties shall encourage and facilitate contact and intercourse among their peoples.

Chapter III: Co-operation

Article 4

The High Contracting Parties shall promote active co-operation in the economic, social, technical, scientific and administrative fields as well as in matters of common ideals and aspiration of international peace and stability in the region and all other matters of common interest.

Article 5

Pursuant to Article 4 the High Contracting Parties shall exert their maximum efforts multilaterally as well as bilaterally on the basis of equality, non-discrimination and mutual benefit.

Article 6

The High Contracting Parties shall collaborate for the acceleration of the economic growth in the region in order to strengthen the foundation for a prosperous and peaceful community of nations in Southeast Asia. To this end, they shall promote the greater utilization of their agriculture and industries, the expansion of their trade and the improvement of their economic infra-structure for the mutual benefit of their peoples. In this regard, they shall continue to explore all avenues for close and beneficial co-operation with other States as well as international and regional organisations outside the region.

Article 7

The High Contracting Parties, in order to achieve social justice and to raise the standards of living of the peoples of the region, shall intensify economic co-operation. For this purpose, they shall adopt appropriate regional strategies for economic development and mutual assistance.

Article 8

The High Contracting Parties shall strive to achieve the closest co-operation on the widest scale and shall seek to provide assistance to one another in the form of training and research facilities in the social, cultural, technical, scientific and administrative fields.

Article 9

The High Contracting Parties shall endeavour to foster co-operation in the furtherance of the cause of peace, harmony, and stability in the region. To this end, the High Contracting Parties shall maintain regular contacts and consultations with one another on international and regional matters with a view to coordinating their views, actions and policies.

Article 10

Each High Contracting Party shall not in any manner or form participate in any activity which shall constitute a threat to the political and economic stability, sovereignty, or territorial integrity of another High Contracting Party.

Article 11

The High Parties shall endeavour to strengthen their respective national resilience in their political economic, socio-cultural as well as security fields in conformity with their respective ideals and aspirations, free from external interference as well as internal subversive activities in order to preserve their respective national identities.

Article 12

The High Contracting Parties in their efforts to achieve regional prosperity and security, shall endeavour to co-operate in all fields for the promotion of regional resilience, based on the principles of self-confidence, self-reliance, mutual respect, co-operation and solidarity which will constitute the foundation for a strong and viable community of nations in Southeast Asia.

Chapter IV: Pacific Settlement of Disputes

Article 13

The High Contracting Parties shall have the determination and good faith to prevent disputes from arising. In case disputes on matters directly affecting them shall refrain from the threat or use of force and shall at all times settle such disputes among themselves through friendly negotiations.

Article 14

To settle disputes through regional processes, the High Contracting Parties shall constitute, as a continuing body, a High Council comprising a Representative at ministerial level from each of the High Contracting Parties to take cognizance of the existence of disputes or situations likely to disturb regional peace and harmony.

Article 15

In the event no solution is reached through direct negotiations, the High Council shall take cognizance of the dispute or the situation and shall recommend to the parties in dispute appropriate means of settlement such as good offices, mediation, inquiry or conciliation. The High Council may however offer its good offices, or upon agreement of the parties in dispute, constitute itself into a committee of mediation, inquiry or conciliation. When deemed necessary, the High Council shall recommend appropriate measures for the prevention of a deterioration of the dispute or the situation.

Article 16

The foregoing provision of this Chapter shall not apply to a dispute unless all the parties to the dispute agree to their application to that dispute. However, this shall not preclude the other High Contracting Parties not party to the dispute from offering all possible assistance to settle the said dispute. Parties to the dispute should be well disposed towards such offers of assistance.

Article 17

Nothing in this Treaty shall preclude recourse to the modes of peaceful settlement contained in Article 33(1) of the Charter of the United Nations. The High Contracting Parties which are parties to a dispute should be encouraged to take initiatives to solve it by friendly negotiations before resorting to the other procedures provided for in the Charter of the United Nations.

Chapter V: General Provision

Article 18

This Treaty shall be signed by the Republic of Indonesia, Malaysia, the Republic of the Philippines, the Republic of Singapore and the Kingdom of Thailand. It shall be ratified in accordance with the constitutional procedures of each signatory State.

It shall be open for accession by other States in Southeast Asia.

Article 19

This Treaty shall enter into force on the date of the deposit of the fifth instrument of ratification with the Governments of the signatory States which are designated Depositories of this Treaty and of the instruments of ratification or accession.

Article 20

This Treaty is drawn up in the official languages of the High Contracting Parties, all of which are equally authoritative. There shall be an agreed common translation of the texts in the English language. Any divergent interpretation of the common text shall be settled by negotiation.

In faith thereof the High Contracting Parties have signed the Treaty and have hereto affixed their Seals.

Done at Denpasar, Bali, this twenty-fourth day February in the year one thousand nine hundred and seventy-six.

Joint Press Communique Meeting Of ASEAN Heads Of Government: Kuala Lumpur, 4-5 August 1977

1. The ASEAN Heads of Government met in Kuala Lumpur on 4-5 August, 1977. The Meeting was attended by the President of the Republic of Indonesia, H.E. General Soeharto; the Prime Minister of Malaysia, H.E. Datuk Hussein Onn; the President of the Republic of the Philippines, H.E. Mr Ferdinand E. Marcos; the Prime Minister of Singapore, H.E. Mr Lee Kuan Yew; and the Prime Minister of Thailand, H.E. Mr Tanin Kraivixien.

2. The Meeting was held in the traditional ASEAN spirit of friendship and cordiality.

3. The Meeting coincided with the Tenth Anniversary of ASEAN. The Heads of Government reviewed the development and progress of ASEAN in its first ten years and, in particular, they examined the progress in the implementation of the programme of action adopted at their First Meeting in Bali on 23-24 February, 1976, as contained in the *Declaration of ASEAN Concord*. The Heads of Government expressed satisfaction that ASEAN countries have made significant progress in building their national resilience through the acceleration and intensification of economic, social and cultural co-operation and the strengthening of the foundation of social justice and equity for all within their individual states. In the context of ASEAN consolidation, as laid down in the *ASEAN Declaration* and the *Declaration of ASEAN Concord* , ASEAN countries have intensified their collaboration in all fields. This has contributed significantly to the solidarity, cohesion and maturity of ASEAN.

4. The Heads of Government reaffirmed their commitment to the *ASEAN Declaration* and the *Declaration of ASEAN Concord* as the basis for ASEAN co-operation. They directed that on the basis of these Declarations, ASEAN countries should further intensify their efforts to strengthen and consolidate ASEAN into a strong, viable and cohesive regional organisation.

Regional Development

5. The heads of Government reviewed developments affecting the ASEAN region. They agreed that the situation as it exists today presents an opportunity for countries in the region to shape their own destiny without the involvement and interference by outside

powers. In this regard they emphasized the importance of developing and improving the relations among Southeast Asian countries on the basis of respect for sovereignty, territorial integrity and non-interference in the internal affairs for the progress, peace and stability of the region.

6. The Heads of Government emphasized the desire of ASEAN countries to develop peaceful and mutually beneficial relations with all countries in the region, including Kampuchea, Laos and Vietnam. In this regard they noted with satisfaction that exchanges of diplomatic and trade visits at high level have enhanced the prospects of improved relations between ASEAN countries and the countries of Indochina. They agreed that further efforts should be made to enlarge the areas of understanding and co-operation with those countries on the basis of mutuality of interests.

7. The Heads of Government welcomed the decision of the Security Council of the United Nations to recommend the admission of the Socialist Republic of Vietnam as a member of the Organisation. They expressed their confidence that in line with the purposes and principles of the UN Charter, Vietnam would contribute to peace and stability necessary for the progress and prosperity of Southeast Asia.

Zone of Peace, Freedom and Neutrality

8. The Heads of Government reaffirmed their commitment to the objectives of the Declaration on the Zone of Peace, Freedom and Neutrality in Southeast Asia. They directed that ASEAN countries should continue their deliberations on the various initial steps already proposed and consider further initiatives which would create conditions conducive for the establishment of the Zone.

9. They expressed their satisfaction at the efforts made by member countries, individually and collectively, to gain the recognition of and respect for Southeast Asia as a Zone of Peace, Freedom and Neutrality. They agreed that these efforts should be continued in order to realize its early establishment.

10. They noted that while these efforts are being undertaken, the efforts by ASEAN countries at economic and social development and the strengthening of the foundation of social justice and equity for all within their individual states by themselves constitute a process that would lead to the creation of conditions conducive for the establishment of the Zone of Peace, Freedom and Neutrality.

Economic Co-operation

11. In reviewing the progress of ASEAN co-operation, the Heads of Government reiterated their commitment to the programme of action contained in the Declaration of ASEAN Concord and directed that efforts should be intensified to attain its goals and objectives. They placed particular emphasis on co-operation in the economic and advancement of the member states of ASEAN is a fundamental element in ensuring political stability of the ASEAN region. In this regard, they commended the ASEAN Economic Ministers for their contribution in intensifying and accelerating the pace of economic co-operation and directed that this should be continued with greater vigour.

12. The Heads of Government noted with satisfaction the progress made in the various fields of economic co-operation as outlined in the Declaration of ASEAN Concord.

13. In the field of co-operation in basic commodities, the Heads of Government noted that ASEAN countries have agreed to accord each other priority of supply and purchase in critical circumstances based on the principle of first refusal. With regard to race, a machinery for consultations on supply and demand to facilitate negotiations has been established. It was noted that for the first year (1977) of operation of the arrangement, the target of 530,000 tons of race agreed upon was exceeded by 400,000 tons in July, 1977. In the case of petroleum, an emergency sharing scheme for crude oil and/or oil products in situations of shortage and oversupply has been agreed upon.

14. The Heads of Government noted that on the implementation of ASEAN Industrial Projects, the feasibility study of the ammonia-urea project in Indonesia had been completed, and the process of joint review of the feasibility study of this project had commenced. They decided that this review be completed as early as possible, so that once confirmed to be feasible, and accepted by member countries, the project could be launched preferably by the middle of 1978. They also noted that feasibility studies would soon be completed on the other ASEAN industrial projects namely, ammonia-urea (Malaysia), diesel engines (Singapore), rock salt-soda ash project (Thailand) and phosphatic fertilizer (Philippines). They also noted that pre-feasibility studies would also be undertaken on other possible ASEAN industrial projects namely, heavy duty rubber tyres, metal working machine tools, newsprint, electrolytic tin plating, TV picture tubes, fisheries and

potash. They directed that these studies be completed expeditiously and agreed that after review and confirmation of the feasibility of each of the first five ASEAN Industrial Projects, steps should be taken forthwith to establish that project as a joint venture of the member countries. The products of the ASEAN Industrial Project will be assured preferential access to markets of the member countries through the various instruments of Preferential Trading Arrangements.

15. The Heads of Government expressed satisfaction on the initiative of the private sector in member countries, particularly through the ASEAN Chamber of Commerce and Industry in intensifying their effort towards the implementation of industrial complementation schemes and projects and industrial development in the region. They reaffirmed their belief that the private sector in the region could play a major role in supplementing the efforts of ASEAN Governments towards achieving greater regional co-operation.

16. Recognising that the acceleration of industrialisation of the region requires the increased flow of technology and investments, the Heads of Government directed that measures be taken to stimulate the flow of technology, know-how and private investments among the member countries, and from extra-ASEAN sources into the region in industrial projects which would enhance national and regional resilience.

17. Recognising the vital role that energy plays in the economy of the member states, the Heads of Government agreed to intensify co-operation in such fields as exploration of energy, research and development of alternative uses of energy, research and development of alternative uses of oil as well as of non-conventional energy sources and the development of training facilities.

18. The Heads of Government noted that the Agreement on ASEAN Preferential Trading Arrangements (PTA) signed on 24 February, 1977, which provides for an overall frame-work for expanding intra-ASEAN trade had been ratified by all member countries. Noting that exchange of preferences on the first batch of products covering 71 items had been agreed upon, they urged that the provisions of the Agreement be promptly and fully implemented not later than 1 January, 1978. They directed that the ASEAN trade negotiations should be intensified and the results achieved be implemented expeditiously. They also noted that other areas of trade co-operation such as the improvement of

intra-ASEAN shipping services, simplification of customs procedures and formalities and harmonization of the system and methods of statistical compilation among ASEAN are being explored.

19. The Heads of Government noted that whilst there have been positive developments in the international dialogue between developed and developing countries on commodity policy, the various elements of the UNCTAD Integrated Programme for Commodities were yet to be negotiated and implemented. They considered the Integrated Programme and in particular the Common Fund, as fundamental to the international effort to overcome commodity problems. They thus reaffirmed their support for the expeditious negotiation and conclusion of specific International Commodity Arrangements under the Integrated Programme for Commodities and called for the early establishment of the Common Fund.

20. The Heads of Government, considering that the stabilisation of export earnings from primary commodities would constitute an important supplementary measure to price stabilisation schemes and to the IMF compensatory financing schemes in the overall effort to stabilise the economies of developing commodity exporting countries such as ASEAN, urged the developed countries to take urgent positive measures to extend to ASEAN, an arrangement for the stabilisation of export earnings derived from ASEAN commodity exports.

21. On the promotion of co-operative economic relationships between developed and developing countries they viewed with concern the spread of protectionist tendencies in developed countries adversely affecting the economic well-being of ASEAN countries and they called on the developed countries to take immediate steps to remove such protectionist measures. It would be in the interest of developed countries to adopt policies which will promote trade between them and ASEAN countries and expand the flow of investments into ASEAN countries.

22. The Heads of Government reaffirmed their commitment to accelerate joint efforts to improve access to markets outside ASEAN for its raw materials as well as manufactured and semi-manufactured goods. They also reaffirmed that investment opportunities in the ASEAN countries should continue to be promoted within the context of the objectives and purposes of their national development plans.

23. The Heads of Government commended the ASEAN Central

Banks and Monetary Authorities for the establishment of an ASEAN reciprocal currency or "swap" arrangement which would provide immediate short term credit facilities for emergency foreign exchange financing to an ASEAN country with temporary international liquidity problems.

24. Recognising the vital role that external financing can play in the realisation of ASEAN Industrial projects, the Heads of Government called on the developed countries to extend financial assistance to ASEAN for these projects on the most favourable terms and conditions.

25. To further promote the flow of trade, investment and business activities among ASEAN countries, the Heads of Government agreed on the need for ASEAN countries to conclude bilateral agreements on investment guarantees and avoidance of double taxation.

26. The Heads of Government took note the progress made in the fields of transportation and communications in the ASEAN region. In particular they observed initial efforts being made by the member countries to bring about regional co-operation in order to achieve efficient intra-ASEAN facilities in transportation and communications, notably:

(a) the development of the ASEAN Submarine Cable System, further studies on the setting-up of the ASEAN Regional Satellite System, the Satellite System for domestic use of ASEAN and border communications between member countries;

(b) the promotion of intercountry mail and border remittance services;

(c) the exchange of specific experiences and training expertise to optimise efficiency of the respective railway organisations, the promotion of transport by road, rail and ferry and the achievement of uniformity of road and traffic regulations;

(d) mutual consultations on matters affecting regional aviation and the adoption of a harmonised approach in the achievement of air agreement with non-member countries; the formulation and establishment of a common stand in any rearrangement of extra-regional flight information boundaries with non-member countries for the optimum benefit of ASEAN having regard to the technical and operational requirements of member countries;

(e) the acceleration and harmonisation in the expansion and modernisation of ASEAN national fleets, the organisation of

ASEAN-based, controlled and oriented shipping conference/s and the promotion of containerization and joint bulk shipment; and

(f) co-operation and mutual consultations in planning efforts.

27. With regard to co-operation in food, agriculture and forestry, the Heads of Governments noted the progress made in the implementation of studies on priority areas of regional co-operation which included the following:

(a) supply and demand for food and other strategic agricultural products;

(b) regional plant/crop protection centre;

(c) fisheries resources management;

(d) forestry resources and conservation;

(e) supply and demand for animal feed; and

(f) agricultural education and training.

28. The Heads of Government noted the importance for ASEAN to develop closer dialogue with developed countries and international organisations in order to expedite progress for co-operation in food, agriculture and forestry.

29. The Heads of Government recognised the desirability of safeguarding the ASEAN countries from possible food shortage by measures such as the establishment of a Food Security Reserve for ASEAN, especially for rice.

External Relations

30. Concerning ASEAN's economic relations with third countries or groups of countries, the Heads of Government agreed that economic co-operation with these countries notably Australia, Canada, Japan, New Zealand, and the European Economic Community be further intensifed and expanded for mutual benefit. They also welcomed the forthcoming ASEAN dialogue with the United States of America. The ASEAN Heads of Government expressed their wish that ASEAN establish closer economic relationship with the West Asian countries.

31. The Heads of Government noted that economic co-operation between ASEAN and the EEC has been initiated in the field of trade, aimed primarily at attaining better access for ASEAN's export products into the EEC. Whilst stressing the need to achieve further improvement in Government welcomed the increasing expansion of economic co-operation between ASEAN

and EEC, the heads of Government welcomed the increasing expansion of economic co-operation between ASEAN and the EEC to other economic fields such as industry, agriculture and rural development, transportation and finance.

32. The Heads of Government noted that economic co-operation between ASEAN and Japan was initiated with the establishment of the ASEAN-Japan Forum on Synthetic Rubber in November, 1973. This has resulted in increased co-operation between ASEAN and Japan on the question of rubber, including financial assistance from Japan for the establishment of a tyre testing and development laboratory in ASEAN.

33. With the establishment of the wider ASEAN-Japan Forum in March of this year and the forthcoming Meeting between the ASEAN Heads of Government and the PrimeMinister of Japan, the Heads of Government looked forward to an expansion of economic co-operation between ASEAN products to the Japanese market, stabilizing prices of and earnings from ASEAN export commodities, financing ASEAN industrial projects, and enhancing ASEAN agricultural and industrial development.

34. The Heads of Government would welcome closer ASEAN-Australia economic co-operation. They noted the progress that has been made in the Protein Projects and Food Handling Projects, established with Australian assistance.

35. With regard to ASEAN-New Zealand economic co-operation the Heads of Government commended the successful completion of the Survey on the End-Uses of ASEAN timber and noted further that three pilot sub-projects on plantation forestry, pine forest development and management of pine plantation have been agreed upon.

36. The Heads of Government appreciated the willingness of Canada to extend assistance to ASEAN. They noted the completion of reconnaissance studies on a Regional Satellite Communication System and on Regional Air Transportation. They look forward to the early commencement and completion of the feasibility studies on these projects and the identification of other areas of economic co-operation such as trade and fisheries.

37. As an additional measure to consolidate and expand ASEAN's formal co-operative relationship with these countries, the Heads of Government endorsed the decision made by the 10th ASEAN Ministerial Meeting to established joint consultative groups with the EEC and other developed countries for consultations on matters of mutual interest. They reaffirmed

ASEAN's readiness to consider the establishment of formal dialogues with other countries groups of countries and international organisations on the basis of mutual benefits.

38. The Heads of Government welcomed the opportunity to meet the Heads of Government of Australia, Japan and New Zealand on 6-8 August, 1977. They viewed these series of meetings as an important development in the co-operative endeavours between ASEAN and these countries, and expressed the hope that these meetings would lead to the intensification of economic co-operation between ASEAN on the one hand, and Australia, Japan and New Zealand on the other.

Co-operation in the Social, Cultural and Other Fields

39. The Heads of Government expressed their satisfaction at the steps taken to realise the goals and objectives of the *Declaration of ASEAN Concord* in the fields of social development and in the cultural and information fields. In this context, they called for closer collaboration among Ministers responsible for Social and Cultural activities to speed up and further enhance co-operation in the Social and Cultural fields, as embodied in the *Declaration of ASEAN Concord*

40. In the field of Social Welfare, the Heads of Government endorsed the Eleven-Point Guidelines adopted by the Ministers responsible for Social Welfare at their Meeting in Jakarta in July, 1977.

41. Taking note of the steps taken to improve social conditions in the region, in particular the initiatives in the field of human resource development and the efforts to integrate women and the youth in the national development process, the Heads of Government agreed on the need for expanded co-operation in this field.

42. They directed that greater concerted action be taken towards the elimination of pockets of poverty, disease and illiteracy, and thus contribute to the enhancement of the dignity of the human person.

43. The Heads of Government commended the initiatives taken in meeting the problems of regional population growth and urged member countries to implement the approved projects on the integration of population and rural development policies and in rural development policies and in this connection to co-ordinate

closely with the United Nations and its Agencies.

44. They affirmed the urgency of implementing an ASEAN strategy to improve community development programmes through increased people's participation in education, training and self-help activities. To achieve these goals, the Heads of Government agreed that ASEAN Member countries shall make available to each other existing facilities and shall utilize fully local resources, human and material.

45. The Heads of Government took note of the steps already taken to curb the abuse of narcotics and the illegal trafficking in drugs by the approval at the Ninth ASEAN Ministerial Meeting of the *ASEAN Declaration of Principles to combat the Abuse of Narcotic Drugs*. The Heads of Government directed that member countries continue to give priority to this problem by taking effective measures to implement the Declaration.

46. The Heads of Government also took note of the adoption by the Ninth ASEAN Ministerial Meeting of the *ASEAN Declaration for Mutual Assistance on Natural Disasters* and urged member countries to take steps to implement the Declaration.

47. They reaffirmed their conviction that economic, social and cultural development are indivisible components of nations and regional stability and a necessary foundation for self-sustaining growth and progress.

48. Nothing that the presence of a large number of refugees from Indochina has resulted in serious problems for some ASEAN countries and recognizing the need on humanitarian grounds to solve this problem, the Heads of Government called on the UNHCR and other relevant agencies to take immediate measures for the expeditious resettlement of these refugees in third countries.

49. In the field of labour and manpower, the Heads of Government endorsed the Seven-Point Programme of Action adopted by the ASEAN Labour Ministers at their Special Meeting in Baguio, Manila in May 1976. They commended the efforts by the member countries in adopting an ASEAN position on the basic needs strategy in the labour field.

50. In particular they endorsed the decision of the ASEAN Labour Ministers to place special emphasis on development policies which are employment-oriented. They directed the Labour Ministers to explore possibilities of undertaking joint projects in the development of appropriate technology in the fields of agriculture, industry and managerial organizational technology.

51. The Heads of Government urged that the present

co-operation in the field of labour and manpower among ASEAN member countries be further intensified in order to improve the well-being of the low-income group and the rural population through the provision of greater opportunities for productive employment with fair remuneration, as enunciated in the *Declaration of ASEAN Concord.*

52. The Heads of Government noted that the ASEAN Ministers of Information at their Meeting in Manila on 22-23 July, 1977 drew up guidelines for the implementation of an ASEAN information policy which supports the fundamental objective of ASEAN to accelerate economic, social and cultural development. They agreed that Information is important to the progress of development in the respective ASEAN countries.

Improvement of ASEAN Machinery

53. The Heads of Government expressed satisfaction with the progress made in streamlining and restructuring the ASEAN machinery. They noted that the necessary adjustment had been made in the organisational structure of ASEAN to enable it to undertake its increasing activities in implementing the programme of action as laid down in the *Declaration of ASEAN Concord.* They agreed that changes in the organisational structure of ASEAN should be effected without altering the status of the ASEAN Declaration as the basic document which embodies the principles and objectives of ASEAN. The Heads of Government directed that efforts be continued to review the organisational structure of ASEAN with a view to increasing its effectiveness.

54. The Heads of Government of Indonesia, the Philippines, Singapore and Thailand expressed their sincere appreciation to the Prime Minister of Malaysia for his direction and guidance as Chairman of their Meeting, and through him expressed their thanks to the Government and people of Malaysia, for the warm hospitality accorded them and for the excellent arrangements made for the Meeting.

Joint Statement of the Special Meeting of the ASEAN Foreign Ministers on the Current Political Development in the Southeast Asian Region: Bangkok, 12 January 1979

Determined to demonstrate the solidarity and cohesiveness of ASEAN in the face of the current threat to peace and stability in the Southeast Asia region, and recalling the Vietnamese pledge to ASEAN member countries to scrupulously respect each other's independence, sovereignty and territorial integrity, and to co-operate in the maintenance and strengthening of peace and stability in the region, the Foreign Ministers of the ASEAN Member Countries met in Bangkok on 12-13 January 1979 and agreed on the following:

1. The ASEAN Foreign Ministers reaffirmed the Statement issued in Jakarta on 9 January 1979 by the Minister for Foreign Affairs of Indonesia as Chairman of the ASEAN Standing Committee on the Escalation of the Armed Conflict between Vietnam and Kampuchea.

2. The ASEAN Foreign Ministers strongly deplored the armed intervention against the independence, sovereignty and territorial integrity of Kampuchea.

3. The ASEAN Foreign Ministers affirmed the right of the Kampuchean people to determine their future by themselves free from interference or influence from outside powers in the exercise of their rights of self-determination.

4. Towards this end, the ASEAN Foreign Ministers called for the immediate and total withdrawal of the foreign forces from Kampuchean territory.

5. The ASEAN Foreign Ministers welcomed the decision of the United Nations Security Council to consider without delay the situation in Indochina, and strongly urged the Council to take the necessary and appropriate measures to restore peace, security and stability in the area.

An Appeal for Kampuchean Independence: Jakarta, 21 September 1983

1. The central issue in the Kampuchean problem is the survival of the Kampuchean nation and the restoration of its independence and sovereignty. The total withdrawal of foreign forces, the exercise of self-determination and national reconciliation are essential elements for the survival of an independent and sovereign Kampuchea. The continuing foreign occupation of Kampuchea and violation of Kampuchean sovereignty, independence and territorial integrity threaten regional and international peace and security.

2. The Foreign Ministers therefore call on the international community, particularly Vietnam and the five Permanent Members of the UN Security Council as well as other states concerned, to join them in intensifying efforts to achieve a just solution whereby Kampuchea can emerge once again as an independent and sovereign nation in fact as well as in law.

3. In order to restore Kampuchea's independence, sovereignty and territorial integrity, the Foreign Ministers further appeal to all countries concerned to refrain from all interference, direct or indirect in the internal affairs of Kampuchea and to respect the neutral and non-aligned status of Kampuchea, which is essential to the legitimate security concerns of all countries in Southeast Asia.

4. Moreover, following the total withdrawal of foreign troops from Kampuchea, the Kampuchean people must be able to exercise their inalienable right to self-determination through internationally-supervised elections in which all Kampucheans shall participate and all political groups in Kampuchea should be encouraged to work towards the goal of national reconciliation.

5. In consonance with the on-going international efforts, the Foreign ministers reiterate their willingness to consult with all parties concerned regarding possible initial steps that could be taken in pursuit of a comprehensive political settlement of the Kampuchean problem. These steps could include the following:

With regard to the declared intention of Vietnam to conduct partial troop withdrawals, such partial withdrawals should take place on a territorial basis, and could begin with withdrawal from the western-most territory of Kampuchea along the Thai-Kampuchean border. These withdrawals should begin as soon as possible in phases within a definite period to be worked out as part of a comprehensive political settlement.

In this context, a ceasefire should be observed in these areas, which should then be constituted as safe areas for uprooted Kampuchean civilians under UNHCR auspices. In addition, peace-keeping forces-observer groups should be introduced to ensure that the withdrawals have taken place and the ceasefire and safe areas are respected. International economic assistance programmes should be encouraged in these safe areas.

6. The Foreign Ministers, conscious of the plight of the Kampuchean people resulting from the ravages of war and mindful of the need for the economic reconstruction of Kampuchea and the rehabilitation of the social and cultural life of the Kampuchean people, hereby appeal to the international community to mobilize resources for a programme of assistance as part and parcel of the comprehensive political settlement of the Kampuchean problem.

An international conference for the reconstruction and rehabilitation of Kampuchea should be convened at an appropriate time.

Declaration of the Admission of Brunei Darussalam into the Association of Southeast Asian Nations: Jakarta, 7 January 1984

The Minister for Foreign Affairs of the Republic of Indonesia, the Minister of Foreign Affairs of Malaysia, the Minister of State for Foreign Affairs of the Republic of the Philippines, the Minister for Foreign Affairs of the Republic of Singapore, and the Minister of Foreign Affairs of the Kingdom of Thailand

Having considered the communication of Brunei Darussalam expressing her desire and interest to become a member of the Association of Southeast Asian Nations (ASEAN);

Having regard to the ASEAN Declaration of 1967 establishing ASEAN wherein it was declared that the Association is open for participation to all States in the South-East Asian Region subscribing to the aims, principles and purposes of ASEAN;

Having regard to the Declaration of ASEAN Concord of 1976; and

Having regard to the unanimous expression by the member states of ASEAN of their agreement to admit Brunei Darussalam to membership;

and

The Minister for Foreign Affairs of Brunei Darussalam representing Brunei Darussalam

Having solemnly accepted the conditions of membership; and

Having agreed to subscribe or accede as the case may be, to all the Declarations and Treaties of ASEAN;

Now therefore, the ASEAN Foreign Ministers and the Foreign Minister of Brunei Darussalam hereby agree and declare as follows:

1. Brunei Darussalam becomes the sixth member state of ASEAN,
2. Brunei Darussalam solemnly agrees to subscribe or accede as the case may be, to all the Declarations and Treaties of ASEAN.

This Declaration of Admission of Brunei Darussalam, done at Jakarta on the Seventh Day of January in the Year One Thousand Nine Hundred and Eighty-Four, shall be deposited with the ASEAN Secretariat.

The Manila Declaration Of 1987

The Sultan and Yang Di-Pertuan of Negara Brunei Darussalam, the President of the Republic of Indonesia, the Prime Minister of Malaysia, the President of the Republic of the Philippines, the Prime Minister of the Republic of Singapore, and the Prime Minister of the Kingdom of Thailand;

Reaffirming their commitment to the ASEAN Declaration, the Declaration of ASEAN Concord, the Declaration of the Zone of Peace, Freedom, and Neutrality of 1971, and the 1977 accord of Kuala Lumpur;

Encouraged by the achievements of ASEAN in the last two decades, particularly in creating a political environment conducive to the development of its members and in carving out a distinct identity recognized and respected in the community of nations;

Having reviewed the current international political and economic situation and having considered the implications for ASEAN of changes over the last decade;

Convinced that economic development and progress are fundamental to the stability and security of the region;

Moved by an abiding faith in the capabilities of their peoples and the potentials for growth of their nations, and by a deep hope in the future of ASEAN;

Endeavouring to advance the achievements of ASEAN as a dynamic and cohesive regional association of states for the well-being of its peoples;

Do Hereby Declare:

1 Member states shall strengthen national and regional resilience to ensure security, stability and growth in the ASEAN region.

2 ASEAN regionalism founded upon political, economic, and cultural cohesion is more vital than ever for the future of Southeast Asia.

3 ASEAN shall pursue regional solidarity and co-operation under all circumstances, especially whenever pressures and tensions of any kind, arising from within the region or from without, challenge the capacities, resourcefulness, and goodwill of the ASEAN nations.

4 Intra-regional disputes shall be settled by peaceful means in

accordance with the spirit of the Treaty of Amity and Co-operation in Southeast Asia and the United Nations Charter.

5 While each member state shall be responsible for its own security, co-operation on a non-ASEAN basis among the member states in security matters shall continue in accordance with their mutual needs and interests.

6 Member states shall strengthen intra-ASEAN economic co-operation to maximize the realization of the region's potential in trade and development and to increase ASEAN's efficacy in combatting protectionism and countering its effects.

7 Member states shall encourage an environment in which the private sector can play an increasing role in economic development and in intra-ASEAN co-operation.

8 ASEAN functional co-operation shall promote increased awareness of ASEAN, wider involvement and increased participation and co-operation among the peoples of ASEAN, and development of human resources.

9 ASEAN shall remain firmly resolved in eradicating the scourge of drug abuse and illicit trafficking which threatens the fabric of its societies and debilitates its peoples.

And do hereby agree as follows:

Political Co-operation

1 ASEAN solidarity shall be strengthened through the adoption of common stands and collective actions on matters vital to ASEAN cohesion and resilience and through close coordination on matters of common interest at the international level.

2 ASEAN shall continue and intensify its efforts in finding a durable comprehensive political solution to the Kampuchean problem in the interest of achieving peace and stability not only in Kampuchea but also for the region as a whole. Positive steps by Vietnam in response to ASEAN's efforts would contribute to such a solution.

3 ASEAN shall persevere in the efforts to find an effective solution to the problem of Indochinese refugees in Southeast Asia.

4 ASEAN shall intensify all efforts towards achieving the early realization of a Zone of Peace, Freedom and Neutrality in Southeast Asia (ZOPFAN) in consultation with states outside ASEAN.

5 ASEAN shall intensify its efforts towards the early

establishment of a Southeast Asia Nuclear Weapon Free Zone (SEA NWFZ) in Southeast Asia, including the continuation of the consideration of all aspects relating to the establishment of the Zone and of an appropriate instrument to establish the Zone.

6 ASEAN shall promote and develop co-operation with states in the Pacific region, both the industrialised and developing states, in recognition of its increasing dynamism and potential. Relations with the developing countries in the region could also be fostered in the context of South-South co-operation.

Economic Co-operation

7 To intensify efforts towards significant expansion of intra-ASEAN trade, ASEAN shall adopt and carry out a package of measures for the improvement of the Preferential Trading Arrangements (PTA). Such measures shall include the progressive reduction in the number of items in the member-countries' exclusion lists and the deepening of the margin of preference for items currently in the PTA. ASEAN shall also relax the ASEAN-content requirement in the Rules of Origin on a case-by-case basis. The standstill of non-tariff barriers (NTBs) shall be implemented and the rollback of NTBs negotiated as soon as possible after the manila Meeting of Heads of Government.

8 ASEAN shall accelerate sound industrial development within the region by making the ASEAN Industrial Joint Venture (AIJV) Scheme more flexible, quicker to implement and more attractive to private investors. It shall also conclude an investment guarantee agreement among ASEAN countries, continue to exchange information on national industrial policies and plans, and take appropriate measures that would encourage the increased flow of technology, know-how and foreign investments into the ASEAN region.

9 In the field of finance and banking, ASEAN endorses the establishment of an ASEAN Reinsurance Corporation by 1988. Other forward-looking measures in this field shall include the use of the intra-ASEAN model of Double Taxation Convention as a guide, liberalisation in the use of ASEAN currencies and improvement in the use of ASEAN currencies and improvement in the efficiency of customs and tax administrators through training programmes.

10 In the area of intra-ASEAN co-operation on commodities, ASEAN shall take joint action to address problems of structural surpluses, seek greater market shares, develop indigenous

resource-based industries, intensify research and development (R&D) programmes and encourage the establishment of producer associations, regional trade associations and commodity exchanges.

11 In the light of the growing importance of trade in services, ASEAN shall enhance closer co-operation in this area.

12 ASEAN shall enhance intra-ASEAN travel and develop a viable and competitive tourism industry. The year 1992, the 25th Anniversary Year of ASEAN, is declared as "Visit ASEAN Year".

13 ASEAN shall enhance co-operation in the field of energy, including energy planning, exchange of information, transfer of technology, research and development, manpower training, conservation and efficiency, and the exploration, production and supply of energy resources.

14 In the field of transportation and communications, ASEAN shall pursue the introduction of Brokers Telegraph System, Inter-ASEAN Bulk Pool System, and Point-to-Point Shipping Services, and the establishment/strengthening of Freight Booking and Cargo Consolidation Centres. The existing transportation system shall be strengthened to ultimately form an overall ASEAN transportation network.

15 ASEAN co-operation in food, agriculture and forestry shall be aimed at improving the standard of living in the agricultural and forestry sectors, sustaining adequate supply of basic agricultural and forestry commodities to meet regional needs; and reducing the differences in agricultural and forestry structures in the region. Future co-operative efforts shall be geared towards greater private sector involvement and more emphasis on human resources development of farmers, fishermen and forestry workers.

Relationship with dialogue partners

16 While ASEAN's dialogues with Australia, Canada, the European Community, Japan, New Zealand and the United States have covered wide areas, member states shall further emphasize market access, trade and tourism promotion, investments, flow of resources, industrial development, transfer of technology, human resources development, and support for ASEAN positions in international fora. ASEAN's dialogues with these countries shall be kept under review to meet these objectives.

Functional co-operation

17 Member states shall, through education, institutional

linkages, and improved flow of information, seek to enhance awareness of ASEAN, inculcate in the people the common socio-economic values and heritage, and promote mutual understanding of the culture, traditions and ways of life of their nations.

18 Intra-ASEAN functional co-operation shall be designed for a wider involvement and increased participation by the women and youth, as well as Non-Governmental Organizations, Inter-Governmental Organizations and ASEAN Inter-Parliamentary Organization.

19 ASEAN shall intensify its co-operation on health, drug abuse prevention and combatting illicit trafficking in drugs, labour, law, population, child survival and welfare, socio-cultural programmes, and science and technology.

20 In the area of environment, ASEAN shall co-operate in promoting the principle of sustainable development and systematically integrating it into all aspects of development and shall focus on the need for policy guidelines to protect ASEAN's common resources and environment.

21 ASEAN shall emphasize developing an intelligent and highly productive workforce by increasing investment in science and technology and by providing effective training in order to facilitate the effective transfer of technology.

Machinery for ASEAN co-operation

22 The ASEAN organizational structure shall continually be improved with a view to enhancing its effectiveness.

Done in the City of Manila of the Philippines, this Fifteenth Day of December in the Year One Thousand Nine Hundred and Eighty-Seven, the twentieth year of the Association of Southeast Asian Nations.

Select Bibliography

Alison Broinowski (ed.), *Understanding ASEAN* (St Martin's Press, New York, 1982).

Nayan Chanda, *Brother Enemy. The War After the War* (Harcourt Brace Jovanovich, San Diego, California, 1986).

Donald K. Crone, *The ASEAN States. Coping with Dependence* (Praeger, New York, 1983).

David W. P. Elliot (ed.), *The Third Indochina Conflict* (Westview Press, Boulder, Colorado,1981).

Bernard K. Gordon, *Towards Disengagement in Asia* (Prentice Hall, Englewood Cliffs, New Jersey, 1969).

Karl D. Jackson *et al.* (eds.), *ASEAN in Regional and Global Context* (Institute of East Asian Studies, University of California, Berkeley, 1986).

Arnfinn Jorgensen-Dahl, *Regional Organisation and Order in South-East Asia* (Macmillan, London, 1982).

Michael Leifer, *Indonesia's Foreign Policy* (George Allen & Unwin, London, 1983).

Michael Leifer (ed.), *The Balance of Power in East Asia* (Macmillan, London, 1986).

James W. Morley (ed.), *Security Interdependence in the Asia Pacific Region* (D. C. Heath, Lexington, Massachusetts, 1986).

Charles E. Morrison and Astri Suhrke, *Strategies of Survival. The Foreign Policy Dilemmas of Small Asian States* (University of Queensland Press, St Lucia, 1978).

Robert A. Scalapino and Yusuf Wanandi (eds.), *Economic, Political and Security Issues in Southeast Asia in the 1980s* (Institute of East Asian Studies, University of California, Berkeley, 1982).

Sheldon Simon, *The ASEAN States and Regional Security* (Hoover Institution Press, Stanford, California, 1982).

Robert Tilman, *Southeast Asia and the Enemy Beyond: ASEAN Perceptions of External Threat* (Westview Press, Boulder, Colorado, 1986)

William S. Turley (ed.), *Confrontation or Coexistence. The Future of ASEAN-Vietnam Relations* (Institute of Security and International Studies, Chulalongkorn University, Bangkok, 1985).

Donald E. Weatherbee (ed.), *Southeast Asia Divided: The ASEAN: Indochina Crisis* (Westview Press, Boulder, Colorado, 1985).

Dick Wilson, *The Neutralization of Southeast Asia* (Praeger, New York, 1975).

Index